# Approaches to Applied Semiotics 3

Mouton de Gruyter
Berlin · New York

# Signs of Music

## A Guide to Musical Semiotics

*by*
Eero Tarasti

Mouton de Gruyter
Berlin · New York 2002

Mouton de Gruyter (formerly Mouton, The Hague)
is a Division of Walter de Gruyter GmbH & Co. KG, Berlin

♾ Printed on acid-free paper which falls within the guidelines
of the ANSI to ensure permanence and durability.

*Library of Congress Cataloging-in-Publication Data*

Tarasti, Eero.
    Signs of music : a guide to musical semiotics / by Eero
Tarasti.
        p.   cm.
    Includes bibliographical references and indexes.
    ISBN 3110172267 (hc. : alk. paper — ISBN 3110172275
    (pbk. : alk. paper)
    1. Music — Semiotics.    2. Music — Philosophy and aesthe-
tics.    3. Symbolism in music.    I. Title.
    ML3845 .T348   2002
    780'.1'4—dc21
                                                  2002070066

*Die Deutsche Bibliothek — CIP-Einheitsaufnahme*

Tarasti, Eero:
Signs of music : a guide to musical semiotics / by Eero Tarasti.
— Berlin ; New York : Mouton de Gruyter, 2002
    (Approaches to applied semiotics ; 3)
    ISBN 3-11-017226-7 Gb.
    ISBN 3-11-017227-5 brosch.

Cover design: Christopher Schneider, Berlin.
Printed in Germany.

# Foreword

This book consists of essays and articles mostly written after the publication of my *Theory of Musical Semiotics* (Indiana University Press, 1994). They have been chosen to fit the series Applied Semiotics, hence their emphasis is more on application than on theory.

Since the appearance of my theory of semiotics, however, much has happened, both in musicology and semiotics. The so-called "new musicology" movement has grown stronger, opening hitherto unexplored avenues of interpretation for musical theory and analysis. In semiotics, new trends have arisen as well, especially in areas dealing with the post-modern, deconstruction, media studies, and biosemiotic. Also, I have been developing a new philosophical theory called "existential semiotics" and recently published a monograph under that title (Indiana University Press, 2000). My forays into these new areas can be traced between the lines of the present book.

This volume is meant to serve as a more or less "practical guide" to musical semiotics, i.e., the study of music as sign and communication. It includes both a history of this relatively new discipline as well as some new contributions of my own devising. Originally the book was much longer, but some chapters, such as those dealing with Wagner, have been removed, to be saved for another volume. I hope that what remains will encourage readers – be they students of music, musicology or semiotics, more advanced scholars, or inquiring minds of any stripe – to learn more about musical semiotics. The field is now undergoing fascinating processes of formation, growth, and diversity. For me, musical signs come alive both through practice – by listening to and performing music – and also through their history and aesthetics. Still, one also needs a theory, a sufficiently complex discourse and meta-language, in order to talk about music's subtle and variegated meanings. My hope is that the present volume goes at least some way toward providing such a discourse.

I am very grateful to colleagues, students, and scholars of the International Project in Musical Signification, launched in 1985 at a discussion in Paris at the French Broadcasting Company and now a well-known academic community. The work done in context of this project has opened my eyes and ears to many new sights and sounds, and hence to many new paths to investigate. I am particularly indebted to Dr. Richard Littlefield in the US, for his extraordinarily devoted editing work, as well as to my other editorial assistant in Helsinki, Paul Forsell, for his great help and hard labor during the years this book was being written.

I dedicate this book to the memory of my friend and senior colleague, Tom Sebeok.

Helsinki, January 28, 2002

Eero Tarasti

# Contents

# Part one:
# Music as sign

# Chapter 1
# Is music sign?

## 1.1 Introduction

Music is said to be the least representational of all the arts. And yet, to take this view means to consider music as an autonomous realm which can be understood only by those who are "musical" and about which only specialists may speak knowledgeably.

The fact is that at the beginning of the twenty-first century we live from morning till night surrounded by musical messages emitted by the electronic communication that envelops us. Not only are all periods of music history present at the same time, but also we can now "enjoy" all music cultures, as blended into what is called "world music". Social groups in postmodern society have characteristic musical styles as part of their "habituses" (Bourdieu 1986) or as a part of the spaces in which they move (Krims 2001). For example, youth cultures cannot be fully understood without knowledge of their musical tastes (Danesi 1994, 1998). The presence of music is so overwhelming that we hardly dare ask whether or not it is communication, or even more specifically, if it is a sign. As Augusto Ponzio (1999) notes, we live not just in a world of communication, but also in one of communication-production. That is to say, not only do we apply, implicitly or explicitly, the *sender-message-receiver* model to all of our transactions, but we also form part of the process of *production-exchange* (circulation, commodification)-*consumption* (Ponzio 1999: 80). The sender-message-receiver model tends to be intellectual and cognitive in nature; it automatically involves signification and meaning the moment one thinks about *what* is communicated. By contrast, the production-exchange-consumption model doesn"t require deep thought: when faced with a commodity, say, in a supermarket, we only need to know if we "like" it or if it "functions" well.

The more philosophically-minded are not satisfied with the communication model, however, but rather see music as an emanation of values, epistemes, power relations (Foucault 1973, 1975), of gender (Kristeva and feminists in the American "new musicology"), of ideologies (Barthes 1957; Frith 1978, 1984, 1988, 1996), as human-animal exchanges (Sebeok 1990; Mâche 1983; Martinelli 2002), or as more abstract, axiological entities. Values have no influence, however, unless they are embodied in our everyday lives and social interactions. In our daily activities, we constantly evaluate things, including the way we communicate with each other. No object or thing has any existence for us unless it means or signifies something. Music thus mediates between values be they aesthetic, ideological, or whatever – and fixed, ready-made objects. In fact, music as a sign provides an ideal case of something meaningful and communicative, and thus of something *semiotical* par excellence.

## 1.2 Music as semiotic: A historical perspective

Oddly enough, few of the great semioticians have said anything about music as a sign. Umberto Eco, in his *Struttura assente*, described music as a system having denotation but not connotation, giving the note "c" as an example (Eco 1971: 97). That is all. He touches on music again only in passing, in his essays on number symbolism in the Middle Ages (Eco 1986: 32). Not one word about music appears in the massive output of A. J. Greimas, nor in that of Yuri Lotman. In contrast, Roland Barthes had much to say about music (1975, 1977). A competent pianist himself, Barthes's essay on the "grain of the voice" remains a classic in studies of vocal expression (see Ch. 7, on "Voice and Identity"). A little less quoted but still inspiring are Barthes's ideas on corporeal meanings – "somathemes", the smallest units of bodily expression – as they occur in Robert Schumann's piano music.

Claude Lévi-Strauss is a semiotician whose name is almost synonymous with music. The latter inspired his monumental study of the myths of North and South American Indians (Lévi-Strauss

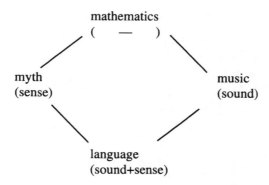

*Figure 1.*

1964–1971). In that study, he introduced his famous model of music and myth, both of which derive from language (Figure 1).

His starting point was language as conceived by the Swiss linguist Ferdinand de Saussure, that is, as a system whose units (words) are divided into two sides: signifier (sound) and signified (sense). For Lévi-Strauss, music is a language without sense (signified), and myth exists independently of its "sounds", i.e., the phonemes of the language in which it is told. Given his structuralist frame of reference, Lévi-Strauss thought that everything meaningful originated in language, and that when we listen to music we feel an "irresistible" need to fill it with meanings. That is to say, the listener *imbues* music with sense.

Such a view of musical signs is known as musical *formalism*, the founder of which was the German musicologist and critic Eduard Hanslick. In his essay *Vom musikalisch Schönen* (1854), Hanslick defined music simply as *tönend bewegte Formen*, 'moving aural forms'. Igor Stravinsky (1947) later rearticulated this view in his Harvard lectures, saying that music had no place for the subjective; it only had to be played. This practical view is shared by many other musicians who refuse to discuss their skills or craft.

Still, music almost never functions without the support of other sign systems. Hence the generally accepted truism, that a sign can only function and be understood against the background of a continuum or "semiosphere" of signs (Lotman et al. 1975), holds for music as well. The semiosphere enables the life of any sign within its domain. Sometimes the semiosphere is a social context. In music, for example, national anthems constitute signs of a larger, social continuum; for instance, *La Marseillaise, Stars and Stripes Forever, God Save the Queen, Rule Britannia*, and the like. Such anthems embody music as a social force. Musical signs can serve as symbols of ethnic and social groups, which distinguish themselves from others by means of their songs. Thus, national anthems are cases of *marked* signs, which arise against the background of the broader field of *non-marked* signs.[1] National anthems are such strong musical signs that we can perceive them as such even in "non-nationalist" contexts, as when quoted in art music. For instance, we recognize *Marseillaise* with all its meanings immediately in Tchaikovsky's *1812 Overture* and at the end of Debussy's piano prelude *Feux d'artifice*; and the political significance of the Emperor Hymn *Deutschland, Deutschland über alles* remains even when it appears in the string quartet by Joseph Haydn or in the finale of Brahms' Piano Sonata in F minor.

Who is this collective "we"? It is those who share a similar cultural and educational background and who thus share a similar musical competence. Music as a sign cannot exist without the competencies necessary for understanding it as such. To illustrate, we take two examples. The first is the subject of J. S. Bach's Fugue in C sharp minor, from Book I of the *Well-Tempered Clavier*:

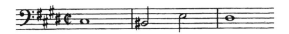

*Ex. 1.*

What does this musical motive mean? An entire five-voice fugue is constructed upon it, and in this sense it represents "absolute" music – no semantics are involved, just the following of syntactic rules of fugal technique. For music listeners of the Baroque period, however, this fugue-subject acted as a meaningful musical sign: it represented the cross and thus the Christ:

*Ex. 2.*

Competent listeners of the time were familiar with this meaning and would have recognized it in Bach's fugue-subject. The same religious meaning is preserved when that subject is quoted, as in the Prelude to César Franck's *Prélude, chorale et fugue*, even though nineteenth-century listeners might no longer have been aware of its original symbolism.

As another example, we take the opening motive of Beethoven's Piano Sonata in E flat major (Op. 81a), *"Les adieux"*:

*Ex. 3.* Beethoven, opening to *"Les adieux"*.

What makes this motive sound both pastoral and melancholy at the same time? The interval sequence of major third-perfect fifth-minor sixth appeared in much eighteenth-century music by composers such as Mozart and Haydn. This particular sequence of intervals referred to courtly "hunting calls" and, by extension, the outdoor-life of nobles. Beethoven knew this, and to that signification he added the intimacy of romantic thought. Normally the "horn fifths" ascend; here, by having them descend and close on a false cadence, Beethoven makes the horn call a symbol of "farewell". This is one way musical signs function: they can be shifted from one context to another, such that they change from signals into symbols. When many such musical signs were linked together in a piece, according to a certain plan or "plot", music became a *narrative* art, a part of story-telling. But it provided different and richer possibilities than did stories comprised of words (novels) or gestures (dance).

We have moved almost imperceptibly from music as a sign to music as narration. Is this a legitimate move? Again, let us take empirical examples as our justification. Nineteenth-century composers habitually provided their music with literary and poetic programs, which were indicated either by the title of the piece, or even by a direct quotation printed in the score. A famous example is Robert Schumann's *Fantasy in C major*, a three-movement piano work of almost symphonic dimensions. As its motto appear these lines from a poem by Friedrich Schlegel: "Durch alle Töne tönet, im bunten Erdentaum…" Schumann thus clearly indicates that the piece should be played and understood in the light of this enigmatic poem. What is that "silent tone" which can only be heard secretly? Some say it is the descending fifth, as a sign evoking the composer's famous spouse, the pianist Clara Wieck. This interval is indeed prominent in the piece. The problem, of course, is that it also appears in countless other works, by Schumann and by other composers as well. The Schumann example illustrates the fact that musical meanings are not lexicographic, but always depend on the context in which they appear.

In the late nineteenth century, the investigation of literary texts as providing music with meaning became the province of musical *hermeneutics*. Later, the musical hermeneuticist Arnold Schering (1936) argued that every Beethoven composition had a "secret" program that referred to some literary work by Goethe or Schiller. For instance, the funeral-march theme of the Allegretto of Beethoven's Seventh Symphony evoked the funeral of Mignon in Goethe's *Wilhelm Meister*; Beethoven's Piano Sonata in A flat major (Op. 110) referred to Schiller's tragedy, *Maria Stuart*; the "Waldstein" Sonata to Goethe's poem, *Herman und Dorothea*; and so on. Schering received much negative criticism for his musical hermeneutics (e.g., by Ringbom 1955). True, composers at that time drew inspiration from the interrelations of arts. For instance, when Beethoven composed overtures to Shakespeare's *Coriolanus* and Goethe's *Egmont*, he naturally wrote music to be understood as "narrative" in nature. But musical narratives do not necessarily follow the same routes as literary ones do. For instance, in *Egmont* the sinister Spanish court is portrayed at the very beginning by ominous, heavy chords. It is difficult to pinpoint what Egmont's musical sign is, but the music's dramatic conflicts portray his struggles for the freedom of the Flemish people. The ending of Beethoven's music, however, is significantly different from that of Goethe's play. At the end of Goethe's play, Egmont is in prison, where in a dream-like vision he sees himself being celebrated as a hero, but then he is executed just as the play closes. Beethoven, however, has a different interpretation of this scene. The execution and the chorale which follows are played *before* the coda. *Then* comes the transcendental glorification, the real triumph of the hero who, at least symbolically, has not died but continues to live in a transcendental form.

Similarly, Ernst Chausson's violin piece *Poème* is based on Turgenev's short story *l'hymne de l'amour triomphant*, according to the composer's biography and even designated as such in the first draft of the piece. Knowing these facts, we hear and experience the piece quite differently from the way we would if we did not know about the program. Still, a musical piece is like a deck of cards: the cards in the literary work and the musical piece may be the same, but the plays we make with them are different. The cases discussed above should suffice to show that music is not just one sign among other signs – it is even a logical consequence of signs, that is to say, a narrative.

## 1.3 Peirce, Greimas, and music-semiotic analysis

At this point, it might be useful to provide some practical semiotic tools for analysis. Yet when applying theories from general semiotics to music, we must take care not to reduce the musical reality to schemes that are alien to its essence. Hence, we first should ask *how* general semiotic concepts would fit the music, or even *if* they fit it at all. To answer this question, a look at some "classical" theories of semiotics is in order.

To simplify only a little, there are two major semiotic schools from which such tools might be adapted. One is the "American" school, which is based on the work of the philosopher and mathematician, Charles S. Peirce (1839–1914). The other is "European", and derives from the work of the Swiss linguist, Ferdinand de Saussure, mentioned above. I hope to show that these branches of general semiotics have relevance to the issue of music as sign, and hence can provide concepts useful for music analysis.

According to Peirce, sign processes are based on phenomenological categories which he called First, Second, and Third. These terms refer to the three phases through which we apprehend reality. Peirce's own example of Firstness comes from music: When we hear a melody as a primal impression at an emotive, perhaps even chaotic level, without recognizing what piece it is or who composed it, and so on – that is Firstness. In Secondness, we might go on to identify the piece. In Thirdness, which involves the most ratiocination, we might draw inferences about its style and structure, what other pieces it resembles, and so on. This triad is reflected at all levels of Peirce's sign theory. A good musical illustration of First, Second, and Third occurs in Marcel Proust's multi-volume novel, *A la recherche du temps perdu*, that inexhaustible source of musical and other aesthetic ideas. The famous "small phrase", which Baron Swann and his beloved Odette listen to together at the salon of Mme.Verdurin, is at first completely unknown to them. This is Firstness, in all its emotional plenitude. Gradually the "small phrase" becomes a sign of the protagonists' love for each other. Swann tries to identify that "small phrase", but cannot find it in any of the musical scores at his home. Then he learns that it comes from a violin sonata written by a composer named Vinteuil. This is Secondness: Swann identifies the melody. (The only technical-musical information that Proust gives about this "anthem" of Swann and Odette's love, is that it consists of seven notes, two of which are repeated.) By the time the love between these two protagonists fades, the tune has entered the phase of Thirdness. It has become a fixed sign, a symbol of their relationship, and has lost its qualities of Firstness.

According to Peirce, the total sign consists of three entities: the *object* to which a sign refers; the *representamen*, i.e., the sign itself; and the *interpretant*, a secondary sign by which we mentally link the representamen to its object. Behind all this looms what Peirce called the "dynamic object"; the latter is an aspect of the real world (e.g., the composer). In music, the object may be a thing or event – for example, a farewell, as in Beethoven's "*Les adieux*". In that case, the representamen would be the music itself (written or sounding), and the interpretant might be something like "sonata form" or a comparison of "*Les adieux*" with other sonatas by Beethoven, and so forth. The interpretant could be any mental sign evoked by the music when the latter is cognised in some logical-rational way.

Peirce further distinguishes three possible situations for each "corner" of his triad: (1) signs in relation to objects: *icons, indexes,* and *symbols*; (2) signs in themselves: *qualisigns, sinsigns, legisigns*; and (3) signs in relation to interpretants: *rhemes, dicents,* and *arguments.* The question for us is, Do any of these concepts apply to music? Certainly they do. The most often used "corner" is the one containing the three basic sign categories: icons, indexes, and symbols. An *icon* (First) is a sign which functions by its *similarity* to the object.[2] In the *indexical* sign (Second), the relationship between sign and object is one of *contiguity.* E.g., a knock on the door is a sign – an index – of the person knocking. Smoke is an index of fire, etc. A *symbol* (Third) is a sign that has no necessary link between representamen and object. Symbols are *arbitrary* and exist merely by convention. Such is the case with numbers and with words: there is no necessary iconic or indexical relation between a living, breathing, quadruped of the canine family and the words "dog" or "chien" or "Hund". The relationship between sign and object is arbitrary.

Do these categories have any relevance to music? To answer this question, let us reconsider the example of the horn signal at the beginning of Beethoven's "*Les adieux*" sonata. It is an iconic sign in the sense that, although played on piano, it imitates the horn signals of late eighteenth-century huntsmen. It is also indexical – because of the deceptive cadence – in the sense that it evokes a certain emotional state, both in the composer who wrote and sent the sign, and in the listener who feels such a sentiment of farewell or at least recognizes it as such. The opening horn call is also a symbol: one does need to learn the language of tonal music in order to understand the meaning of this sign. Otherwise it would be nothing more than acoustic arousal.

There is more to the semiotics of music than just listing various cases of icons, indexes, and symbols. For music can also *internalise* all these "external" signs. Thus, any sign evoking an earlier sign by virtue of similarity can be called an "inner icon" of the first-heard sign. Any sign related to another sign by contiguity or proximity is an inner index of it. And when any musical element attains the status of signifying the whole piece – e.g., the "Fate" motive of Beethoven's Fifth Symphony – then it becomes a symbol..

The above examples give us reason to think that Peirce's categories seem to apply to music, and in Chapter 8 we shall apply them to the analysis of improvisation. Though one could go deeper into all of his categories, I shall end our present discussion of Peirce by considering signs in themselves as applied to music. As mentioned above, these are *qualisigns* (Firsts), *sinsigns* (i.e., single-signs; Seconds), and *legisigns* (Thirds). A qualisign is any quality perceived directly in a sign; for instance, a pianist's touch on the keys; a singer's vibrato; and the like. A sinsign is any individual sign recognized as an entity produced by certain "legisigns", the latter serving as the "model" for the sinsign. For instance, "*Les adieux*" is a sinsign (token) of sonata form in general (type).

If Peirce's "American" semiotics seems to fit music, what about "European" notions of semiotics, such as that of A. J. Greimas? Greimas (1917–1992) was a Lithuanian-born linguist who emigrated to France and became famous as professor of semantics at the Ecole des Hautes Etudes en Sciences Sociales in Paris. His seminars stimulated one of the most sophisticated schools of thought in the history of semiotics. Greimas's first major book, *Sémantique structurale* (1966), contained the seeds of many of his later concepts. At the same time, it revealed the roots of his semiotics to lie in the structural linguistics of Saussure, Lévi-Strauss's structural anthropology, and in the work of pioneers in narratology, especially that of the Russian formalist Vladimir Propp.

In his early work, Greimas concentrated on "seme-analysis", i.e., the study of the smallest units of meaning in a text, and went on to propose that all meaning stems from what he called "isotopies". The latter are deep-level semantic fields that enable us to read a text or a part thereof as a coherent whole. To illustrate, he analysed a short story by Maupassant, entitled *Deux amis*. The story takes place in 1871 in Paris, then under siege by the Prussian army, and begins with these words: *"Paris était bloqué, affamé et râlant. Les moineaux se faisaient bien rares sur les toits, et les égouts se dépeuplaient. On mangeait n"importe quoi"* ("Paris was closed, hungry and dying. The sparrows were scarce on the rooftops, and the gutters were empty. People were eating anything at all"). The quoted passage consists of short phrases, articulated by periods and commas. Yet nobody reads it piecemeal, stopping at every comma and period, but rather as a continuous whole. Because it is a portrayal of Paris in a certain condition, "Paris" serves as the isotopy of the passage, making the latter a coherent textual segment. According to Greimas, we usually become conscious of isotopies only when they suddenly change or when two different isotopies are present at the same time. The latter situation can obtain even in a single word (e.g., puns, oxymorons), and many anecdotes and witty discussions are based on such *complex isotopies*, as Greimas calls them. For instance, Oscar Wilde's play, *On the Importance of Being Earnest*, plays on the double meaning of the word "Earnest", as referring either to a person Ernest or to the virtue of being sincere.

As with Peirce, certain of Greimas's concepts also apply to music. Take, for example, the beginning of Beethoven's Piano Sonata in E flat major (Op. 31 no. 3):

*Ex. 4.*   Opening from Beethoven's Piano Sonata, Op. 31 No. 3.

Like the Maupassant text quoted above, this musical passage consists of short phrases separated by pauses. But no one listens to it in that way. Rather, one hears a continuous build in tension toward the cadential tonic six-four chord, and thereafter a humorous resolution to the tonic via the dominant. This basic dominant-tonic tension – the most essential aspect of functional tonality – forms the isotopy of the Beethoven passage. Does music have *complex isotopies* as well? Again, the answer is Yes. Consider the coronation scene in Musorgsky's opera *Boris Godunov*. There, two chords are united by the enharmonic reinterpretation of the note G flat as F sharp. Hence, the note has two meanings simultaneously. Moreover, this move fits well with the narrative: the enharmonically related chords symbolize the internal conflict of Godunov, who does not want to be crowned Czar. At the same time, the music iconically describes the bells of the Kremlin (see Ex. 8a on page 37).

Greimas believed the unfolding of every text to be governed by an achronic, "semiotic square". The latter arises from an opposition between two terms, or "semes", s1 and s2; for instance, man/woman, left/right, day/night, nature/culture, life/death, and so on. These two primary terms, s1 and s2, can be logically "negated", which produces two new terms, or "logical possibilities", within the same semantic field: non-s1 and non-s2. When all four terms are projected onto the same chart, one has a flexible logical tool for analysis:

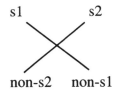

*Figure 2.*

This scheme can be used on any level of analysis as a practical tool. Later, we shall see how it may be used in various music-analytic contexts.[3]

For now, we turn to another aspect of Greimas's semiotics. From Vladimir Propp, Greimas borrowed the *actantial model*, which consists of six protagonists or "actors" typically found in folk tales: *sender, receiver, subject, object, helper*, and *opponent*. Greimas formalized Propp's model into "functions", the latter being performed by the protagonists. One of two situations begins every story: either the subject is *conjuncted* with (S ^ O) or *disjuncted* from (S v O) its object. For instance, if a man owned property, he was *conjuncted* to money (S

^ O). On the other hand, if he lacked property, then he was *disjuncted* from it (S v O). Most of the folktales studied by Propp begin with the latter situation. Starting with this initial "lack", as Propp called it, the rest of the story consists of attaining – being conjuncted with – fulfilment. This situation clearly obtains in music that is obviously narrative, say, in opera. For example, at the beginning of the *Ring of the Nibelungen*, the ring is stolen. The Rhine-daughters are *disjuncted* from their object. At the end of the opera, they get it back; i.e., they are *conjuncted* with it.

A radical phase in the development of Greimas's thought took place in the 1970s when he constructed a theory of *modalities* as the forces most important for shaping semantic and semiotic processes. In linguistics, "modalities" are the ways in which speakers animate or colour their speech with subjective feelings, emotions, beliefs, hopes, fears, and the like. For instance, in French, one does not say, *Il faut que je vais à la banque* (It is necessary that I go to the bank). Rather, one says, *Il faut que* j"aille *à la banque.* When using the verb *falloir* (to have to) to express the modality of "must", then it is necessary to indicate that modality by using the subjunctive verb-form in the dependent clause (here, *aille* instead of *vais*).

The two basic modalities are "being" and "doing", to which five others can be added: "must", "know", "can", "will", and "believe". These modalities are vital to musical as well as verbal discourse. Music, which often eludes fixed, lexicographical definition, is semantic by virtue of the modalities. The modalities can form part of the inner qualities of the music itself, or they can be activated "externally" by how the music is performed. (For more extensive discussion of the modalities in music, see Tarasti 1994.)

In the early 1980s, Greimas organized all his central notions into a formalized theoretical system which he called a "generative course" (the latter inspired by Noam Chomsky's "generative grammar"). Greimas's entire system is applicable to music, and has strong parallels with Heinrich Schenker's music-analytic model, a similarly "axiomatic" and generative system, invented in the 1920s and 1930s, but institutionalised after WWII in Anglo-American as the dominant model for the analysis of tonal music, particularly in the USA (see Littlefield 2001: chap. 2).

We have thus far shown how two important schools of "classic semiotics" – those of Peirce and Greimas – are relevant in determining whether or not music is a sign. The evidence clearly suggests an affirmative answer. But if music is a sign, how do we *understand* it as such? This question requires close examination.


## 1.4 Understanding / misunderstanding musical signs

Consider the difference between these two questions: Do you like Brahms? Do you understand Brahms? One can *like* music; it can be enjoyed without being *understood*. Though some think that music can be enjoyed only if it is understood, is that, in fact, the case? Many people who make music, for fun or professionally, can remember the exact moment and the particular music which opened the door for them into the magical world of tones. At such a moment – the "awakening" of the musical self – music that has been heard earlier only by habit, situation, education and the like, suddenly undergoes a qualitative change. It touches one, it comes alive, it begins to "speak" and "move". Now the message has been *understood*. The music acts as a key that unlocks the door to an unknown world. It has become "existential". We are somehow convinced that this message is "true", "authentic", and crucial to our being.

Even if we adopt the view that there is no such thing as one "correct" way to understand music, we should nevertheless try to grasp this primal phenomenon as semiotical. Still, the ways in which music is understood are contingent, and vary over time. If on the one hand, Proust viewed music as highly representational – as a journey from star to star – then on the other hand, others, like Hanslick, claimed that music portrays nothing (see section 1.2, above). Moreover, various "isms" have left their mark on music. For example, during the "Modernist project" (Taylor 1989), music was construed paradoxically. It reflected man's alienation from the cosmos by functioning as an arbitrary, conventional sign system, as simply a construct. Little regard was given to what it might stand for or what messages it might carry. At the same time, music came to serve a Utopian function, as the only means of regaining our primal, lost unity with the surrounding cosmos.

Following this distinction, there are two kinds of music: *organic* and *inorganic*, discussed at length in Chapter 4 (below). In the former, the listener identifies music as a kind of "living organism" which imitates "natural processes", and by such identification participates in the experience of unity. The opposite holds true in inorganic music, such as that written using serial or other "pre-programmed" techniques. Inorganic music emphasises man's separation from nature and takes a critical distance from the society that has produced it.[4]

By contrast, in the age of romanticism (discussed further in Chapter 2), which continued amidst the modernist project and still thrives in our own postmodern time, an aesthetic of expressivism took pride of place. Nature spoke to humankind intimately, and by listening to its voice, one could reconnect with the cosmos. This view obtained particularly in music, whose "voice" spoke to the heart of the universe. For example, in Schopenhauer's view, music was the emanation of Will, understood as the driving force of Nature itself.

The modernist and romantic aesthetics have been briefly outlined, in order to point up the contingency of musical meanings. The next chapter provides a more thorough overview of those "isms" and their effect on the historical development of musical semiotics. To end the present chapter, I present fourteen theses on what constitutes "understanding", and how such theses affect our thinking about musical signs.

## 1.4.1 Theses on understanding / misunderstanding musical signs

Consider the basic situation of any communication and signification:

subject *S1* $\longrightarrow$ sign $\longrightarrow$ subject *S2*

In the above process, S1 produces a sign that is received by S2. It does not matter whether or not subject S1 "understands" the sign, only that he or she express something when producing it. Subject S2, however, either understands or misunderstands the sign. The latter can occur in two ways: (1) Either subject S2 misunderstands the sign because he or she uses a code or sign-system – what Husserl called *Bedeutungszeichen* – other than the one used by S1. (2) Or S2 misunderstands the sign because he or she does not receive it as an expressive sign (*Ausdruckzeichen*). In either case, S2 fails to access the world, and hence the intentions, of subject S1.

Music, too, can be misunderstood, and in the same two ways just discussed. On the level of *Bedeutungszeichen*, we know from music history that the "Church modes" emerged through misunderstanding(s) of the ancient Greek modes. Similarly, if a pianist plays a wrong note, or if the instrument is out of tune, we notice it immediately. Misunderstanding can also occur on the level of interpretation and expression (*Ausdruck*). When the Tokyo Symphony Orchestra performs Sibelius's symphonies, a Finnish listener may experience a kind of cross-cultural clash. One should hasten to add that this is *not* a negative phenomenon. Rather, new interpretations emerge in precisely this way. If the interpretation is artistically convincing, then it justifies itself.

Let us assume that subject S1 is a composer and that S2 is a listener. In order for the sign to function, the two subjects must share common codes, i.e., possess a similar musical competence. Moreover, it is futile to discuss music unless the speakers involved have sufficiently similar competence. The former two examples concern "external" communication, but music also functions as "autocommunication", which involves a kind of self-understanding. The act of listening to or performing music returns one directly to oneself, to one's inner world, and causes changes at the physiological level, in neural and other bodily processes. In this case, we are dealing with *existential* understanding (cf. Tarasti 2001). During such activities, we come to understand not only music, but also ourselves and the world, because music, in its essential temporality, is perhaps the perfect metaphor and model of human life: birth, death, and what happens in-between. By music we *transcend* our existential situation. Music returns us to the primal moment of narration:

*hic, nunc, ego.* At the same time, it liberates us from that moment. Herein lies the power of musical self-understanding.

## 1.4.2 Theses on processes of understanding

(1) *Understanding is to see the general through the particular.* Scientific explanations usually seek to infer general concepts from particular instances. One attempts to view a phenomenon – an idea, behaviour, person, work of art, or whatever – as a variant of a larger paradigm, and to locate the variant in question within the latter. This process often involves conceptualising the object in question. In such cases, to "understand" is to give something a name or description (e.g., medical diagnoses, psychoanalytic evaluations, and so on).

But do we better understand an artist only in terms of context, say, that of a narrative of illness? For example, Wagner was a narcissist who had attacks of *pavor nocturnus.* That said, do we better understand his music? This species of understanding is in fact a kind of *argumentum ad hominem*, especially when one is trying to understand the signs left by a person. In Peircean terms, such a case exemplifies the token being seen via the type, the qualisign via sinsign, the sinsign via legisign.

One often tries to understand composers or pieces of music by placing them into a broader context, as when a Mozart symphony is viewed as exemplifying Viennese classical style. As another example, Sibelius, Tchaikovsky, de Falla and others often receive the label of *"nationalist"* composers. Their music is heard above all as representing their respective nations; they do not "speak" the proper (i.e., German) language of tonal music, but rather display exoticism, folklorism, nationalism, and the like – in a word, Otherness. By thus constraining how those composers' works should be heard, one misunderstands the message of their music. Similarly, when we view (or hear) a composition only in terms of the composer who wrote it, we limit the possible ways of understanding his or her music. A typical example of the latter is to interpret a composer only through his or her gender, similar to the way Marxist musicologists see music as a sign of social class. Present-day theories of how musical signs reflect gender are as little-developed as are Marxist theories of how musical signs reflect society (cf. Chapter 5, below).

(2) *Understanding is the shift from knowing* (Wissen) *to becoming familiar with* (Kennen). On this view, knowledge becomes personal, subjectively felt. In music, mere knowing is not enough. One understands music only through playing, composing, singing, or other "hands-on" activities. Music constantly must be reborn; for every generation, it must become an aesthetic contemporaneity. Thus, musical understanding is also a perpetual challenge. There have been periods in which the status of knowing and doing have been reversed. In medieval times, for example, to be a "musician" meant to be a theoretician, who, with knowledge of physical and mathematical laws, mastered music speculatively. *Musica practica* – the actual performing of music – took second place.

(3) *Understanding is to see a text or sign as a node in a network of other texts or signs.* Above, we defined "semiosphere" as a continuum of signs, which makes possible the understanding of individual signs within its domain. Here we broaden that discussion a bit and focus on the notion of "intertext", a term coined by Julia Kristeva (1969). A good illustration of this concept is a passage in the last chapter of Nietzsche's *Gay Science*. There the "musicality" of the prose is foregrounded, and musical enunciation is imitated by a gradual acceleration in tempo. Its intertextual counterpart is not difficult to guess: the Finale of Beethoven's Ninth Symphony. This relation is made quite obvious by the indexical sign that Nietzsche provides – *"Nicht diese Töne ..."* – which is a direct quotation from Schiller's *Ode an die Freude*. Nietzsche's text constitutes an iconic-indexical intertext of Beethoven / Schiller. Consequently, to understand a musical text or sign means to join it to other signs, musical or otherwise – to a "chain of interpretants", as Peirce called it. To misunderstand is to relate a phenomenon to the wrong interpretants. Music, while "absolute" and autonomous, is also connected in many ways to the other arts and to the culture surrounding it. Sometimes the key to musical understanding lies precisely in this interartistic network.

(4) *Understanding is to see the enunciate* (what *is said*) *in relation to enunciation* (how *it is said*). Some believe that to "contextualise" a phenomenon is to understand it. Misunderstanding, in this case, would be to reify or mystify the object, by taking it as a given and thus ignoring the conditions of its production

This is a rather one-sided view. For music does not yet exist as mere "enunciate", that is to say, as notes alone. It must become manifest via "enunciation", that is, via live performance. Authentic musical form is not the one we distinguish in a score, but the one we experience while listening to it. A skilful composer does not write "paper music" but envisions the musical enunciation, i.e., the performance. Sometimes composers – such as Wagner, Richard Strauss, Gustav Mahler – even have a particular instrumentalist or singer in mind, a preferred enunciator, when writing their music. When composers write concertos for solo instruments, they often collaborate closely with the future "enunciators" of their music.

(5) *Understanding is to reduce performance to competence; it is to construe something as a consequence of something that precedes it.* In order for semantics to be possible, one must first master the semiotic level; in order to speak a language, one must know the grammar. Misunderstanding is the lack of such competence (though a lack which can perhaps be compensated for).

It is difficult to study empirically the more or less random meanings assigned to music by "incidental" listeners. Musical meanings are understood only by competent listeners. This last statement must not be understood normatively, however. One does not *need* to understand music at all; it can be enjoyed even if it is not understood conceptually. We can also understand music even if we cannot verbalise our experience of it. Musical semiotics, however, tries to analyse the musical signs and sign-processes that enable us to experience and understand music. In such an enterprise, words are indispensable.

(6) *Understanding is simply to do away with misunderstanding.* A musical work, style, or composer may for many years be misunderstood to the point of going unnoticed, then suddenly be (re)discovered. A typical example was the popular re-evaluation of J. S. Bach, thanks to Mendelssohn, at the beginning of the nineteenth century (although

in professional circles he had always been appreciated). Music listeners may accept a cliché about a composer, but then awake to find that it was an illusion. For instance, on the basis of his prose writings alone, many in Wagner's lifetime hated his music, although they had not heard a bar of it. Conversely, an anti-Wagnerian can abruptly turn pro-Wagnerian, upon hearing the miracle of the Bayreuth Opera House.

(7) *Understanding is more an event of* parole *than of* langue. Saussure drew a distinction between *langue* and *parole*. The former refers to language as a system, i.e., as the grammar or "rules" of a language. *Parole* refers to the real manifestations or "speech acts" of a language. The *langue / parole* distinction holds in some music as well. For example, twelve-tone serial techniques serve as a *langue* – a grammar that dictates what notes can be used, and where. The understanding of such music is rare, however, since most listeners cannot recognize the "rows" nor tell if they are grammatically "correct".

(8) *To understand is to move from "surface" to "deep" structures.* This is the dream of the structuralists: the notion that those aspects of a text that are most immediately available to the senses are ruled by or eventually lead back to a controlling, deep structure (e.g., Greimas's "semiotic square"). One variant of this surface / deep-structure hierarchy is that "being" is more fundamental than is "appearance". Because something can be made to look other than what it really is, understanding consists in revealing the "being" that looms behind the "appearance". To understand an ideology is to see "through" it, to the person or group that tries to legitimise their power by means of ideological discourse.

Swiss musicologist Ernst Kurth (1947) argued that music does not consist of tones, but only *appears* through them. The more profound, essential aspect of music is the tension and kinetic energy behind the notes. On the other hand, we know that even the slightest change in the acoustical side (signifier) of a musical sign also produces a change in its content (signified). Here we witness the clash of two musical aesthetics: If music were mere sensory stimulus, then music would be the same as its "appearance"; behind it there would stand no "being". But if music is the expression of something, its basic movement is from the immanent, deep content – what Kristeva calls "genotext" – towards the manifest aural shape ("phenotext"). Roland Barthes applied Kristeva's terms to music: some singers only perform phenotext, understood as the cultural, the aesthetic, the stylistic; whereas other singers emphasize the genotext, i.e., the entire body. In Barthes's view, when listening to a song, one should hear the lungs expand and contract, the heart beat, the muscles grow taut then relax, and so on.

(9) *Understanding is reorganizing the elements of a certain field.* Another structuralist argument, this view sees understanding as a game or puzzle. In Hermann Hesse's novel, *The Glass-Bead Game*, music is portrayed as just such play, and Lévi-Strauss (1967–1971) reads the Oedipus myth as if it were a musical piece, by isolating its similar elements (paradigms) and rearranging them into something like an orchestral score. Jean-Jacques Nattiez's paradigmatic method of melodic analysis follows a similar procedure (1975, 1990). With this method, we can at least analyse, and hence somewhat understand, the musical substance of a piece of music, if not its functioning.

(10) *Understanding is based on morphology over time; it is to see how things unfold, one from the other.* This represents an evolutionary view, such that to understand someone's behaviour is to show the development which led to that person. It is to "live through" the history of an individual or a society.

Music is the supreme temporal art. Hence musical significations cannot be experienced all at once, but must be taken in over the time it takes for the music to unfold. Musical narrativity is based on this process (cf. section 1.3). Usually a piece begins with a certain lack, which can be of a purely musical nature; for instance, a gap in a scale, an asymmetrical motive, a syncopated rhythm, and so forth. This problem is often left hanging, so to speak, until resolved at the very end. The irresolution of this situation creates suspense or tension that prevails throughout the whole piece, propelling the latter toward resolution. For example, refer again to the slow introduction to Beethoven's "*Les adieux*". There the note A flat is systematically avoided, saved for the dramatic effect that it produces at the *attacca* beginning of the Allegro.

(11) *Understanding is a paradigmatic event in which one sees the alternatives.* This view of understanding demands awareness of the resources available. To understand is to see all the alternatives before

choosing to act. In music history, we take into account the stylistic possibilities available to composers, or as Leonard B. Meyer (1973) says, "what might have happened". In playing or conducting music, we try out alternative ways of rendering a phrase or section, any of which may be possible within a certain style. In this way, we seek to reach the essence of a particular piece or passage.

(12) *Understanding is to see the real nature of things. It is to reduce a phenomenon to statistical facts, to confirm it by scientific experiment.* This argument is almost anti-semiotical in nature, because semiotics claims to do nothing more than elaborate models and hypotheses of reality. For semioticians to model a phenomenon in "hard-science" terms is a kind of mystification, since we deal primarily with human, cultural, and social behaviours – not physical laws. Music is not based on natural or physical law, although such has been argued many times (e.g., music as an elaboration of the overtone series). Rather, various cultures choose – from the continuum of tones, noises, and sounds offered by nature – those which they consider to be music.

(13) *Understanding is basically an internal, cognitive process by which the subject comes to understand him- or herself.* There are many varieties of self-understanding. Yet most people do not understand themselves until they see how others view them. Self-understanding may be almost entirely a social event (see Bakhtin 1988; and Mead 1967). By and large, musical taste is related to the social aspect of self-understanding. Musical taste is not a private issue, but a sign of a life style. Hence musical taste reflects one's concept of "me" (on types of listeners, see, e.g., Adorno 1973).

(14) *Understanding is a shift from "I" to "not-I", this shift forming the basis of all morality and ethics.* Empathy and compassion are based on the ability to put oneself in another's shoes, to adopt the position of another subject. This is the mystical event in many a moral philosophy.

Does music have such a moral impact, by helping us understand the Other? Music can "speak" for a given ideology, and many contemporary musicologists, especially in the United States, view music as thoroughly ideological. If one adheres strictly to this view, then if a composer or performer subscribes to a "bad" ideology, the latter will always appear in the music itself. This theory does not hold true, however. For music is largely indifferent to the ideologies or political-historical situations in which it is realized. In fact, ideology often limits the possibilities of music, such that those ideologies which are viewed as "progressive" and "good" often produce aesthetically poor works. Significant works and performances cannot be rejected aesthetically simply on the basis of their background ideologies. For instance, take Furtwängler's interpretations of Wagner, recorded during wartime in Berlin. Recordings of those performances prove that they were superbly executed, despite the political-ideological context in which they took place.

Thus far, and unfortunately so, semiotics has paid little attention to the understanding of signs (for an exception, see Tarasti 2001). To do so, we must move in a more hermeneutic and phenomenological direction. Obviously, both understandings and misunderstandings of music are possible. Moreover, *by music* we come to understand many aspects of our existence. In this way, musical semiotics can play a crucial role in general semiotics, the latter understood as research into humanity's general symbolic and semiotic capacities. The following chapters show in more detail how musical understanding takes place, how it relates to other arts, and how we can describe these processes by an appropriate metalanguage and analytic method.

# Chapter 2
# Signs in music history, history
# of music semiotics

## 2.1 Introduction

In Western civilization the period from the nineteenth century up to
modern times has witnessed the breakthrough and flourishing of semiotics in the proper sense. Nevertheless, in music history, which seems
to follow its own inner laws, no phenomenon emerges unprepared,
and the foundations of a style and of compositional techniques can
always be traced back to earlier periods. Considering music history in
the light of semiotics, one has to state straightforwardly that the "semi-
oticity" of music, either implicit or explicit, depends almost entirely
on what one considers semiotics to be and how one defines it. In this
chapter, which, after a short look backwards, focuses on the period
from Romanticism to our time, the semiotic nature of music is defined
in a relatively flexible way, borrowing concepts and terms from various schools, even ones which are contradictory in their mutual relations. The emphasis here lies on material that is empirically given. It is
the data of music history that I will try to describe in the light of semiotics. Therefore I may take sign categories like icon, index, symbol,
etc. from Peirce, adopt notions like seme, isotopy, modalities, disengagement / engagement from Greimas, employ Lotman's view on culture as a text, Eco's distinction between structures of communication
and signification, and integrate all these approaches into the framework of the present chapter. In other words, I am not yet strictly applying my own theory of musical semiotics, but taking a more general and
"objective" point of view.

It would be erroneous to think that music became a semiotic phenomenon only with Romanticism, when it was experienced as an index
for the personal emotions felt by a composer. Also in the Baroque era,
music was said to signify, when it produced detailed figures that conveyed *passions de l'âme* (see Descartes 1649), i.e., affects of a univer-

sal character, not the personal feelings of the sender of the musical message.

We can interpret the shift from the Renaissance to the Baroque on the basis of dichotomies such as the following (Renaissance / Baroque): (1) one style / many styles; (2) moderate interpretation of a verbal text ("madrigalism") in vocal music / absolutizing the verbal text (such that the affects contained in it determine the music); (3) equivalence of parts / polarity of parts; (4) diatonic, modal melodies moving in a narrow range / chromatic, major and minor melodies, moving in a broad range; (5) modal counterpoint (chords result from voice-leading) / tonal counterpoint (lines written against a chordal background); (6) intervallic structures (dissonances counted from the bass) / chordal structures (dissonances counted from the tonic or key tone); (7) permanent tempo (with the heartbeat as the basic pulse) / variation of tempos (with extremes of fast and slow); (8) unidiomatic composing (i.e., the same music, regardless of the instrumentation) / idiomatic composing (different instruments and voices having their own character, so as to let various vocal and instrumental styles emerge).

In each of these dichotomies one sees reinterpretations and re-evaluations of the semiotic processes underlying music. For example in Orlando di Lasso's motet *Tristis est anima mea* sadness is depicted by a descending series of chords in fifth relations (Ex. 5). Such devices later developed into "madrigalisms", i.e., text interpretations through musical symbols. For instance, in vocal music by Marenzio, Gesualdo and Monteverdi, one can hear "departure" portrayed with chords in third relations (Ex. 6). In such musical techniques the semiotic nature of music is already quite conspicuous: music is used as a sign which stands for something to someone.

One can describe the shift from Baroque to Classicism and from Classicism to Romanticism with similar dichotomies. Baroque / Classicism: polyphonic lines and counterpoint / homophonic texture (i.e., melody is most prominent; other parts serve as its accompaniment); dance suites with fugue as a central technique / sonata form; and so on. The Austrian musicologist Guido Adler illustrated the differences between Classicism and Romanticism with the following

*Ex. 5.* Orlando di Lasso, *Tristis est anima mea* (late sixteenth century); sadness depicted by descending series of chords in fifth relations.

*Ex. 6.* Chords in third-relations symbolizing "departure" in Renaissance madrigals.

oppositions: Classicism – which Adler understood somewhat unusually as including not only composers of the Viennese Classics such as Haydn, Mozart and Beethoven (whom he called *"neuklassisch"*, neo-classical), but also some Renaissance and Baroque composers (whom he called *"altklassisch"*) – was characterized by complete congruence of parts; equivalence of formal processes; economy and mastery of technical devices; limiting of expressive power so that a certain level of beauty is never exceeded; integration of the best aspects of earlier styles (Adler 1911: 225). In contrast, Romanticism revealed itself in the blending of forms; the conscious rejection of classical norms; indulgence and seeming loss of control; coloristic effects and tone painting; a programmatic attitude (in contrast to pure or "absolute" instrumental music); and so on (Adler 1911: 228). Adler's characterizations enable us to see that shifts from one style to another are not merely surface phenomena of music, but are related to deep epistemic changes in their proponents' worldviews.

Ernst Kurth defined the difference between the polyphony of the Baroque age and the homophonic style of Classicism in the following way: Polyphonic music, whose development coincides with the rise of Protestantism and whose roots extend to the Middle Ages, emerged from the occidental religious urge to strive for the transencendental. Its forms reflect the desire for the infinite and the search for redemption. Accordingly, a polyphonic, linear art emerged, which aimed at an elevating and sublime contrapuntal texture. In contrast, Classical art touches the earthly human consciousness, by emphasizing worldly pleasures and by placing man at the center of things. From the laborious suspiration and rich inner elaboration of polyphony, the classical style freed itself and entered a world of animated song and play. Classical melody – which is based on the *Lied,* with its symmetrical and periodic structures consisting of two-, four-, and eight-bar phrases – finds its boundaries within ourselves, whereas polyphonic lines strive for infinity. Polyphony aims at mystical development towards the distance, whereas classical homophonic melody draws expressivity as a particular inner quality into itself *(Innigkeit)* (Kurth 1922: 174–187).

Consequently, for the whole period of Viennese Classics, and to a large extent also during Romanticism, the Classical *Lied*-type melody became the basic model of melodic expression. During this time, melodies developed into virtual "actors" and became protagonists of musical discourse, thus providing music with "anthropomorphic" features. This is the basis of "actoriality" in music (see Greimas and Courtés 1979: 79; Tarasti 1991e, 1992b, 1992d).

As can be seen from the above style distinctions, it is extremely difficult to separate implicit from explicit musical meaning. Their treatment depends almost entirely on the theory that is chosen as the starting-point. Nevertheless, Western musical practice provides ample evidence of the profoundly semiotic nature of music. A competent music listener very soon recognizes if a performer has or has not realized the semantic differences between different styles. As early as the Baroque era, François Couperin said: *"Nous écrivons différemment de ce que nous executons"* ["We write in a different way from what we perform"] (quoted in Veilhan 1977: iii). In other words, music must not be interpreted by slavishly obeying the notation, that is, the visual signs of music, but by trying to attain the conceptual, aesthetic, axiological and epistemic realities which lie behind those visual signs. Music is as inseparable from these cognitive cultural constructs as are the other arts.

## 2.2 Signs in music itself

### 2.2.1 Romanticism

Instead of focusing on events which connect music with external reality, one can concentrate on purely musical processes. The former are "extrinsic musical processes", the latter "intrinsic" ones. As an example, take the opening "Fate" motive of Beethoven's Fifth Symphony. Its intrinsic properties are the nucleus for the subsequent music, and its extrinsic properties have been taken to signify Fate knocking at one's door. Concerning the intrinsic sign processes of music, the shift between the ages of Classicism and Romanticism did not entail an abrupt qualitative change. The tonal basis of music had been firmly established in previous centuries.

When the nineteenth century began, the tonal system had already become a hierarchy in which every element was subordinated to the tension between tonic and dominant. Therefore, tonality could not be considered merely as a harmonic entity, but constituted a principle that also determined rhythm, melody, and form. Nothing could make the normal syntagmatic order of the chords I-III-VI-II / IV-V / VII-I (including the false cadence V-VI) unstable at the beginning of the Romantic era, even if with Romanticism the universal tonal language of music was starting to break down. On the one hand, this gradual collapse was triggered by sign processes intrinsic to the music, when each composer was constantly developing new ways to roam further from the center – that is, the tonic – of the musical "narration" (Greimas and Courtés 1979: 79–82 call this phenomenon *débrayage,* disengagement). It thus became more and more difficult to return to the tonic, till finally composers stopped trying to do so altogether. On the other hand, this dissolution of tonality also took place due to the relationship of music with outer reality.

How is tonality to be interpreted in a semiotic sense? Its existence as such can be taken as the deep structure of the immanent narrativity of music. The minimal condition for a story is that something becomes something else. As discussed in Chapter 1.3, Greimas describes this phenomenon with the formula S v O; i.e., the subject is "disjuncted" from an object, but regains that object in the course of the narration, i.e., becomes conjuncted wiht it: S ^ O. In this framework, the chordal movement from tonic toward dominant means "disjunction" from an "object", i.e., the tonic chord; and there also occurs a return, or "conjunction", with the object at the end. Greimas's "subject" and "object" are "actants", i.e., *dramatis personae,* which he extracted from the *Morphology of the Folktale* by the Russian formalist Vladimir Propp (1928). In folktales they normally appear along with other actants, such as helper, opponent, sender and receiver. To Greimas the concepts of subject and object have additional philosophical implications (see Greimas and Courtés 1979: 3–4). Narrativity can also become manifest on the surface level of musical discourse as a particular style or "gesture", in which sense it has most often been understood by traditional musicologists (e.g., Dahlhaus, Adorno, Newcomb, Meyer).

As early as the age of Classicism, music developed into an "absolute" or intrinsic sign language, and its highest manifestations, the symphony and sonata form, even penetrated the domain of opera. Nevertheless, music was also able to convey extramusical meanings on its surface level by means of "topics". In the Classical style, these refer to signs from the lower musical styles, such as functional music, military music, dance forms and so on, which are embedded in the surface texture of a musical piece (see Ratner 1980). Topics could also include musical styles from an earlier period, such as Baroque counterpoint in the *gebunden* style (with suspensions) or the "learned style". In some cases such a *topic* might have a direct indexical connection to a certain emotional state, as in dramatic "Storm and Stress" passages featuring diminished seventh chords or in the *empfindsamer* (sentimental or emotive) style, in which instrumental music imitated the expressivity of vocal music. Even graceful court culture was depicted by a topic of its own, the *galant* style, with its many ornamentations.

In the Classical style, however, the presence of *topics*, as signs referring to extrinsic reality, did not yet disturb the tonal hierarchy. When Roland Barthes (1964) compared a Classical literary text to a well-ordered linen-cupboard, he could just as well have been describing the music of that time. The topics served only to animate the basic tonal unfolding of a piece. In Romanticism, however, the relationship between music and the other arts intensified, and the impact of literature and painting could be felt more and more deeply in musical texts. First of all, Romanticism elaborated its own topics. In Franz Liszt's piano works, for example, the following topics can be distinguished (according to Grabócz 1986): (1) the Faustian question "why?", i.e., the search for something; (2) pastorality; (3) pantheistic sense of nature (4) religiosity; (5) storm and macabre struggle; (6) sorrow; (7) heroism. But more traditional aesthetic categories could also appear as musical topics; for example, the "sublime", as conveyed by slow, rising scale passages as found in the slow movement of Beethoven's Fifth Piano Concerto, the slow movement of Bruckner's Eighth Symphony, in the Grail-motive of Wagner's *Parsifal,* and the slow movement of Sibelius's Violin Concerto (see Tarasti 1992a). The semiotic mechanism through which such topics could be heard and distinguished operated with a mixture of iconic and symbolic (arbitrary or conventional) processes. The iconic form of a Faustian question and its topic may be based on ascending speech intonations accompanied by certain bodily gestures; these are iconically imitated in music by a rising melody that does not reach its culmination but is interrupted, thereby causing expectation on the part of the listener. Pastorality was created through the use of particular instruments and timbres, which evoked the pleasures of rustic life. In addition, the lilting, dotted *Siciliano* rhythm in compound meter was felt to be pastoral, in the same way as open fifths were considered an imitation of bagpipe drones in *musette* movements of Baroque dance suites. Thus, semiotic mechanisms for the musical enactment of various topics were abundant indeed. Even mythical associations could become recurrent topics, and composers used them consistently, and without collusion; for example, D minor as a demoniac key (beginning as early as Mozart's Piano Concerto in D minor) and as a balladic key, as occurs in Brahms, Liszt, Chopin, Wagner, and Glinka (see Tarasti 1979). In some cases the topics could be of a literary or philosophical origin; for example, the principles of dream and ecstasy, as formulated by Nietzsche in his *Die Geburt der Tragödie aus dem Geiste der Musik* (1872), also appeared as common topics in the music of the period.

Nevertheless, these topical signs of Romanticism applied only to individual, discrete signs of a musical piece, be they certain chords, melodic motives, rhythmic cells, or instrumental timbres. The syntactic combinations of the topics continued to take place according to the Classical tradition. The most conspicuous influence which the new emphasis on expressivity had on the structure of music could be found in the cogency of themes. They were characterized by the following attributes: (a) relatively simple chordal background; (b) clear-cut form; (c) a sufficient number of characteristic elements. These units of a theme may be considered "semes" as regards the content, and "phemes" with respect to the acoustical manifestation (these terms come from Greimas and Courtés 1979: 276 and 332–334, the former meaning the minimal unit of signification, the latter the minimal unit of phonetic expression). From these thematic units there emerged the compositional principle of "developing variation" (Schoenberg 1975: 164), which has also been described as the pervasive thematicity of music (Réti 1962). This refers to a method of composition by which one derives from a single theme an unlimited number of other themes, such that an entire composition could be integrated as a series of variants of the same theme, which thus achieved the status of a "type" or Peircean "legisign".

In the age of Romanticism, the idea of thematicity continued and became even more important as a cohesive force, at the same time as the tonic-dominant hierarchy was growing weaker (witness the surge of third-related key relationships). At the same time, themes began to carry extramusical messages – they became signs of certain narrative protagonists popular in the time of Romanticism. When a theme is taken to be the description of the character of a certain actor, then it loses part of its structural value as having possibilities for further development. The Romantics started to privilege themes that were *Lied*-like and hence could be cognized fully on first hearing, thus having an immediate impact by portraying their object iconically, indexically, and symbolically. But themes could then no longer be used so efficiently as a unifying force for the musical texture. Schubert's *Wanderer-Fantasy* is a case in point.

In the latter half of the nineteenth century, when functional harmony dissolved, themes assumed more crucial roles in musical form, as a fulcrum for the listener amid the constant modulations. This is the function of Wagnerian leitmotives in his late style's "musical prose" (Danuser 1975), which he considered an art of continuous transition.

Harmonically, Romantic music started to become an indexical enactment of emotions. The emotional values of dissonance and consonance – euphoric and dysphoric moods – gradually began to change. Dissonance, as a constant, unresolved, and pervasive tension, was no longer experienced merely as unstable or disturbing, but as sweet and tempting. In his *Oper und Drama,* Richard Wagner described his harmonic devices with the phrase *"Liebe bringt Lust und Leid"* ["Love brings pleasure and suffering"], thus exemplifying a mixed sensibility: "[…] so that the musician would feel himself inclined to move from the key corresponding to the first feeling to another, second feeling. The word *Lust* […] would in this phrase contain a completely different tone than in the other one […]. The tone with which it was sung would necessarily become a lead-tone determining another key, in which the word *Leid* is expressed" (Wagner, *Gesammelte Schriften,* vols. 10–11: 260). By "lead-tone" Wagner here does not mean the seventh scale-degree, but takes it as referring to an entity that bridges modulations to another key (i.e., another "isotopy", in the sense of Greimas). Moreover, if the aforementioned phrase were to be continued by another one such as: *"Doch in ihr Weh webt sie auch Wonnen"* ["However, into its woe it also weaves delight"], then the word *webt* would contain a modulation back to the first key, to which we would return being one experience richer. In Wagner's example, one and the same melodic phrase therefore subtly conveys several emotional states (cf. Greimas and Fontanille 1990, on the "modulations of passions"), and it functions as an index to euphoric and dysphoric feelings. In another essay, *Über die Anwendung der Musik auf das Drama,* Wagner takes a further example from Elsa's dream in *Lohengrin* (cf. the Nietzschean dream topic), in which seven different keys are passed through in a period of eight bars, which end by returning to the beginning key (Wagner, *Gesammelte Schriften,* vols. 12–14: 297; see Ex. 7).

*Ex. 7.*   Richard Wagner, *Lohengrin*, modulations in Elsa's Dream.

With this example Wagner illustrates his principle that one must stay within the same key as long as there is something to say in it. Such utterances by Wagner are rare, regardless of the fact that Romantic artists wrote abundant prose. For they tended not to reveal their professional secrets, that is to say, how they really wrote music or what the intrinsic sign processes were in their compositions. In their prose they moved almost exclusively on the level of musical signifieds, paying little attention to signifiers.

The role of harmony in Romantic music can justly be portrayed as a signifier / signified relation, in the sense that the audible harmonies were emanations of the human psyche, and particularly its "will" (Schopenhauer 1879 II: 582). Harmonies thus clearly possessed a sign content – a signified – which motivated them. For instance, in Wagner's operas certain chords acquire a symbolic value when they express or describe some narrative topic. In *Lohengrin* the mere A major tonic conveys the sphere of the Grail; in the *Ring des Nibelungen* the chords of the Walhalla motive are firmly anchored in D flat major; the sword motive mostly appears in C major; and so on. At the same time, the chords retained their syntagmatic and paradigmatic dimensions: they could easily produce tension when they were joined together syntagmatically, while at the same time attracting the ear by their color. Regarding this latter aspect, composers had many paradigmatic variations on their palette. As a typical illustration, one can take enharmonically altered chords, in which the coloristic effect is created by the alternation of two distantly-related chords. The chords in Boris's coronation scene in Musorgsky's opera *Boris Godunov* (Ex. 8a) and the brass signals in Rimsky-Korsakov's *Scheherazade* (Ex. 8b) function according to this principle.

In some cases the chords can be both tense and coloristic (see LaRue 1992), as in the death motive in Wagner's *Valkyrie,* in which the effect of gloom, fear, and strangeness is created by his combining

*Ex. 8a.* Modest Mussorgsky, *Boris Godunov*, enharmonic devices in the chords depicting Boris's coronation. ·

*Ex. 8b.* Nikolai Rimsky-Korsakov, *Scheherazade*, enharmonic enharmonic chord alterations in fanfares.

the tonic chord of D minor and the dominant seventh chord of F sharp major. The major / minor alternation could in itself function as a sign, as occurs in Brünnhilde's greeting of the sun, with its consecutive A major and A minor tonic chords (*Siegfried*, Act III).

In general, harmonic development in a piece of music was often meant to express the unconscious. Naturally, Wagner's famous Tristan chord, of which there are innumerable analyses and interpretations, is in the first place a tension-bearing chord with its appoggiaturas and ambiguity as to key, but it also serves as a symbol of longing throughout the whole opera. Interpreting "life as a prelude to some unknown song of which death plays the first notes" (so goes Lamartine's poem), the Romantics thought that music existed precisely to express such an expectation.

In late Romanticism, chordal appoggiaturas remained unresolved to an ever greater extent, as in the extremely dissonant, "catastrophic" chords of Mahler's symphonies, where they also function as signs of extremely contradictory and agitated emotions. It is characteristic of Wagner's late style that he uses many diminished seventh chords. It is noteworthy that their resolutions, too, are often surprising and irregular. The result is music that sounds as if it were in constant transition, in which one can never know at the beginning of a phrase in which key it will end. (An analogous phenomenon in literature at the turn of the century was Prousts's novelistic style, a kind of "Wagnerian" prose.)

As one culmination of Romantic distance from the tonic, Alexander Scriabin developed his famous *Prometheus* chord, which, in various transpositions, constituted whole pieces. Although compositions based on this chord were aurally experienced as one continuous and unbroken dominant function, Scriabin's idea was to treat it as if it were a tonic. By writing music in which extremely centrifugal elements were heard as new centers, he came close to atonality. According to him, the Prometheus chord could be reduced to smaller units of "second articulation", so that they consisted of the softness of a diminished fourth (= major third), the hardness of the pure fourth, and the conflicting, demoniac qualities of the augmented fourth (= tritone). In semiotic terms, the chord was made up of several different phemes and semes, i.e., minimal units of musical expression and content.

Despite all this, the compositions of the Romantic age still obeyed the principles of tonality in the building of global form. In some cases the harmonic deep structure, i.e., the succession of the chords and their scale-degrees, is reflected and repeated as melodic structure on the surface level. For example, the famous central motive of Schubert's *Erlkönig* is at the same time the essential bass line of the tonal course of the whole piece (as Kielian-Gilbert 1987 has shown). Similarly, the notes written for the "light organ" in Scriabin's *Prometheus* provide an harmonic analysis of the whole piece (as remarked by Yuri Kholopov).

In constructing extensive musical texts and syntagms on the basis of such tonal deep structures, the Romantics also often employed the old principle of *horror vacui* by creating long "implication structures" (Meyer 1973: 114 passim) or *Linienphasen* (line phases; Kurth 1922: 23). Romantic melodies were based to a great extent upon the background harmonies. Often a melody was no more than the linearisation of some harmonic idea. An example is the transition theme in Chopin's *Scherzo in C sharp minor*, before the *coda*. As a counterbalance to the regular and symmetrical periodicity of the Viennese Classics, Romantic melodies tended to express a certain "kinetic" energy in their continuous movement, with the Wagnerian "endless" melody as the ideal. In addition, melody was characterized by the expansion of range, dynamics, and by large, expressive and dramatic intervallic leaps. On the other hand, melodies served as signs of the actors in musical narration. Many gestural themes by Liszt are of this kind; for, example the main motive of his piano piece *Vallée d'Obermann* can be taken as a portrayal of the character of the hero, the musical interpretant of the main figure of the novel by Etienne de Sénancour (1892). While the weak aspect of such gestural themes was that they could not be developed but only repeated (as Adorno 1952: 35), they enabled the listener to follow such narratives in sonatas and symphonies through psychological identification with the actorial gestures. The heroes of Berlioz's or Mahler's symphonies are not at all the composers themselves: the subjects of enunciation and the enunciate have to be separated. Nevertheless, in many cases Romantic composers consciously strived to erase this distinction. For instance, Wagner rearranged important events of his life in his autobiography, *Mein Leben*

(1963), so that the invention of central themes or ideas in his work coincided with biographically notable dates: the Good Friday music of *Parsifal* would thus have been written on a Good Friday, and the idea for the prelude to *Rhinegold,* which depicts streaming water, would have come to him while he was listening to the waves in the canals of Venice.

Thus, in musical communication melodies had an emotive function, in Jakobson's sense (1963: 214). They forced one to pay attention to the experiences of the sender of the message, the composer himself. Some biographical studies have revealed connections between the creation of melodies and events in the lives of composers, such as the *idée fixe* of Berlioz alluding to his love; the "Christ" theme of Sibelius's Second Symphony evoking his trip to Rapallo, Italy; or Janáček's string quartet *Intimate Letters* referring to his love affairs. The age of Romanticism favored just such a naive way of listening to melodies.

The Romantic period emphasized originality in the construction of melodies, yet did not exclude musical quotation (cf. Karbusicky 1992). For instance, Brahms cited the *Emperor Hymn* in the Finale of his Piano Sonata in F minor, and Wagner borrowed the main theme of Liszt's *Faust Symphony* as a motive of Sieglinde in the second act of *Valkyrie.* Especially important were quotations from folk music, which formed a genre of its own and helped create national styles. All these cases represent attempts to embed iconic signs in music. National iconicity thus became a very important sign category in music, by which one could establish connections not only between folk and art music, but also between a composition and a place of birth, country, climate, nature, or general spiritual atmosphere.

Moreover, Romantic melodies, even in instrumental genres, were often closely related to those of vocal music. Although his melodies were not meant to be hummed like an aria by Bellini, Chopin's *cantabile* melodic style formed a kind of intertext in his works, by referring to *bel canto* singing gestures. (By "intertext" I understand a section or phrase which in one text evokes another text, be it of a musical, visual, literary or any other nature; see Kristeva 1969: 443). On the other hand, the virtuosity of various instruments gave rise to special *Spiel-*

*figuren* melodies (cf. Besseler 1957), such as one finds in Paganini and Liszt .

In the area of rhythmic-temporal qualities of music, too, Romanticism tried to break with regularity and conventionality. Syncopation (e.g., Beethoven's *"Appassionata"*, third movement) and caesuras (especially the long *fermate* pauses in Bruckner symphonies) acquired a special symbolic value. Romanticism was mainly, however, a period of long, slow movements and *rallentandos*. We find a sign of this kind as early as with the *ritardandos* at the beginning of Beethoven's Piano Sonata in E flat major (Op. 31 No. 3). Such passages serve as "anti-indexes" in music, inasmuch as they retard the normal temporal process. Romanticism favored not only such extreme *ritardandos* but also the other extreme, of frantic, forward-rushing rhythmic climaxes (e.g., Chopin's Piano Sonata in B minor, last movement).

Nonetheless, the rhythms of Romanticism were still bound to the motions and movements of the human body. Roland Barthes has shown how the syncopated pulses of Schumann's piano music are based upon special *somathemes,* the smallest units of bodily rhythm. The body "speaks", as it were, through such units (see Barthes 1975). Schumann's *C-major Fantasy* typifies the Romantic attitude toward time: the abrupt alternations of accelerandos and adagios in the first movement, the extremely energetic figuration based on repeated dotted rhythms in the second movement, and the extraordinarily slow and halting music of the third movement. It is precisely such formations, freed from the chains of periodic rhythms, which Ferruccio Busoni took as progressive elements in Beethoven and Schumann, namely, those moments in which they anticipated "absolute music": "In general, in the introductory and passing movements, preludes and transitions the tone poets came closest to the true nature of music, where they believed that they had left symmetric relations without notice and seemed to breathe unconsciously and freely ..." (Busoni 1916: 11).

Any rhythmic elements can become marked features that assume various sign functions in musical discourse (see Hatten 1994). As early as Beethoven, and even earlier in Haydn, pauses form an essential part of the musical text. The main motive of the last movement of the *"Waldstein"* Sonata effectively illustrates three typical features of

Romanticism: the expansion of a melody to cover three octaves, the pause filled by the bass note c before the upbeat in the upper part of the melody, and the timbre which for some listeners evokes a sunrise.

In the Romantic period, timbre served a special sign function, not just in the development of orchestration techniques, but also by playing a special *Klangfarben* melodic role. Richard Wagner believed that the orchestra had a specific *"Sprachvermögen"* or speaking ability (Voss 1970: 27). The orchestra was needed in order to realize the poetic intention; and the instruments, considered as extensions of the human voice, also correlated closely with actors' gestures.

On the other hand, Wagner's orchestration aimed at idealizing timbre, by making the source of the sound disappear (e.g., in Bayreuth's opera house, among other places, the conductor and the orchestra were not visible to the audience). The physical sender of the sound had to be concealed so that the sound could create a perfect illusion. In Wagner's scores every instrument has its particular basic meaning – a denotation – which has been compared to that of the words of a language (Voss 1970). Yet in operatic art, the orchestration must serve the dramatic situation, which provides the instrumental denotations with connotations that in turn depend upon the context. Hence, in Wagner the violins playing in their upper register is symbolic of the Grail, of sublimity, of religiosity, depicting the modality of *"süsse Wonne"* (sweet joy). The violas have a forlorn, sad meaning; Berlioz, too, defines the tone of the violas as one of deep melancholy (Berlioz and Strauss 1904: 67). The violoncellos express passions, but also need and disaster. The contrabasses depict gloom and foreboding. The flute provides light effects, but does not occur very often in Wagner as an independent musical actor. The oboe refers to naivety and innocence, but also to sorrow, nostalgia, and pastorality. The English horn depicts sadness and plaintiveness (in Berlioz it signifies dreaming and the evocation of distant events, as in Marguerite's aria in the *Damnation of Faust*). The clarinet in Wagner represents love and eroticism. The horn, an instrument of hunting, refers to nature in general. It depicts solemnity and rejoicing, and for some interpreters of Wagner, it signifies the call of a "lost paradise" (see Claudel 1970). The trumpet is an instrument of heroes and rulers; according to Liszt it is "brilliant" and "radiant", but also provides a tinge of religiosity. The trombones portray festivity, nobility and sublimity. The harp serves as an index of a certain local or historical color (as in the singing contest of Wartburg in *Tannhäuser*). In sum, orchestration is crucial for creating meanings in music. It animates the musical structure and furnishes it with semiotic modalities.

### 2.2.2 Modernism

For music, the rise of Modernism, as against the late Romanticism and Symbolism of the turn of the nineteenth to the twentieth century, meant semiotically the dissolution of the unified tonal language inherited from Classicism. When tonality collapsed, the central force that had held music together collapsed with it, and "disengaged" tendencies were set in motion. Nevertheless, narrative elements based on tonality have maintained their importance in many musical areas, particularly in popular and media music (cinema, TV, video, multi-media), which had expanded to all countries of the world by the end of the twentieth century. In addition, a transition from what Marshall McLuhan called a "cold" to a "hot" society took place (see Charbonnier 1970), and the changes that occurred in all areas of communication with growing rapidity also took place in the language and style of music (cf. Chailley 1977).

   In the Classic-Romantic period, communication was thought to be a simple transmission of the musical message from the composer to a listener who had learned the right codes and could understand the "musical language". Now this unidirectional chain was broken. From a semiotic perspective, the greatest dilemma of Modernism seems to be that the listener cannot receive both its code and its message at the same time. Without any familiar point of reference in the music, any level of "first articulation", its reception becomes awkward. Modern music corresponds to the worldview of "modern" man, who finds himself to be a "decentered" subject, ejected from the center of being. This explains the anti-narrative tendency in many styles of contemporary music.

The dissolution of the old tonal language came about through these changes (LaRue 1992): (a) *Expanded diatonicism*, understood as the inclusion of larger and larger chords of superposed thirds and the free exchange of major and minor forms of the same key. (b) *Chromaticism*: beginning with Wagner's *Tristan*, composers started to use chromatically altered chords so that the leading tone lost its indexical function completely, and any tone could lead to any key whatsoever. (c) *Neomodality*: a generalization of the development of national musical styles. However unique they may be, on the harmonic-technical level even such different national music styles as those of France and Finland may resemble each other, due to the presence of modal elements (in the musical sense of "Church modes" and other non-major/ minor-based harmonic components), such as I-bVII or Vb3-I or IV-i. Also, "exotic" scales came into use, as the consciousness of music cultures outside Europe increased. Debussy's fascination with pentatonic scales, for example, can be traced to his hearing of Javanese gamelan music at the Paris World Exposition in 1899. Musical language opened up to intercultural exchanges. For instance, Béla Bartók (1957) systematically exploited folk music modes and developed a theory of how to harmonize peasant melodies in accordance with their original spirit. (d) *Structural dissonance*: this refers to the habituation to dissonances, starting with the added sixth and leading to the acceptance of dissonant chord structures, such as the tonic MM7 at cadences, as one finds in the music of Debussy, Villa-Lobos, and many others. (e) *Bitonality and polytonality*: these occur when two or more superimposed keys prevail over long sections of music, as two or more simultaneous "isotopies" (i.e., levels of meaning). An example is the simultaneous use of F major and F sharp minor in *Botafogo*, one of the pieces in Milhaud's *Saudades do Brasil*. In some cases polytonality arose from the presentation of incongruous yet overlapping events, as in Charles Ives's symphonic triptych, *Three Places in New England*. With bitonality a new way of listening to music also developed, which, often anachronistically, reinterpreted harmonic configurations in earlier styles (Milhaud would hear certain musical passages by J. S. Bach as "bitonal", e.g.). (f) *Atonality*: this refers to the conscious avoidance of tonality by the favoring of antitonal (hence, centrifugal) forces by means of the negation of repetition. All twelve notes of the octave became equivalent; their intrinsic hierarchy disappeared altogether. A serialized tonal language emerged, based upon the "row", its inversion, retrograde, and inversion of retrograde, as well as their transposition to all the remaining pitches. These elements constituted a matrix that functioned as the basis for the work of composing. The main pioneers of the serial school were Arnold Schoenberg and Anton Webern.

The matrix of serial music can be compared to the elements of second articulation in language, i.e., phonemic units, the only difference being that the elements of a twelve-tone matrix do not form recognizable lexicographical units. On the mere basis of aural perception, it is impossible to discern which row is used and when. No figures are repeated, and the music remains fixed in its "design" (David Lidov's term), yet it remains weakly articulated despite the fact that it is based on a certain "grammar". With multi-serialism, not only pitches but other musical parameters were also serialized. Olivier Messiaen's *Mode de valeurs et d'intensités* (1948–1949) was one of the first compositions to realize ideals of comprehensive serialism.

The development of serialism and multi-serialism reduced composing to a mere process of calculation and led to the loss of the physiological level of music – its "somathemes", topics, and other conventional properties. There has been much debate about whether serial music was a language at all. For Lévi-Strauss (1964: 32–34), it was not a language, since the first level of articulation had been erased entirely. According to Jankélévitch (1961), "Orpheus does no longer return" in serial music, which is thus doomed to sink into a meaningless state. It is hard to imagine how a completely serialized piece of music might be analyzed semiotically.

Some of the earlier dodecaphonic music retained familiar elements from earlier periods on some levels of articulation. A good example is the "row" *cum* main theme of Alban Berg's Violin Concerto, which consists of a chain of traditional, arpeggiated triads (save for the last two notes). In spite of being serialized, this row still has strong tonal implications, as does some of the dodecaphonic music of Einojuhani Rautavaara (cf. Sivuoja-Gunaratnam 1997).

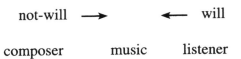

*Figure 3.*   Daniel Charles's principles of will and not-will in musical
            communication.

In the years following World War II, serial composers sought to gain complete control over all musical parameters. Nevertheless, aurally, their works sounded improvised and random. In this way serial music faced a problem that, as Bukofzer notes (1947), the Baroque age had already encountered: should music be based upon "inaudible form" or on "audible structure"?

Notwithstanding this problem, the idea of a grammar ruling over music came into fashion at the beginning of the twentieth century. The Russian formalists – in literature, film, painting, as well as in music – argued that the inspiration of the artist was no longer relevant; what mattered aesthetically were the artistic devices used in producing a work of art. Later, Igor Stravinsky (1947) argued that music could not reflect anything as subjective as a human soul. As early as the 1920s Vassily Kandinsky had already attempted to construct a universal grammar of all arts whose elements were lines, points, and planes. According to him, these arts included dance and music; for example, he analysed the beginning of Beethoven's Fifth Symphony on the basis of these concepts (Kandinsky 1926). Music inspired the architect Le Corbusier to elaborate a semiotic system of architecture based upon the smallest units, which he called "modules" (Le Corbusier 1951–1958). This approach, which used the smallest significant units to form larger texts through a kind of *ars combinatoria,* was already structuralism in its purest form.

Nevertheless, twentieth-century music history cannot be interpreted as a progressive march toward serialism, despite the fact that many composers and critics in the 1950s and 1960s took this as the only "progressive" line. In the 1920s, Neoclassicism emerged, which sought to restore the stylistic characteristics of the Classical and Baroque eras, such as reduced instrumental forces, a kind of distanced or restrained expressivity, as well as myths of antiquity (an example is the collaboration of Jean Cocteau with Igor Stravinsky). Above all, Neoclassicism respected the virtues of clarity and transparency, made ironic use of musical devices inherited from such composers as J. S. Bach and Pergolesi, and favored playfulness, hilarity and lightness. In this sense, the Neoclassicists (such as Poulenc, in his *Concerto for Two Pianos*) could be taken as precursors of the Postmodernists of the 1980s. The manifestations of Neoclassicism were manifold. Musically it could appear as a pandiatonicism inspired by folk music, as a kind of petrified folklore as exemplified in the reconstructions of Mexican Indian music by Carlos Chavez, or *Kanteletar* arrangements by the Finnish *Lied* composer Yrjö Kilpinen. It could also appear in the phonetic treatment of a text, by ignoring the meaning of the word level, as exemplified by Stravinsky's method of Latin versification in his *Oedipus rex*. Even Ferruccio Busoni could be taken as a representative of "young classicality" (Beaumont 1985), in his desire to utilize musical expressions of the past by putting them into firm and durable forms.

In the 1960s, avant-garde composers became familiar with structural linguistics and found inspiration in semiotic sources. Thus, Luciano Berio's *Sinfonia* contains not only semiotically polyvalent collage techniques, but also borrowings from Claude Lévi-Strauss's structuralist texts (e.g., *Le cru et le cuit*). Pierre Boulez, a representative of a strict serialist school, also aimed to elucidate the rhythmic devices of Stravinsky's *Sacre du printemps* (1971 and 1986). Umberto Eco (1968) attempted to articulate the difference between *"pensée structurelle"* – i.e., serial thought – and *"pensée structurale"* (structural thought): whereas the former kind of thinking creates structures, the latter only discovers them. The last-mentioned way of thinking became a kind of episteme behind the music of the 1980s and early 1990s. The shift from structuralist thinking, with its orientation towards the object, to the cognitive age, with its emphasis on the subject, is also manifested in the sign processes of music itself. As a reaction to the extreme rationalism and reductionism of the serialist school, two new trends appeared in music: so-called *musique pauvre,* with John Cage as its main apologist, and minimalism. John Cage rejected the serialist idea of maximal control, since the more one controls the music, the more one is controlled by it. Cage's philosophy of freedom was also influenced by medieval mysticism, oriental doctrines, as well as the American transcendentalists Thoreau (1854) and Emerson (1836; cf. 1979). Daniel Charles has aptly described Cage's music as *"musique du non-vouloir"*, music of not-will (Charles 1987–1988). The less the composer's will tries to dominate the listener, the more room there remains for the will of the listener in the musical process.

Cage wanted to permit each person, as well as each sound, to be the center of creation (Charles 1981). His musical ideal was the peaceful symmetry of Satie's pieces, an ideal also realized in some music of the latter half of the twentieth century, particularly that of the Arvo Pärt. *Musique pauvre* characteristically plays with the dialectics between scanty yet present elements and elements which are absent but implied by the former. For instance, Cage's *Music of Changes* (1961) consists only of a series of pointillistic sound events, whose coherence and consistency remains entirely the responsibility of the listener. Such music activates the listener's modal activities, forcing him or her to fill with modalities the gaps in the aural musical form (on Minimalism, see Tarasti 1988a).

Minimalism, too, tries to put listeners into a state in which they merge with the musical process (Reich 1981). Minimalism's excessive diatonicism and endless repetitions of triadic figures are not historical allusions to the historical period of tonal music, but a phenomenon analogous to the tests that psychologists use to study people's cognitive perception of music (Deutsch 1982). Minimalist music is an "ecstasy" of repetition, in the sense in which Baudrillard (1987) describes the "ecstasy" of communication in the modern world. Whereas repetition functioned in earlier music as an articulating principle against a background of non-recurrence (entropy), it has now lost this marked character. Hence even the slightest changes during these endless repetitions can be experienced as factors that shape the form – as *"différances"* in the Derridean sense of both differences and deferrals (cf. Derrida 1967). In this context, repetition can no longer perform the task which the Russian formalists assigned it, i.e., to serve as an agent of surprise. Despite the active figuration on the surface level, Minimalist music gives the impression of being extremely static, a succession of reified "now"-moments. Semiotically speaking, these moments represent pure durativity, in the sense that they have neither beginning nor end and, in fact, no temporal articulation at all. In this sense, Minimalism, too, is totally anti-narrative.

Minimalism has abandoned narrativity, as Postmodernism has given up belief in what Lyotard calls *les grandes récits*, or master narratives. Minimalists such as Steve Reich and Philip Glass find music completely subjectless. In Arvo Pärt a modicum of narrativity remains; nevertheless, all his works sound as if under the hidden rubric of "the last story". In spite of their abundant repetitions, Pärt's works are like expanded cadences. They maintain the illusion of narrativity by means of musical signs and allusions, symbols, indexes, and icons, such as minor-mode keys, bells, sounds of a string ensemble, canonic techniques, and so on.

In the history of twentieth-century music, electronic music forms its own line of development, even if it could be taken as a continuation of experiments in man-machine communication started as early as in the Baroque era by Kircher (1650). Tape music facilitated *"musique concrète"*, i.e., the use of everyday noises as material for compositions. As early as 1915 Russolo had classified various sounds in his *The Art of Noises*. Even earlier, the real anvils which Wagner used in *Rheingold* in order to depict the work of the Nibelungs in Nibelheim were an instance of the use of noise in music. Various techniques of sound synthesis also made possible the transformation of such natural noises as the murmur of the wind, the rush of the waves, the sound of falling water, and so on. Undoubtedly, noises in music are elements of the first articulation (Martinet), i.e., words that have a certain denotation on the basis of their recognition. Still, how one can create a continuum or syntagm out of such signs, and finally even music with a plot, remains a fundamental question raised by tape music. Semiotic aspects of electronic music have rarely been pondered systematically (for an exception, see Grabócz 1991–1992). Most often research in this area has focussed on ways of producing new sound material, and not on its signification or its aesthetics (see, e.g., the classical treatise *Traité des objets musicaux* by Pierre Schaeffer [1966], as well as the ongoing research conducted at IRCAM). A special style of contemporary music is that of "spectral music", which experiments with synthetic transformations of overtones, turning the composer, who uses computers and synthesizers as a "chisels", into a kind of musical sculptor who can delete certain regions from the natural tones and work on what remains. A typical feature of spectral music, such as that of Murail, Grisey, Scelsi, and Saariaho, is its extremely static quality, such that the starting point is sometimes only a single instrument playing one note, which is electronically varied in many ways. This kind of music seems to subsist on the "subsemantic" level of "protointonations" (Leman 1992).

The electronic communication technology of the twentieth century not only made all the style periods of Western art music simultaneously present but also brought extra-European music cultures to the fore. Thanks to recordings made by music anthropologists and to ease of travelling, composers of art music have, to an ever greater extent, been exposed to all kinds of popular and folk music. As examples one could take Ligeti, who in the 1980s was influenced by African music, Reich by oriental music, Messiaen by Indian music. The overwhelming abundance of messages flowing from all sides has relativized tonal languages. Music listeners have become passive receivers who, with radio and TV channels turned on all the time, listen to music only with one ear. Music has become mere sound *dans les coulisses*, a landscape, a tonosphere. Adam Krims (2001) has studied this aspect of music as a commodity. At the same time, the triumph of tonal music has continued in film music. Hollywood composers and producers of music for TV-series have preserved the denotations of certain leitmotives and topics of the Classic-Romantic style period, which they transform according to their needs. The same elements are used in the "mood music" of doctors' and dentists' waiting rooms, in stores, airports, and elsewhere. Through these pervasive musical practices, almost the whole population of the globe has become sensitized to the tension-detension mechanism of tonal music. It is almost impossible for a contemporary person to attain the freshness of Firstness when encountering music.

## 2.3 History of musical scholarship in the light of semiotics

In the area of music theory and analysis, German-speaking academe produced two remarkable music scholars who may be considered as proto-semioticians: the Austrian Heinrich Schenker (1868–1935) and the Swiss Ernst Kurth (1886–1946). Schenker's theoretical system was formed on the basis of historical research into musical performance practices and composition sketches (particularly those of Beethoven), and guided by German philosophy (e.g., Goethe's morphology). According to Schenker, the great composers (all of whom were German-speaking representatives of the Classic-Romantic period) improvised their musical works out of a deep structure which he called the *Ursatz* (the resonance of the term with Goethe's *Urpflänze* is probably not coincidental). The *Ursatz* in turn was based on nature itself in the form of the first tones of the overtone series, which together constitute a major triad, the *Urklang*. By various operations, the composer moves from this chord to the *Hintergrund* (background) through the *Mittelgrund* (middleground) to the V*ordergrund* (foreground), the latter level being the one on which music is actually heard (see, among others, Neumeyer 1988 and a deconstructionist interpretation of Schenker by Littlefield 2001).

This typically "structuralist" idea was the foundation for Schenker's method of music analysis. Schenker did not consider his method as a science but as the practice of an art. Its great merit was that it took a composition's structure as a continuum in which every event was significant and had its rightful place. Thus, temporally separated tonal events became meaningful when they formed a part of the *Urlinie,* the fundamental melodic line whose descent creates the tensional course of a piece. This method accounts well for the fundamentally kinetic nature of music. Schenker could be criticized, however, for excessive axiomaticity and reductionism, in that he always reduced music to the same *Ursatz,* thus leveling style differences between musical pieces and between individual composers. After his death, Schenker's approach was taken up in the United States, where it became a dominant method of analysis. When musicologist Fred Lerdahl and linguist Ray Jackendoff published their seminal work A *Generative Theory of Tonal Music* (1985), it became obvious that Schenker's model was very similar to Noam Chomsky's "tree-model" of linguistic phrase structure. Yet in fact, it was Leonard Bernstein, in his *Unanswered Question* (1976), who first suggested the parallel between generating a piece of music and a linguistic utterance. As early as the 1960s semioticians had supposed that language and music were analogous phenomena since they both consisted of chains of acoustic signals (cf. Posner 1988), and this view was reinforced in Schenker's model.

Ernst Kurth's "energetic" conception of music has only recently been considered a precursor of musical semiotics. His views have proved particularly useful as a counterbalance to the segmentational and taxonomic methods of semiotic music analysis in the 1980s. Kurth stressed the energetic, continuous nature of music, not the separate, discrete signifiers, i.e., the signs perceived by the auditory sense. What mattered for Kurth was the signified, the kinetic energy pulsating behind the notes. He even spoke of notes as having "a will to a chord". In this sense he joins the philosophical epistemes of the turn of the century, e.g., Henri Bergson's view of two kinds of time: *temps d'espace* (space time), which could be physically measured, and *temps de durée* (duration), which was phenomenal, experienced time (see, e.g., Bergson 1975). Kurth also emphasized the temporal nature of music; for him, the pertinent aspect in music was the experience of movement. In his *Grundlagen des linearen Kontrapunkts* (1922), a study of J. S. Bach's melodic style, Kurth stated: "The experience of movement which is felt in a melody is not only a kind of subsidiary psychological phenomenon, but it brings us to the very origin of the melodic element. This element, which is felt as a force flowing through tones, and the sensual intensity of the sound itself, they both refer to the basic powers in the musical formation, namely to the energies, which we experience as psychic tensions" (Kurth 1922: 3). Kurth can be considered a semiotician in three senses. He taught (1) that the sound stimulus of music always functions as a sign for something (semantics); (2) that attention must be paid to what happens in the mind when one is listening to music (cognition); (3) that analysis starts "inside" and moves toward the "outside", i.e., from deep structure to the surface (structuralist and generativist approach). Kurth's basic analytic units are the *"Bewegungsphase"* (motion phase) and the *"Linien-zug"* (line course). A musical segment lasts only so long as there is enough power in its initial impulse to keep the motion going. Kurth's theory thus revolutionizes traditional segmentational criteria and might be applied successfully to contemporary works hitherto considered to be non-segmentational; for example, pieces using field techniques and those with freely pulsative movement (from Ligeti to Penderecki to Minimalism), and spectral and computer music. Kurth did not develop an explicit analytic procedure, though his theories always remained closely connected to musical practice; for example, his treatise *Romantische Harmonik and ihre Krise* (1923) deals with Wagnerian chromaticism, and his most extensive analyses are of Bruckner's symphonies (1925).

Other great music theoreticians from German-speaking academe have found less acceptance. Hugo Riemann (1849–1919) was considered out-dated in the context of 1960s structuralism, since he believed in the myth of tonality as a principle of nature. Alfred Lorenz (1868–1939) was regarded as a scholar whose system did violence to music, when he forced entire Wagnerian symphonic textures into medieval bar-form (two *Stollen* followed by one *Abgesang).* The fault in his analysis was that its basic units could be stretched to be as long or as short as necessary to fit his external categorizations. Nevertheless Lorenz's main work, *Das Geheimnis der Form bei Wagner* (1924–1933), was one of the first attempts at a complete analysis of Wagner's music that was not limited to merely hermeneutic interpretation. Moreover, Lorenz provided several insights about leitmotive technique, melodies, and other aspects of Wagner's music.

Lorenz also inspired the Finnish musicologist Ilmari Krohn to create his own theory and system of music analysis, which was based, as Lorenz's was, on rhythmic units. Krohn's efforts to apply his system to Sibelius's symphonies proved unsuccessful, however, particularly his attempt to reduce Sibelius's music to Wagnerian leitmotive technique and to find programmatic associations for each of his symphonies (Krohn 1945). More significantly, Krohn's method of classifying folk tunes inspired Béla Bartók in his investigations in folk music. Krohn's brother Kaarle, and uncle Julius, a literary scholar, together with the folklorist Antti Aarne, created a model for classifying folk tales, which was later adopted by Vladimir Propp (see Aarne and Thompson 1961; Propp 1928).

The musical hermeneutics of Arnold Schering (1877–1941) can be taken as a semiotic attempt to analyze musical signifieds. As pointed out above (Chap. 1.2), however, Schering (1936) clearly exaggerated when arguing that behind every instrumental piece by Beethoven stood some literary program borrowed from Goethe or Schiller. He was nevertheless correct that, in a composer's mind, a program sometimes functions as scaffolding. Yet as soon as the composition is accomplished, the music begins to live by its own power. From Henri Bergson's philosophy there emerged another line of research, likewise postulating temporality as the central musical parameter. Among others, phenomenologist Gisèle Brelet examined musical performance in his *l'interprétation créatrice* (1951), and came to the conclusion that melody originated in natural language. Earlier, Vincent d'Indy (1851–1931), in his *Cours de composition musicale* (1897–1900: 30), had theorized that melody emerged from different ways of uttering a verbal phrase, such that the syllables became "musicalized". In his example, the phrase *Il a quitté la ville* could be pronounced neutrally, interrogatively, or affirmatively, its intonation being determined by two kinds of accent, "tonic" and "pathetic". Thus d'Indy anticipated later theories on the modalities of language and music.

On the basis of language inflection and influenced by Kurth, Boris V. Asafiev (1884–1948) developed his intonation theory, which became the prevailing theory and analytic method in Eastern Europe for many years after World War II. Asafiev was a prolific writer who also published under the pseudonym Igor Glebow. His main work, *Musical Form as a Process*, translated into English in 1976, was written during the siege of Leningrad, which partly explains its sometimes incoherent structure. When Asafiev died in 1948 he was the only musical representative in the Academy of Sciences in the Soviet Union. Asafiev's basic concept was "intonation", which paired any musical element – interval, chord, rhythm, motive, timbre – with its emotional value or content. In its aim to unite musical signifiers and signifieds, this theory was inherently semiotic. He also emphasized the mobile character of music, and presupposed that intonations formed chains of functions such as *initium* (beginning), *motus* (movement), and *terminus* (ending, cadence). He hypothesized that "stores" of intonation were formed from characteristic musical passages, and that these repositories of intonations remained in the collective memory of listeners. These stores contain the bases of the way people feel in a given period, such that music could be sensed as "true speech". When people's thinking changes, new intonations arise. Asafiev studied such an intonation crisis in connection with the French Revolution.

The sociological aspect of Asafiev's theory anticipated later ideas in the Tartu School of Semiotics, although it was burdened with the conservative view of folk music as a kind of "primary modelling system" that determines the development of art music (this thesis was used in Zhdanov's negative criticism of Shostakovich and Prokofiev). In the West, Asafiev remained almost completely unknown, until music semioticians in the 1970s rediscovered his work. His theories were adapted to modern narratology by Viatcheslaw W. Medushewski, who distinguished between protointonation – an expressive shape, such as a cry or exclamation, without any compositional articulation – from musical intonation in the proper sense. Medushewski has also presented typologies of inner, first-person narrators in music, such as a lyrical, dance-like, or meditative "I". Asafiev's theories have been further applied by Joseph Kon, Yury Kholopov, Yevgeny Nazaikinsky, and have influenced the work of Jaroslav Jiranek (e.g., his *Grundfragen der musikalischen Semiotik* [1985]), and Hungarian academician Jozseph Ujfalussy (e.g., 1968). Moreover, some present-day studies of popular music reflect the influence of Asafiev, as in the theory of "hooks" of popular song (Frith 1978, 1984 et al.) and the "affect analysis" of popular music (Tagg 1979).

In the United States musicology gained in stature when, fleeing Nazi oppression, many German scholars emigrated there from Europe. According to the specialties of these musicologists, strong interest developed in the study of performance practices of early music, in archival research, and in ethnomusicology. However, few new works appeared dealing with analytic methods and philosophical-aesthetic interpretation of music. Scholars were often satisfied with European models, as Schenker's popularity shows. Nevertheless, some figures stand out as pioneers of musical semiotics in the US.

As a precursor of modern ethnomusicology, Charles Seeger pondered deeply the semiotic problems of music, and it is unfortunate that his epoch-making essay "On the Moods of a Music Logic" (1960) was left out of discussions of musical semiotics in the 1960s and 1970s. In that essay, Seeger presented a structuralist model of analysis in which various musical parameters were divided into their smallest units, called "moods", which could be combined into larger entities. Seeger also studied the semiotic nature of transcription in ethnomusicology as a prescriptive or descriptive procedure, and dealt with issues of value in music (Seeger 1977).

The term "semiotics" rarely appears in Leonard B. Meyer's extensive work in music analysis and aesthetics, though he nevertheless dwells on semiotic problems. His distinction between referential and embodied meanings in music analyzes the eternal problem of music aesthetics: the nature of musical meaning and its place as either inside or outside the music itself. Meyer's most outstanding analytical work is *Explaining Music* (1973), in which he presents a model of analysis based upon the concept of implication. He argues that our musical expectations are determined by certain melodic archetypes, such as symmetry, axis, triad, the "gap-fill" principle, and so on. On their basis, the beginning of a piece of music implies a certain continuation and end. His analysis, e.g., of Wagner's *Tristan* prelude and Beethoven's sonata *"Les adieux"*, illustrates this theory convincingly (see also, Treitler 1989 and Rowell 1983).

Susanne K. Langer (1895–1985) numbers among the foremost American semioticians (cf. Sebeok 1991: 42–44), but her musical aesthetics, advanced in her book *Philosophy in a New Key* (1942), is rarely mentioned in connection with musical semiotics. According to Langer, music does not present symptoms (indexical signs) of feelings, but rather their "logical expression" (symbols). Via her teacher Ernst Cassirer, her theories have at last taken their position within the semiotic tradition.

Some theoreticians in the United States have developed Schenker's theories in a semiotic direction; for example, Eugene Narmour, particularly in his book *Beyond Schenkerism* (1977). In the latter, he clearly shows the deficiency of Schenker's method in explaining the dramatic and narrative strategies of individual pieces. In this same line are writings by David Neumeyer and Richard Littlefield (1992). Narratological studies of music in the proper sense began in the 1980s, when musical narrativity began to be explored as a historical phenomenon of Romanticism (cf. Newcomb 1984 and Abbate 1991). However, they did not apply the rich concepts developed by European narratological studies in the other arts.

When one turns to the area of musical semiotics proper, as it developed in Europe in the 1960s, it is often hard to distinguish traditional musicologists from semioticians of music. A typical example was the Swede Ingmar Bengtsson, who began his career as a music historian and style analyst and only later became interested in musical semiotics and non-verbal communication (see Bengtsson 1973).

## 2.4 Main lines in the development of musical semiotics

Musical semiotics, as a field relatively independent of both semiotics and musicology, started to develop as early as the 1950s and 1960s. Like general semiotics in those days, musical semiotics, too, was structuralist in its strong allegiance to linguistic models. In his *Structural Anthropology* (1958), Lévi-Strauss declared that linguistics had caused a "Copernican revolution" in the human sciences, suggesting that the "rigorous" methods of structural linguistics and phonetics could be used in other disciplines as well, and that they promised a level of exactness comparable to that of the natural sciences.

The first noteworthy application of linguistics to music was Nicolas Ruwet's studies in the interrelationships of language and music, and particularly his analyses of the Prelude to Debussy's *Pelleas* and of medieval *Geisslerlieder* (Ruwet 1972). Reading a myth as one would read a musical score – an idea borrowed from Lévi-Strauss's (1958) analysis of the Oedipus myth and now turned back to music – Ruwet invented the paradigmatic method of analysis. Similar musical motives were placed in a chart one under the other so that one could see at a single glance their distribution in a whole piece of music. From the beginning, the problem of singling-out paradigmatic units received much emphasis, and criteria by which to carry out segmentation were discussed at length. Jean-Jacques Nattiez adopted distributional analysis from Ruwet and established it for a long time as *the* music-semiotical analytic method (Nattiez 1975 and 1990). As early as in his paradigmatic analysis of Debussy's Sy*rinx*, however, Nattiez already remarked that, in the end, it was impossible to know in advance which were the pertinent levels of paradigm, since they varied in the course of the piece, and that before starting to analyse a given piece one had to know several other works by a composer in order to obtain the style competency required for selecting the correct paradigms. This presented a considerable obstacle for the validity of the method, because the goal was to develop a completely "automatic" set of algorithms, such that a computer could carry out the analysis. Moreover, the method seemed to fit only monodic music well. In more complex music, such as J. S. Bach's fugues, in which the texture was not only linear but also harmonic, the method was more difficult to apply. The paradigmatic method aimed to derive a generative grammar for musical texts. Focusing on the styles of some relatively restricted and simple musical works, one could formulate generative rules by which new, style-coherent, grammatically well-formed melodies could be produced endlessly by computer; in a test situation, the latter were indistinguishable from the "authentic" melodies. Such applications were performed on children's songs in Germany by Thomas Stoffer (1979), in Sweden by Johan Sundberg (1992; Sundberg and Lindblom 1970), in Italy by Mario Baroni and Franco Jacoboni (1978) as well as by Rossana Dalmonte (1981) on Bach's chorales and Legrenzi's arias, and also later by Lelio Camilleri and his colleagues at the Florence Conservatory, Margo Ligabue and Francesco Giomi (see Camilleri 1992), in Canada by Ramón Pelinski (1981) and by Jean-Jacques Nattiez on the music of the Inuits, and in Finland by Erkki Pekkilä (1988) on folk music. The generative method culminated in the work of Lerdahl and Jackendoff (1985), when they systematized the inherent tonal rules of Mozart's style.

Yet neither Ruwet's nor Nattiez's paradigmatic procedure took into account the fact that musical signifiers were also supposed to have another side, that of signifieds. If one considers the minimal semiotic requirement to be that music have at least two levels, those of expression and content (Hjelmslev), signifier and signified (Saussure), that it is something which "stands for something to someone" (Peirce), then musical semiotics necessarily has to pay attention to musical significations as well. Nattiez improved his paradigmatic model by re-casting the musical message or text itself as the "neutral level", to which he added the levels of creation (poiesis) and reception (aesthesis), which altogether comprise what Jean Molino called the "total musical fact". In addition to musical production and reception, musical semiotics also had to clarify the implicit criteria used in the paradigmatic analysis itself. Nattiez's own analysis of Wagner's "Tristan chord" and its various interpretations well illustrates this strategy (1990: 216–238). Nattiez applied his tripartite model to Chéreau's and Boulez's Wagner interpretations (1983), then considerably improved it in his *Musicologie générale et sémiologie* (1987) and *Music and Discourse* (1990).

At the same time as linguistics was entering musicology through the work of Ruwet and Nattiez, other, no less important trends in musical semiotics were occurring, albeit ones which, due to language barriers, were not so conspicuous in the international context. The first international congress on musical semiotics, held in Belgrade in 1973 and organized by Gino Stefani and others, brought attention to a whole group of such musical semioticians (see *Actes du 1er congrès international de sémiotique musicale* 1973). Many of them had the profile of a traditional musicologist, to whom semiotics came more or less naturally. Thus, when one evaluates theories of musical semiotics, one should always take into account the underlying musical culture, tradition, experience and education. This helps one to understand the strengths and weaknesses of the theory in question. For example, Stefani, the leading contemporary Italian semiotician of music, was influenced by his education in Catholic liturgical music and music of the Baroque era. In his numerous works (e.g., 1974, 1976, 1977, 1982. 1990), Stefani remains close to the everyday practices of music. He wants to develop a musical semiotics that can be used in music education, music therapy, and cultural animation. His theoretically most cogent work, *La competenza musicale* (1982), is based upon the distinction between two models of musical competence: popular and erudite. The model contains five levels altogether: work, style, musical techniques, social practices, and general codes, which are present to varying degrees in the aforementioned competences. Lately, Stefani and his wife Stefania Guerra Lisi have developed a new approach to the application of semiotics, based on the "globality of languages", understood as musical universals of prenatal origin. Pupils of Gino Stefani, such as Luca Marconi, Marco Beghelli, and Dario Martinelli, have become influential among the younger generation of music semioticians.

From a very different direction comes the musical semiotics of two Czech scholars, Jaroslav Jiranek and Vladimir Karbusicky, both of whom have a structuralist background. But whereas Jiranek leaned more toward Asafiev's intonation theory (and earlier, the Marxist model), Karbusicky chose Peirce's sign theory as his starting point. In 1968 these scholars took separate paths. Jiranek remained in Prague, and Karbusicky joined the faculty at the University of Hamburg. Karbusicky's *Grundlagen der musikalischen Semantik* (1986), one of the most essential readings in the field, is based upon Peirce's concepts of icon, index, and symbol. He considers music to be an indexical expression of emotions and has conducted experimental studies in musical meaning to prove up this assumption. Peirce's theory has also been applied to music by the Canadian David Lidov (1980) and the American Robert S. Hatten (1987), who also has developed a theory of markedness in his analyses of Beethoven (1994). Wilson Coker (1972), William Dougherty (1993), Kofi Agawu (1991), David Mosley and Naomi Cummings also belong to this line. To return to musical semiotics in Eastern Europe, one must mention Polish scholars such as Mieczyslaw Tomaszewski, who has developed a highly original semiotic-hermeneutic approach in his Chopin studies, Michal Bristiger in his researches in music history, Anna Czekanowska in ethnomusicology, and the younger scholars Danuta Mirka and Maciej Jablonski.

A special school of musical semiotics sprang from the theories of the Lithuanian-born semiotician Algirdas Julien Greimas. I myself have applied his *semanalyse* to mythical meanings in music, trying to show that the interaction of myth and music, in Lévi-Strauss's sense, has also taken place in the context of Western music (Tarasti 1979). Music may well receive its sense from myths, and a whole network of mythical meanings can be outlined as such, including semes like the nature-mythical, hero-mythical, magical, fabulous, balladic, legendary, sacred, demonic, fantastic, mystic, exotic, primitivistic, national-musical, pastoral, gestural, sublime and tragic. My later narratological inquiries – mainly based on Greimas but also utilizing concepts drawn from the theories of Peirce and Lotman – have dealt both with programmatic and absolute music. My theory of musical semiotics is based upon four phases chosen from Greimas's generative course: (1) isotopies; (2) spatial, temporal, and actorial categories and their engagement / disengagement; (3) modalities; and (4) semes / phemes. Perhaps the most important and original of these levels is the one dealing with musical modalities: "will", "know", "must", "can", and "believe". These modalities, which originated in linguistic-semiotic theories, can be defined in purely musical terms as well (see, e.g., Tarasti 1992d and 1994a).

Other scholars, too, have applied Greimas's concepts to music. For example, Ivanka Stoianova (1978) developed an original theory combining psychoanalysis, intonation theory, and semiotics. Márta Grabócz (1986, a Hungarian musicologist and student of Jozseph Ujfalussy, has applied the concept of isotopy to Liszt's piano music and to electronic compositions. Especially noteworthy are her studies of electronic music by François-Bernard Mâche (Grabócz 1991–1992). Moreover, the Greimas's method still prevails in his homeland, Lithuania.

Daniel Charles is one of the outstanding music philosophers of France, specializing in Heidegger, on one hand, and on John Cage's Zen philosophy, on the other. Greimas's pupil, composer Costin Miereanu, now a professor in Paris I, has maintained the Greimassian approach in his theoretical writings. Furthermore, Greimas has inspired other younger scholars, particularly those at Aix en Provence, who have gathered round Bernard Vecchione (1986 and 1987). Other notable scholars there include music sociologist Jean-Marie Jacono, Christine Esclapez, and Christian Hauer.

In ethnomusicology, semiotic ideas have been used by scholars such as John Blacking, who studied the musical semantics of South African Veda music in his *How Musical Is Man?* (1976). Charles Boiles clarified how meanings were united with music by the Tepehua Indians (1973). Simha Arom has studied the music of the pygmies (1969). Yoshihiko Tokumaru has applied semiotics to Japanese traditional music (1980), and Shuhei Hosokawa has investigated contemporary Japanese culture, as in his analysis of the Walkman (Hosokawa 1981). Also notable in Japan is the teaching and theoretical work of Satoru Kambe in Tokyo.

Raymond Monelle of Edinburgh, in his *Linguistics and Semiotics in Music* (1992), provides an overview of musical semiotics in all its breadth to British academe, though as early as the beginning of the 1980s, nearly all the most important introductions to music analysis published in the Anglo-Saxon world already contained at least one chapter on musical semiotics (cf. Bent 1987; Dunsby and Whittall 1988). Monelle's latest book, *The Sense of Music* (2000), applies deconstructionist ideas to music. The pioneer of the discipline in Britain was David Osmond-Smith, who developed a theory of inner iconicity in music (1975) and applied semiotics to the study of modern music (e.g., Berio).

The most extensive research project in musical semiotics today is conducted under the title "Musical Signification". It includes about 300 scholars from all over the world, and brings together music semioticians of all stripes, both traditional musicologists and ethnomusicologists, computer theoreticians, cognitive scientists, psychoanalysts, historians and many other music researchers. The project was founded in Paris in 1985 by a group of scholars including François Delalande, Costin Miereanu, Marcello Castellana, Gino Stefani, Luiz Heitor Correa de Azevedo, and myself. So far it has held seven international congresses: in 1986 in Imatra, 1988 in Helsinki, 1990 in Edinburgh, 1993 in Paris, 1995 in Bologna, 1998 in Aix en Provence, and Imatra again in 2001he papers of these symposia have been published through various international and academic publishing houses (among others, see Tarasti [ed.] 1995; Stefani, Marconi, and Tarasti [eds.] 1998; Miereanu and Hascher [eds.] 1998). The project has become the world's largest gathering of music semioticians and has contributed to establishing this new discipline in colleges and universities around the globe. The project also includes an international doctoral and post-doctoral seminar which is organized annually at the University of Helsinki. In these seminars training is given to future doctors in musical semiotics. Anthologies and papers from the doctoral seminars are regularly published in the series *Acta Semiotica Fennica* by the International Semiotics Institute at Imatra, in collaboration with Indiana University Press.

Musical semiotics has also expanded into Latin America. For example, José Luiz Martinez and Luiz Fernando de Lima, both of whom received their doctorates from the University of Helsinki, are representing musical semiotics in Brazil – to which we have to add the work of Heloísa Araújo de Duarte Valente, Lia Tomas, and others. In Mexico, seminars have been held at UNAM in Mexico City by Susanna Gonzalez Aktories, Mario Stern, Ruben Lopez Cano and others.

To sum up, during the last thirty years musical semiotics has become part of "normal" musicology. At the same time, it has gained its freedom from the control of general semiotics and has focussed on the autonomy and originality of musical discourse. Recently, cognitive studies have turned semiotics into one of their special branches, which investigates the counterparts of musical processes in neural network models of the human brain.

One notes a general tendency to abandon more and more the simple generative models of rules for linear configurations, in order to search for new types of theoretical schemes. This has been encouraged by results in the semiotics of other fields, such as deconstructionism, psychoanalysis, feminist studies, critical studies, and so on. On the American scene, musical semiotics has been appropriated by the so-called "new musicology". One may even speak of the "emancipation of musical signs" (see Ch. 5), which has delivered American scholars from their earlier, rigidly positivist models and led them to more interpretative and hermeneutic reflections. Without the theoretical groundwork laid by semioticians this important turn would not have been possible.

Many scholars (e.g., Imberty 1976 and 1981) who practiced semiotics in the area of experimental psychology of music have quite naturally ended up in the cognitive sciences. Yet, conversely, one can consider the cognitive approach as but a sub-discipline of semiotics. It is in fact a rather recent invention, when viewed in light of the 2000-year history of semiotics in Western civilization.

In any case, semioticians of music are no longer outsiders, neither in general semiotics nor in musicology. The latter has in fact tacitly adopted many concepts introduced by semioticians, such as the distinction between the subject of the enunciate and that of the enunciation (Dahlhaus made this distinction, erroneously thinking he had borrowed it from the Russian formalists).

Concerning the publishing channels of musical semiotics, the journal *Musique en jeu,* in which Nattiez published his first articles, must be mentioned for the 1970s. Later, music semioticians had to publish their essays either in general musicological journals, such as IRASM, *Analyse musicale, Music Theory Spectrum, Indiana Theory Review, Music Analysis,* and the like, or in semiotic journals; on the latter, see the special issues on the semiotics of music in *Semiotica* (1976 and 1987), *Zeitschrift far Semiotik* (1987), and *Degrés* (1987–1988). *Eunomio*, edited by the Italian musicologists Paolo Rosato and Michele Ignelzi. is a journal totally devoted to the semiotic analysis of music. Nevertheless, the number of dissertations underway in many parts of the world, the increasing appearance of new books on the subject, and the widening variety of theoretical approaches available to scholars working in the field show that musical semiotics is continuing to grow both in quantity and quality.

# Chapter 3
# Signs as acts and events:
# On musical situations

*"Everything is being.*
*Time is only a filter*
*set upon it."*

So far we seem to agree that music signifies. Yet here the unanimity stops. For if we assume the simplest definition of a sign, that it is *aliquid stat pro aliquo*, then one gets myriad responses to the question, What does music stand for? For modern cognitive science, music represents a mental process, to such an extent that the sign itself fades from sight and what remains is only the simulation and modeling of the neural network – a solipsistic situation in which neural cells "communicate" with each other. Nevertheless, as Umberto Eco stated in his *La struttura assente*, "if we could imagine that signs might be conceived "intuitively" by handling them with direct contact between two spiritual beings, without resorting to social conventions, then semiotics would not have any meaning." In this canonical view, the very premise of semiotics is provided by precisely such "social conventions", without which a sign could not exist. A sign appears as a code, which is a symbolic system and which is intended to transmit information between a sender and a receiver. All forms of communication function by sending messages, which are in turn based upon codes. Furthermore, every act of communication is based upon a pre-existing "competence", since all speech (*parole*) presupposes language (*langue*).

For many years the study of musical signs followed the same path as general semiotics, in its efforts to reduce a musical sign to a normative, constraining set of rules, whether it be a generative grammar, style norms, or various classes of signs as defined by general semiotics (icons, indexes, legisigns, semes, isotopies, etc.). All of "classical semiotics" – says Roland Barthes in his *Eléments de sémiologie* – has been heading in this direction. And insofar as it is the goal of science to look for invariants, this procedure seems to be the correct one.

Yet general semiotics has lately moved in another direction, namely, toward the study of unique, individual phenomena. In this case, one need not try to reduce the object to a code system, but may conceive of it in a more phenomenological and hermeneutic way so as to understand its originality. In music, one evidence of this different direction may be seen in the many criticisms of Schenkerian analysis for its inability to elucidate the style of an individual composer or the message of a single work. Other, more traditional models of music analysis have undergone similar attempts to guide them away from universality, and toward more particularity. For example, the concept of a composer's unique "strategy" within a general musical style has been elaborated in the work of Eugene Narmour and Robert S. Hatten. The emphasis is no longer on general codes, as evidenced by techniques and social practices, but on the style of a single opus, as in the model of musical competence developed by Gino Stefani. Raymond Monelle's deconstructionist analyses have also endeavoured to indicate the uniqueness of individual texts. He locates textual "ruptures", which momentarily reveal the universe of unarticulated semiotic, the pre-symbolic world of gestures and desires: suddenly the phenotext, be it song or dance, lets the genotext emerge through it and out into the foreground. But let us return briefly to more traditional modes of research, to point up the differences between them and the approach that will be outlined later in this chapter.

Leonard B. Meyer's monumental *Style and Music* (1989) provides a good example. The book launches with the statement that a style comes from "a series of choices made within some set of constraints", which are code-determining norms that a subject must accept if he/she wants to communicate. Yet even this is intermingled with the particular moment and with choice, by virtue of the fact that such constraints determine "what might have happened" in a particular context in which a choice is made. Meyer lists these constraints starting with the most general ones (laws, rules, strategies) and proceeding to the most specific ones (dialects, idiolects, and intraopus styles), thereby reaching what is really unique in music. Meyer states that some composers are original in inventing new rules, whereas others apply the old rules in novel ways. Nevertheless, the essential point in evaluating music is to know "what a composer might have chosen as well as what he actually chose". Music that is completely accidental or aleatoric cannot be approached at all from this angle, because in such cases "what *is*" cannot be distinguished from "what might have been". Alternatives are irrelevant in such a "style". Because such music is not a consequence of human choice, it does not belong to the area of style, but is like a phenomenon in the natural world: it simply exists.

Meyer, while clearly trying to understand the individual moments in music, still continues to emphasize the aspect of constraints, or socially coded systems. Although he finally admits that choices in turn presuppose intentions, the intentions can be reduced to goals: "Furthermore, the existence of intentions ... entails the existence of goals... The choices of composers can be understood and explained only in light of intentions generated by goals – goals that are implicit in the constraints of the style and are largely set by the ideology of the culture." Therefore Meyer proceeds as do most classical semioticians, inasmuch as he underlines the importance of *langue*, the dependence of everything on cultural code systems.

Yet there are alternatives to this procedure which as yet have received scant attention by music analysts. One alternative is to shift from mere observation of a musical utterance (text), in order to scrutinize the whole situation of communication, taking into account the fact that every sign is an *act* performed by some subject. In general, communication involves a dialogue between subject and utterance. Efforts in this direction have been made in psychoanalytic and feminist-oriented analysis, where scholars have theorized how the human body is projected into music (see Ch. 5).

From this physiological and bodily perspective another avenue opens up, which connects music to the prevailing epistemes of a culture, to its dominant canons, to the stylistic constraints of musical discourse. In the non-musical realm, Michel Foucault follows such a path in his analysis of Velázquez's painting, *Las meninas*. Foucault's analysis is at the same time a dialogical inquiry, inasmuch as the spectator is drawn into the representational system of the painting. Leonard Meyer has said that the value of music is determined by its "relational richness". Foucault reveals in the Vélazquez painting just such an exceptionally rich, internal network of the interrelations of its parts.

*Las meninas* represents the painter himself in the act of painting the sovereigns of Spain. In the picture, the princess, accompanied by her maids and dwarfs, has come to look at the painting. Foucault starts at the neutral level (in Nattiez's sense) of the painting, its quasi-objective zero point, making observations upon which his subsequent interpretation is built (in truth, however, Foucault's analysis relies on a hermeneutic pre-understanding that would have been impossible without the great philosophical competence of its writer). He pays particular attention to the gazes of the persons in the painting: the princess turns her head towards the right side of the picture, but her gaze is directed straight ahead at the spectator standing in front of the painting. A vertical line dividing the canvas into two equal halves would pass between the child's eyes, and her face is a third of the total height of the picture above the lower frame. Here, beyond question, resides the principal theme, the true object of the painting.

According to Foucault, however, the painting has not one but two centres of reference. The princess is standing precisely in the middle of an X, but there is also another way to articulate the painting; namely, with a vast curve, its two ends determined by the painter on the left and the male courtier on the right. The centre of that curve would coincide with the princess's face and the gaze of her maid of honour. But the movement of the princess is frozen by a sight that would be totally invisible if the persons in it were not seen in the depths of a mirror: the line issuing from the mirror crosses the whole area of the represented depth. The other line is shorter, coming from the princess's eyes and crossing only the foreground. These two medial lines converge at a very sharp angle, and the point where they meet, which seems to jut out from the painted surface, occurs in front of the picture, more or less exactly at the spot from which *we are observing it*. This point thus unites the three functions of looking at the picture: the gaze of the model, the gaze of the observer of the painting, and the gaze of the painter.

Finally, Foucault argues that perhaps *Las meninas* embodies the very essence of Classical representation, and defines the space which the latter opens to us. The painting renders the necessary disappearance of that which is its foundation – the person it resembles and the person in whose eyes it is only a resemblance. Such representation, freed from the relation that was impeding it, can offer itself as representation in its pure form.

Foucault's interpretation shows how an analysis of an artwork can step outside a rigorously textual approach and at the same time reveal, by observing the communicational relations within it, how the work reflects the epistemes of the age, the latter's archaeology of knowledge and feeling. Music analysis has not yet reached such a level, but it might be approached in the manner of Foucault. Perhaps some musical commentators from an older generation instinctively came close, as did Sir Francis Tovey in his best moments, but they did not adhere to a rigorous model, nor did they theorize their methods.

Some theories totally contextualise the existence of a musical sign. Music is viewed merely as a transaction according to the traditional model of communication, though enriched by all kinds of filters provided by modern technology (Pierre Schaeffer advanced such a model). Some, like Pierre Bourdieu, contextualise the musical sign as a way of living in a sociological context; others, as a transmission in modern media society. Such investigations neglect the inner structure of signification in music and forget the dimensions hidden within the sign itself. One wonders if there exists a starting point from which a musical sign would appear at the same time as both *communicational* and *significational*, to borrow Eco's terms (see Ch. 8.2–8.4).

My own efforts to go beyond the narrow communication model have drawn inspiration from Marcel Proust's conception of music in his *A la recherche du temps perdu*. In the volume entitled *La prisonnière*, music is portrayed as a rich interaction between all participants in the communication. Essential to the Proustian scheme is the disruption of the unidirectional, linear-chain model, since in real communication our exchanges dart back and forth and do not proceed in just one direction. In such an analysis, music already appears as a certain *situation* rather than as a fixed object.

I have looked for music analyses in which something similar would happen on the level of the message itself (utterance); i.e., analyses not treating music as a linear-syntagmatic chain but as a compound situation comprised of many various elements. The only analysis of this kind that I have encountered is Jean Barraqué's reading of Debussy's *La mer*; even though, due to the lack of a proper metalanguage, its realization is deficient as compared to its objectives. Barraqué tries to demonstrate how great works attempt to find their own fates and come to the non-predeterminacy of musical time: "... les grandes œuvres devraient s"inventer un destin propre et par-là, aboutir à une non-préfiguration du temps musical". ["... the great works had to invent a destiny of their own, and by doing so, resulted in the unpredictability of musical time."] Debussy's music perfectly exemplified a new formal conception which Barraqué called "open form". Through this music Barraqué believed to have found an analytic method that went beyond the limits of traditional form analysis, perhaps to the level of generalization: "En effet, dans *La Mer*, la technique musicale est réinventée, non dans les détails du langage, mais dans la conception même de l'organisation et du devenir sonore (selon une démarche que l'on pourrait rapprocher de celle de Mallarmé). La musique y devient un monde mysterieux qui, á mesure qu"il évolue, s"invente en lui-même et se détruit." [Indeed, in *La mer*, musical technique is reinvented, not in the details of the language, but in the concept of organisation and of sonorous growth (in a fashion comparable to that of Mallarmé). In *La mer*, music becomes a mysterious world, which, as it evolves, both invents and destroys itself.]

Barraqué thought it necessary to create a new type of aesthetic analysis which departs from "a more profound technical investigation, but is especially capable of revealing for each work its original direction (yet without ignoring its situation in history)." Thus here Barraqué introduced the same program as what I have above set as the goal of "new musical semiotics", namely, the effort to discover the individuality of a work and to break free from a slavish and rote-like syntagmatic analysis. Barraqué states that "in Debussy the form can not only be conceived as a succession or a progressive acquisition by the connection of ideas, but rather via the amalgams, elliptical courses, oppositions of forces which are not based on literal thematic structures but imply a movement from one to the other through poetic transformations in which the situation of the object-themes create zones of neutrality." Here we see our term *situation* in its proper place. But in the realization of his analysis Barraqué resorts to traditional notions like exposition, development, recapitulation, coda. Nevertheless, within them he speaks about musical "states" and differences between note-tone and sound-tone (*note-ton*, *note-son*), i.e., music as a syntactic enunciate or as an enunciation. Barraqué thereby aims for a dialogical model of musical analysis that captures the interaction between the text and how it is heard.

My own efforts have brought me to the threshold of what I call *existential semiotics* (Tarasti 2001). This by no means heralds the rebirth or return of existentialist philosophy. Rather, I am continuing in the direction of musical research such as that of Floyd Merrell, who in his *Peirce's Semiotics Now* (1995) seeks to underline the individuality of signs. Likewise, in Barthes's *Elements of Semiology* (1967) signs are classified according to categories such as signals, indexes, icons, symbols, signs, allegories. He distinguishes five species of relationship between any two elements, the last of which is the case in which a sign has an existential relationship to its user. In Barthes's view, Wallon, Peirce, and Jung consider some categories of sign to have precisely such an existential function. Wallon believes that the signal is such a sign, Peirce says the same of indexes, and Jung of symbols. In Greimas's theory the existentiality of signs would be a kind of deixis, a reference to I-, here-, and now-moments, i.e., to a *situation* that prevails for a person at a given time and place.

Does the consideration of the situations of signs lead to positive analytic results? Or does it take us to what perhaps deserves no study at all, or in Eco's words, only to what a certain sign has meant to some subject? Despite this danger, it seems to me that only by using the notion of *situation* can we analyze musical semiosis in all its complexity and uniqueness.

*Situation*, as an existential semiotic concept, first of all refers always to a certain particularity. Of course different kinds of situations can always be typified, but typologisation still presumes that the situational phenomenon has first been investigated as its own entity. Situation cannot be explained as a causal chain of events, but rather as a continuous intermingling of happenings that represent various modes of being in the real contexts in which they occur. One's situatedness is the same as Heidegger's concept of *in-der-Welt-sein*. Situation is that part of the world with which one enters into a relationship. One relates to the world via his/her situation. Situation is the whole of all those phenomena, objects, and states of affairs under which and by which a person's organic and conscious existence is realized. Situation always consists of a play-space of various factors. One's situatedness could be compared to a tone, which is always realized as a combination of pitch, duration, and timbre. All of these qualities exist in sound waves, but at the same time they are all components of one entity, the tone. The same holds true for people, who are at the same time organic process, consciousness, and the facticity of being in history, culture, and the objective world.

Because of its capaciousness, the concept of situation leads to a considerably broader view on the conditions of semiosis, signification, and communication. The three aspects of a situation – the world itself (*Dasein*), organic process, and consciousness – are mutually dependent, not in the manner of causal chains, however, but as a continuous microdialectics. It is difficult to conceive of the organic process as somehow becoming thinner and more transparent, leading to a consciousness; or, contrarily, that consciousness gradually "condenses" into something organic – in semiotic terms, that the signifier of a sign would be a condensation of the signified, or conversely, that the signified is a thinner, transparent version of the signifier, the physical aspect of a sign.

When studying the structure of a situation, one must examine not just all the manifestations of its "facticity", that is, the "objects" and "texts" offered by a culture, which classical semiotics mostly investigates. One must also elucidate the historicity of a situation and its fateful twists and turns. Our goal is to clarify the logic of the inner events in a situation, but not as though the predictability of events were our sole quarry. Not everything must be, nor should be, anticipated. A person is neither a robot nor a natural phenomenon, whose manipulation would constitute the ultimate goal of research.

An entirely different *semiotic* program takes shape on this basis, which is not very far from Peirce's triadic sign categories. If *representamen* refers to organic process, to something physical, the *object*, in turn, to facticity, to that sign content which stems from outside, from "reality", then the *interpretant* would imply the consciousness, as a concept which in our minds unites sign with object. This new program takes a negative view toward linear causality and dissolves it into three dimensions of an existential sign: its facticity (being in *Dasein*), its physical aspect as an organic process, and its role in the consciousness. Next I consider what consequences this concept of situation might have for analysing music.

## 3.1 Situation as communication and signification

Even in musical research, the general communication model has been exploited in many ways. According to this model (discussed in Ch. 1.1), a message goes from a sender (composer) to a listener, via a performer and/or instruments, as an acoustic stream of sounds. In this process one has to distinguish between code, channel, and context, with their corresponding functions. This model should be replaced by a model of narrative action, which in itself constitutes a step towards the universe of signification. A musical situation should be taken as the crossroads of signification and communication, the place where physical/implied author and physical/implied listener meet (cf. Chatman 1978). The whole world of a text unfolds between the implied composer and the implied listener. This means that Beethoven as a physical person and Beethoven as an "implied composer" are two different things. In the same way, Duke Razumovsky as a physical listener and as the implied listener postulated by the implied composer "Beethoven", the master of the Classical style, are two different entities. Moreover, in the work itself there is a (musical) narrator, who organizes musical events according to a certain kind of logic, while taking into account a possible audience. For instance, the narrator in the song "An die ferne Geliebte" presumes a distant beloved to whom the musical story is addressed. In the sonata *"Les adieux"*, a narrator arranges the events into a plot which he assumes that his audience will "decode" correctly.

One can go still further: in a composition a theme-actor can appear, which functions in a purely musical sense, in such that it influences another theme-actor that serves as a recipient of this action, thereby establishing the relationship of agent/patient. For instance, in the first movement of *"Les adieux"*, the beginning of the introduction opens with the horn motive that in turn influences the motive in the *attacca* beginning of the Allegro. Therefore narrative music – and in this case all music is theoretically "narrative" – has the following type of structure:

## Narrative composition

$$C \qquad iC(N/iN1,2...n \longrightarrow iA1,2...n/A)iL \qquad L$$

in which:

C = physical composer
iC= implied composer
N = narrator
iN= implied narrator, or theme-actors as agents
L = physical listener
iL= implied listener
A = audience
iA= implied audience, or theme-actors as patients

Consequently, in music, as well as verbal texts, there exist many embedded levels of narration, i.e., chains of composer-narrator/ listener-audience or agent/patient. When speaking about situations, one has to remember to separate them carefully from each other.

Situations can also be those of the real world. Composers and listeners are subject to historical and organic processes: they get ill, they enjoy themselves, they make political and other decisions, they struggle to survive, they consume music as a part of certain way of life, and so on. When Albert Wellek once rejected studying the "mere sociology of musicians", he meant precisely this level of musical situations, on which anthropologists in particular always first encounter their informants before they start to "get into" whatever culture they are studying. Naturally, investigations of this physico-cultural level are important to studies of musical communication, but a semiotic analysis cannot stop there. By simplifying the aforementioned model, emphasis goes to the following "boxes" of the chain:

$$\boxed{\text{composer}} \rightarrow \text{implied} \rightarrow \text{message} \leftarrow \text{implied} \leftarrow \boxed{\text{listener}}$$
$$\qquad\qquad \text{composer} \qquad\qquad\qquad \text{listener}$$

In this second scenario the focus shifts one step, toward the inner core of musical signification. In the movement from composer to implied composer, and from listener to implied listener, representation is launched in music: elements of outer reality are internalized so as to form factors that wield influence inside the musical discourse. For instance, the implied composer is someone with a certain competence, who provides his musical message with signs that the implied listener can presumably receive and decode correctly:

$$\text{composer} \rightarrow \boxed{\begin{array}{c}\text{implied}\\\text{composer}\end{array}} \rightarrow \text{message} \leftarrow \boxed{\begin{array}{c}\text{implied}\\\text{listener}\end{array}} \leftarrow \text{listener}$$

Finally, the musical message itself can be interpreted as a model, as a microuniverse whose elements stand in various relationships to each other. In some cases this involves a kind of reflection from the two outer circles. But just as often the transformation may have taken place as early as on the previous level of implied composer/listener, and does not therefore communicate anything directly from the social, historical or physical situation (from so-called "reality"). The "model" represented by the message, with its purely musical "communications" and actions, can even be deliberately antithetical to the pre-suppositions of the implied composer and listener. In any case, the distinction between these three degrees of agents/patients forms the first step towards clearing up much conceptual confusion in music analysis.


## 3.2 Situation as act and event

The principle of pragmaticism, as advanced by Peirce, William James and others, holds true for the analysis of situations: "Considering what effects that might conceivably have practical bearings, we conceive the object of our conception to have. Then, our conception of these effects is the whole of our conception of the object". The notion of "situation" is useful if something new follows from it in the practice of semiotic and musical research, say, some new way of seeing, hearing, and dealing with phenomena.

At the same time, inside the musical discourse one has to scrutinize the actions of various agents, subjects, and actions which produce and maintain situations. Situation might be easily identified with a space: the space at a given moment as perceived by a given actor. In music, situation always implies an actor; no situation can exist without an actor somehow pertaining to it. Therefore, what is crucial for a musical work is the way it draws listeners into the situation and forces them to participate in it. Situation is thus an *act* (i.e., an *active* situation) or an *event* (i.e., a *passive* situation) on the part of a musical subject. Situation is either created by the implied composer or narrator, or it occurs to him/her. The strategy of the avant-garde "open work" was for the situation to be created not by the enunciator (composer) but by the enunciatee (listener). The work could be virtually incomprehensible, but the implied receiver-listener recreated it (or was supposed to do so) by providing it with significations.

For describing musical situations the logic of act and action proves appropriate. Such logic was elaborated by, among others, Georg Henrik von Wright in his study *Norm and Action* (1963). Wright does not use the term "situation" but rather speaks about "occasions" that provide the possibility either for an occurrence of a general event or for doing an act. Acts, in turn, concern changes in the facts of the world. There are three types of both worldly and musical facts: (a) states of affairs – for instance, "Beethoven composed nine symphonies" or "Each year the Teatro Comunale in Bologna performs several operas"; (b) processes – say, "performing a musical work"; (c) events – for example, "The slow introduction to *Les adieux*" is followed by an *attacca* Allegro" or "Ten years ago Teatro Comunale performed Busoni's *Doktor Faust*". In brief: in a state of affairs something *happens*; in a process, something *is happening*; in an event, something *happened*.

In this classification, an *event* always means change. This could be a shift from one state to another (as from exposition to development in a sonata form), or from a state to a process (musicians start to play after tuning), or from a process to a state (musicians stop playing when the piece ends). Or the change could take place within a process (for instance, musicians playing in duple meter suddenly shifting to a triple meter, while the process of playing continues).

Unlike an event, an *act* cannot be identified as a change in the world. Rather, to act is in a sense always to intervene in the course of affairs. For example, to write a composition or to perform it is undoubtedly an act. There are both individual and general acts. For instance, a general act could be the performance of "*Les adieux*", and the corresponding general change (event) would be that the sonata was performed at all. An individual act would be that "Claudio Arrau played "*Les adieux*" in Rome in 1970", the individual event being that it was performed in that year in Rome. The logical difference between acts and events lies in their activity or passivity: an act always requires an acting agent.

*Acts* have to be distinguished from *actions*. It is, for instance, an act to perform "*Les adieux*", but it is an action to be able to perform it. Events occur and processes continue; acts cause the occurrence of events, and actions make processes continue.

The following schemes symbolize the four types of elementary changes and non-changes: pTp, pT-p, -pTp, and -pT-p. Correspondingly, there are four types of elementary act: d(-pTp) means the doing of p; d(pT-p) means the destruction of p; d(pTp) means the preserving of p, i.e., the world does not change regarding the feature given by p in the two consecutive situations; and d(-pT-p) means the forbearance of p. We derive an equal number of supplemental cases when the "doing" is negated, such that one speaks of letting something go undone.

The logical distinctions made by von Wright also hold true for musical communication, and particularly for the narrative model sketched above. Take, for instance, the difference between individual and general events and acts. In the first movement of a classical symphony the subordinate theme usually emerges when the dominant key is reached – that is a general event. But when it happens in a particular case, say, as in Sibelius's Second Symphony, then it is an individual act of the composer. When a given composer does it – Sibelius or Bruckner or whoever – it reflects something existential, because the composer could also have chosen to do otherwise. When the case of this subordinate theme is seen as a rule or norm, then its realization is an event. This explains why a sign as an individual act never blends with what the sign is as an individual event. Classical semiotics treats signs as individual or general events, whereas existential semiotics deals with them as individual acts.

Following von Wright, we could say that a situation provides an occasion for an event or an act to occur or be accomplished; for instance, only if the window is closed can it be opened. A musical example: only in a situation that includes both exposition and development can we hear the development *qua* development. Thus musical forms, in the sense of traditional schemes, serve as situations for the occurrence of certain things. Therefore the concept of situation can be transcendent: it can be a *possible* vision, scheme, or abstraction, which may or may not be realized.

The choices which Meyer describes as "those which might have been realized" are based on just this premise: they form counterfactual situations, which constitute their own network "beneath" the surface of reality. If, for instance, the series of events a......p......q has occurred, then one can always think of what might have happened if, instead of p, -p had appeared; or instead of q, -q had taken place. In other words, beginning from moment a, there emerges a network of

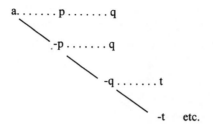

*Figure 4.*

alternative chains of events which might depict the possible ways a composer or listener acts.

In order for such a network of possible stylistic choices to take shape, it should have observed at least once that *a* can be followed by *p* or -*p*. In other cases, -*p* cannot be taken as a true alternative. How we conceive the range of possibilities is a consequence of what we observe on the surface of the reality. One cannot "dive" under it. Heidegger's notions of *Dasein* and *Da-sein* draw attention to this difference: *Dasein* represents the whole situation with all its possibilities. *Da-sein*, however, refers only to the being-there of the surface reality.

Contrarily, one could argue that not all new possibilities within a given style have ever occurred in reality, although they can well be imagined. Still, *situation* includes everything that might have happened as well as the remembrance of those choices, acts and events that were actually fulfilled at one time.

Hence when studying any composer in terms of existential semiotics, one has to examine the situations in his/her music which appear as acts, events, and processes. The musical logic characteristic of a given composer manifests precisely as a particular relationship between musical acts and events. For instance, the emergence of a motive or theme, which we would easily be tempted to take as a musical act, is in fact an "act" of a subject in a fictive musical narrative. It means the situation of -*pTp*; but it can be also destroyed, say, by thematic liquidation, yielding the situation *pT-p*. *P* could also be preserved; for instance, what was originally an individual actant, a musical sign as an act, may become a process (this happens often in Sibelius's music). Finally, one may inhibit or prevent something from emerging: *-pT-p*. For instance, in this last case the implied composer might do something that transgresses normative constraints, such as not letting the music take shape according to a traditional scheme (that was Debussy's strategy in his *La mer*, as analyzed by Barraqué). This is experienced as the lack of a certain solution in a musical situation, which the implied listener would expect according to the norms. Here, behind the individual existential musical situation, looms the normative *langue*. One must therefore distinguish between two cases: a situation as a transcendental norm, scheme, grammar, which exerts force yet is not actual; and the actual situation, the music as heard. Musical signs which are actually present on the "surface" I call *act-signs*; and possible or virtual signs, *trans-signs*.

One may discern act-signs and event-signs in music. In cases of the former, the creativity of *parole*, the individual signification bursts forth from a rupture in the musical text. In the case of event-signs, we have a more passive following of stylistic constraints and *langue*, a submission to the "rules" of communication. How an act differs from an event in a musical situation is illustrated by the following examples.

In music one may shift from act to event or from event to act. The Larghetto movement of Beethoven's Second Symphony begins in the galant style, with an *Empfindsamkeit* topic. Yet soon the movement starts to develop from a mere event into an act, when unexpectedly the motives lead to more dramatic conflicts that allow the idea of Beethovenian development to emerge. The implied narrator does not yet commit a norm-breaking act, but stands on the threshold of doing so (Ex. 9a).

A similar example is provided by the end of the last movement of Beethoven's "Pastoral" Symphony, where in bars 188–205 one first hears a simple coda over the following chord progression: I-VI-V/V-V-I. This exemplifies a normal cadential "event" at which one arrives following the constraints of the piece and style rather than as any kind of "act" of the narrator. But when the cadence repeats, it is expanded, and changed into colourful ninth chords. This rupture in which the "note-tone" is transformed into "sound-tone",[5] according

*Ex. 9a.*   Beethoven, Second Symphony, Larghetto, bars 1–4.

*Ex. 9b.*   Beethoven, Second Symphony, Larghetto, bars 148–151.

to Barraqué's distinction, affords a musical act: I-VI-V/V-V7-I9/7 = V7/IV-V-I (bars 219–237).

Sibelius's symphonic logic illustrates the opposite device: a shift from an act to an event or process. Very frequently in his symphonies a characteristic thematic unit, at its first occurrence, appears as an "act" bearing a particular significance. Later, due to multiple repetitions, it is brought to the state of mere event or process. It is "de-actorialized", as it were, and transformed into sheer musical space or line. This technique appears already in his early works such as *En Saga* and the *Forest Nymph*.

Of course, some composers employ a narrative technique in which the same theme actor is led through different situations and events. The theme itself neither "does" anything nor changes into anything, but passively undergoes various events in these changing musical milieus and situations – a device much favoured by the Romantics (cf. the slow movement of Beethoven's Fifth Symphony or Schubert's *Wanderer Fantasy*).

Contemporary music holds even greater possibilities for variation. For example, Magnus Lindberg's composition, *Action, Situation, Signification*, tries to articulate the interrelationships between the musicians' activities (*action*) and the concrete, static sounds of nature (*situation*). Serving as inspirational sources for this piece are Pierre Schaeffer's *Traité des objets musicaux* (1966) and Elias Canetti's *Fire, Mass and Power* (1995). In this work by Lindberg, ideas borrowed from Canetti have been transformed into serial numerical principles that govern the musical substance, while the sound-picture of the work as *musique concrète* alludes to external reality. The work refers to five basic elements: sea, rain, fire, wind, and earth. Each element has its own identity, its own rhythmic configurations, and pitch collections. The sea is represented by oscillating repetitions. Rain is distinguished by its constancy; fire is irregular; and changes in direction and intensity allude to the wind. "Sea", "Rain", "Fire", and "Wind" are the main movements of the piece, and each one follows the same pattern: initially the situation is a diffuse jumble of disparate materials. Toward the end of each movement the texture thins out, until only the sounds connected with the symbol (natural element) in question remain. At this point, *action* becomes *situation*. This illustrates, in our theoretical framework, a shift from a field of acts to that of an "event".

### 3.3 Situations as intertextuality

The examples presented above have foregrounded diachronic, linear elements of situations. Yet, situations also have synchrony. Almost all narration is more or less intertextual, and every text or part thereof refers to some other text. Every text must be read through the lens of other texts, since all texts inevitably absorb other texts, transforming them within in the (virtual) totality of intertextual space. This is also generally true of music, where intertextuality designates the constant recycling of previously used musical materials, genres, etc. At the more particular level of specific works, intertextual references have

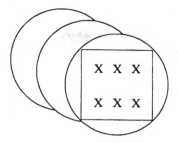

*Figure 5.*

long formed a standard technique, starting with ancient music: the "parody" Mass, the use of *cantus firmus*, and other kinds of borrowing. Listeners to music have always already heard something, and they bring those earlier experiences to bear in conceptualizing what they hear in the present. Behind musical act-signs loom two kinds of transsigns: remembrances and possibilities. They constitute a musical situation with its own paradigm of sub-situations (Fig. 5). Whether these sub-situations exert the constraints of Peircean legisigns, or whether they exemplify certain types (Goodman), depends somewhat on the choices made by the subject, the implied composer.

Behind the symphonies of Brahms and Bruckner we distinguish Beethoven's symphonies as their points of reference, their sub-situations. The closer we come to contemporary music, the richer and more complex becomes the intertextual network. In a classical music text (understood in Adler's sense), the intertexts and subtexts are not necessarily heard. Rather, they belong to the assumed musical competence of the implied listener, upon which the narrative program of the musical work can be built. The use of musical *topics* is based on just such a notion of immanent textuality.

Leitmotive technique in Wagner's music, particularly towards the end of the *Nibelungen Ring*, relies largely upon musical situations that function by means of intertextual references. The leitmotives form a kind of panchronic sign-paradigm, which has presumably been stored in the memory of the implied listener. The implied composer, Wagner, trusts in his implied listener. He builds whole scenes according to the idea that the musical form is dictated by an earlier situation, which as an intertext can be transformed. He uses this technique of intertextual situations, for instance, in the story of Siegfried at the end of *Götter-dämmerung* as well as in the finale of the *Meistersinger*. This finale is an expansion of the prelude to the whole opera; hence the overture serves as the sub-situation of the latter. Correspondingly, Siegfried's narrative is a condensation of the scenes of the murmuring forest and Brünnhilde's awakening, which serve as its sub-situations.

Regarding leitmotive technique as such, one finds a positive answer to the question of whether they follow any system: the system obtains in the relationship between the motives and their situations. This can be illustrated by the following diagram of a scene in the *Nibelungen Ring*:

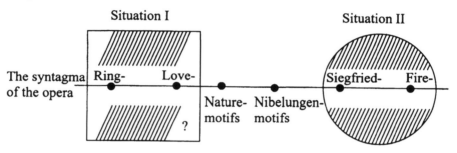

*Figure 6.*

How are situations segmented and articulated in Wagnerian opera (and in general)? How long can a musical situation last, and how do we know when it starts and ends? How can we tell when situation I becomes situation II? The criterion for answering these questions can be, as Boulez remarked concerning Wagner, a purely musical form; but it can also be a situation determined by the drama. Some leitmotives pertain to such situations, while others fall outside it. In Greimassian terms, they are either *engaged* or *disengaged* in a given situation. For instance, the leitmotive tables in the piano score or in *Das Buch der Motive* (published by Schott) display signs detached from their real situations. These signs can of course be analysed independently, but the essential question is how they function when engaged in a situation. One of the fundamental issues, then, is whether a sign produces a situation, or a situation produces a sign.

In the diagram, the area with diagonal lines and a question mark in refers to the fact that motives (signs) alone do not fill the musical situation, but are only distinguished therein as individual actors. What, then, is that other texture? How do musical signs grow out of it? Is there always something, in a given situation, which catalyzes a leitmotive? I leave these questions unanswered at present. For now, let us note that gradually the use of situations and intertexts becomes more and more explicit during the course of music history. They become textual irruptions, outbreaks of individual significations in the form of musical acts. In postmodern music, intertexts are no longer invisible or unheard genotexts. Rather, they are made audibly perceptible when one gleans maximally contrasting elements from the memory paradigm of the implied listener and realizes them as act-signs. The borrowing techniques in Luciano Berio's *Sinfonia* consist not only of separate motivic citations but also the overlapping of entire situations, thus representing a kind of explicitly synchronic intertextuality (Mahler versus the Swingle Singers).

## 3.4 Articulation of situations

To end this chapter, I examine how individual situations are articulated. First, the linear-syntactic model dissolves, as a pragmatic consequence deriving from the notion of situations. It is replaced with another type of organization, describable in the semiotic terms of Charles S. Peirce. As discussed in Chapter 1, he based his semiotics on three phases by which persons are in contact with their surrounding reality and in which signs take their shapes. The first phase is that of Firstness. Peirce says: "Firstness means unanalyzed, instantaneous, immediate feeling, direct "suchness" dependent on nothing else beyond itself for its comprehension..." Firstness is thus timeless; it is the present experienced emotionally and all at once.

Applied to musical situations, this involves a case in which all the elements are experienced as more or less simultaneous and unarticulated, according to their qualisigns:[6]

In the phase of Secondness one meets the "Other"; sameness is broken; an experience takes place which distinguishes between action and reaction, stimulus and response, change and resistance to change. Secondness contains elements of polarity, comparison, struggle. If a First is something that *might* be realized, then a Second *is* a hard fact, the facticity of *Da-sein*, something which really happens. Thus we are always in Secondness when we orient ourselves in time and place, when we make a decision, or experience a surprise. Unlike Firstness, Secondness does not occur in the here-and-now. "Secondness is the predominant character of what has been done".

In other words, our musical situation is clearly articulated into elements which have been realized, which we really hear in a musical piece, but which at the same time, by the act of comparison, refer to remembrances and possible signs, to the whole universe of counterfactual alternatives that might have happened if the implied composer had made alternative choices. In this phase musical act-signs and trans-signs become distinguishable, some of them as the "surface" of the reality, and others remaining as a virtual intertextual space or network (Figure 7).

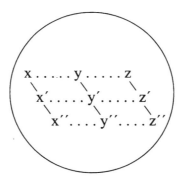

*Figure 7.*

In Thirdness, the feeling of continuity and the rules of action prevail. Thirdness is oriented toward the future, and thus helps us to predict what is coming. It represents logical thinking, order, law, and is thus a principle opposed to chance and chaos: "The thread of life is a Third". The same could be said about music, since in our musical

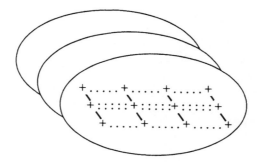

*Figure 8.*

situation the elements are arranged according to the principle of narrative sequences, thereby becoming a signifying continuum. At the same time, a whole situation can be compared to other entire situations which serve as its intertexts. In Thirdness, situation is provided with temporal articulation as a chain of continuous becoming. Only on this level does the whole field of intertextuality emerge as a series of possible sub-situations (Figure 8.)

Composers can repeat situations, sometimes to the point of obsession. A composer might have a particular way of building musical situations in the alternation of acts and events, such that, ultimately, he or she writes one and the same piece throughout his/her life. Proust spoke about the individual voice, which carries through the whole output of a composer and through all the "performances" of an interpreter. Perhaps the repetition of these situations and their solutions are in the end what constitutes a composer's "style".

Insofar as anything represents the universal in a unique situation, it is also an existential choice. We only have to remember that the existentiality of musical signs is determined by purely musical criteria acting in the musical *Dasein*. Correspondingly, existentiality is determined in narrative communication as an implied interaction between composer, performer, listener. And it is a long way from each of these to the real existential situations in which flesh-and-blood composers, performers, and listeners live in the social-cultural context of their time.

# Part two:
# Gender, biology, and transcendence

# Chapter 4
# Metaphors of nature and organicism in music:
# A "biosemiotic" approach

## 4.1 On the musically organic

A crucial part of the aesthetics of Western art music deals with the concepts of the organic and organicism. In a still broader context, music is connected to the episteme of "nature". According to Claude Lévi-Strauss, by music we become conscious of the physiological roots of our being. In learned music, a special "pastoral" style was developed to portray nature. For example, many musical topics of the classical style relate to nature and the outdoor life, such as the horn signals in Weber and at the opening of Beethoven's *"Les adieux"*. When Adorno said that "Sibelius's music is all Nature", this statement referred to many things, but for him it was mainly a negative aesthetic category in the musical-social situation in 1937. Closer inspection shows, however, that Jean Sibelius's work ranks alongside the "Nature music" of Beethoven's "Pastoral" Symphony and the overture to Mendelssohn's *A Midsummer Night's Dream*. The inconsistency in Adorno's thinking was that, when Sibelius evoked nature it was doomed immediately, but if Mahler did so, then it represented the progressive Hegelian *Weltlauf*.

Nature appears in so many ways in the aesthetics of Western art music that only Arthur Lovejoy, in his classic essay "Nature as Aesthetic Norm" (1948), has attempted to list them all. Nature can mean human nature, the cosmic order, imitation of nature, truthfulness, objective beauty, simplicity, symmetry, balance, the primacy of emotion, spontaneity, naivety, primitivism, irregularity, avoidance of symmetry, expression of the artist's voice, the fullness of human life, savagery, fecundity, evolution, and so on. All of these categories obtain in music.

Along with the development of the idea of absolute music – which meant instrumental music – there emerged the idea of the symphony and symphonism. This notion was in turn intimately related to the idea of organic growth. This aesthetic norm took hold, becoming an influential value in the entire tradition of symphonic music. In some countries, to write a symphony is still considered the high-mark of a career, whereas in others, such is no longer the case. (Debussy once left a concert hall in the middle of a Beethoven symphony, complaining "Oh no, now he starts to develop.")

According to Ernst Kurth there were two important lines of development in the history of Western art music. One was the periodic formal principle, based on the lied and the march and developed by Viennese classicism. It is characterized by clear-cut two-, four-, and eight-bar units, out of which more expansive musical forms can be composed. The other principle was linear art, independent of any strict measures and bar lines, which started with Palestrina's polyphony and culminated in J. S. Bach's melodies, an example being the freely undulating lines of the Chromatic Fantasy. These two principles were the basic forces of musical formation. And as we have said, for Kurth music was kinetic energy. The aurally manifest form (signifier) of music was not essential; music only appeared by means of or was represented by it. Thus, all music approaches the status of "nature" if one interprets the latter in a Bergsonian way as *élan vital*, or living energy. For Kurth music was "organic" when it followed a free motor impulse. Quadrangular, periodic rhythm was for him artificial, a kind of "cultural" filter overlaid upon nature, even though it was based on the "binary" corporeality of actions such as singing and marching.

At approximately the same time as Kurth, another music theoretician from the Germanic area, Heinrich Schenker, developed his own conception of tonal music, which was also based on "nature". Nature was for Schenker the triad, produced by the natural overtone series, which he called the "chord of nature" (*Urklang*), whose intervals were filled by a primal melodic line plus a bass, together forming the *Ursatz* (cf. Ch. 2.3, above). Prolongation of the latter by means of artistic improvisation produced the only "good" music. Good music – that is, the only music worth analyzing and listening to – was of course tonal music and particularly German tonal music. Schenker drew his concept of organicism from Goethe and the latter's doctrine of the metamorphosis of plants.

Kurth and Schenker represent two different views of organicism in music. According to Kurth, organicity or "kinetic energy" arises primarily in the ebb and flow of the linear, horizontal movement of music, or in semiotic language, in its *syntagmatic* structure. By contrast, for Schenker the organic appears in the vertical movement from a deep structure towards the surface, from *Hintergrund* to *Vordergrund*, that is to say, in music's *paradigmatic* structure. From the syntagmatic perspective, the organic nature of music obtains by a certain arabesque movement. *l'art nouveau*, for instance, would be an ideally "organic" style period, with its twining arabesques in leaf-like shapes. From the paradigmatic view, organicism is seen as the inner growth and unfolding of music. Stefan Kostka, in his *Materials and Techniques of Twentieth-Century Music*, defines the organic in music, as opposed to the inorganic:

> A traditional painting depicts something, and if the painting is a good one, every part of the canvas contributes to the effectiveness of the visual message that the artist is trying to convey. In traditional literature every passage has its purpose – fleshing out a character, setting the mood, developing the plot, and so on. The same is generally true of music in the European tradition: the composition is considered to be greater than the sum of its parts, a work of art in which each passage has a function that is vital to the overall plan of a work. Think of any tonal work that you know well, and imagine what it would be like if its parts, themes, transitions and so forth were randomly rearranged. It might be interesting to see how it would turn out, but the piece would almost certainly not be as effective as a whole. (Kostka 1999: 152–153)

Kostka goes on to emphasize that twentieth-century music evidenced a widespread reaction against the traditional organic view, that is to say, the idea of a composition as a teleological process. He singles out Stockhausen's "moment" form as the antithesis of organicity.

In a broader sense, however, the organicism of music can be connected with the general problem of arbitrary, conventional articulation versus iconic or indexical articulation of a sign system: all *grammars*, including musical ones, are in Saussurean theory arbitrary and constructed, based on a set of particular rules. These rules can be made explicit and thereby artificially generate music according to the model, or *langue*.

Contrary to this approach – which exemplifies the idea of nonorganic form – is the view of music as a *design* or *Gestalt*, terms used by the Canadian composer and music semiotician, David Lidov. Grammar, as a set of static rules, can never be organic. Only design or gestalt can be related to something living. In support of this view, we can note that reformers and inventors of musical grammars, such as Schoenberg, rarely number among "organic"-sounding composers.

This leads us to ask, At what point do we experience music as organic? Does organicity, when experienced consciously, no longer seem as organic as it did before? In other words, is the organic an unconscious category, as Réti viewed the motivic process to be? Organicity sometimes appears to be the consequence of a certain activity of the musical enunciator, whether composer or interpreter. If too much deliberation goes into the composition, then the resulting music is no longer organic. Only when composition takes place in a trance or under inspiration is the result organic. Such a case would involve a special dialogical relationship between the utterance and the act of uttering, between the text and its producer.

Yet even this definition does not help clarify what "organic" means as a quality of a musical text. Why is one composition organic and another one not? One explanation is that all mechanical repetition and potpourri-like formations are inorganic. Boris Asafiev advanced this idea in his intonation theory. As late as in Beethoven's symphonies "a composition became an organically and psychologically motivated whole, which unfolds as growth and development" (Asafiev 1977, 2: 489). As an example Asafiev points to the overture to Wagner's *Die Meistersinger*. It is a hidden symphony, whose parts – sonata allegro, andante, scherzo, and finale – blend together in such a way as to follow each other logically. They occur, one after the other, as various phases of a cycle, as a single line of development (Asafiev 1977, 2: 490). Asafiev also calls such an organic form "dialectic".

If such a fusion is to be taken as "organic", then it is exemplified by such pieces as Liszt's B-minor Sonata, Schubert's *Wanderer Fantasy*, Sibelius's Seventh Symphony, as well as the blending together of the first movement and scherzo in the latter's Fifth Symphony. Carl Dahlhaus echoes Asafiev in his interpretation of Beethoven's symphonic form, when he insists that musical form is not like a mould that can simply be filled with individual themes (Dahlhaus 1985: 369). Beethoven did not compose "in" form but "with" form. He may, for example, shift transitional material or aspects of the main theme into a subordinate theme. The difference between Schubert and Beethoven is thus clear. In Schubert the form is associative, potpourri-like, but in Beethoven it is "developing variation" (which term Dahlhaus borrows from Schoenberg): the listener experiences connected, similar motives as a musical logic, the counterpart to mere association.

In semiotic terms, syntagmatic linearity alone does not suffice – neither inner iconic similarity nor mere inner indexicality. The musical form has to be experienced as goal-directed, *als zweckmässig*, in Kant's terms, otherwise the music is not organic. Asafiev, too, pays attention to the goal-directedness of music, distinguishing between two types of *telos* or finalities in symphonic literature: either the cheerful and free fusion of the personality with the cosmos (Beethoven) or spiritual pain and isolation amidst the crowd, oblivion, and tragic destruction. For Asafiev, musical finality is achieved when a leading idea is revealed, which captures the attention and out of which successive waves of development emerge (1977, vol. 2: 483). This Asafievian ideal is almost literally realized in Sibelius. In the Fifth Symphony, for example, a constant struggle takes place between these two forms of finality, and until the very end the listener remains unaware of which solution the composer has chosen.

Thus, in order for music to be organic, it requires more than motivic and thematic unity; it must consist of more than fortuitous variation. Nor is it enough that these variations follow each other indexically and smoothly. Music has to progress towards some goal or *telos*; music must be directional. As a temporal art, all music has finality, of course. But here we do not mean the common temporality of music but temporality as "marked" (cf. Hatten 1994). In organic music, musical time is organized towards a certain goal.

How does a listener know that the music has a goal and a direction? Leonard B. Meyer, in his *Explaining Music* (1973), presents a theory of melody that emphasizes well-formed melodic shapes. There are certain musical-cognitive archetypes, the breaking or deficient fulfillment of which causes the listener to remain waiting for the right solution, the correct design (cf. Ch. 1.4.1, thesis 10). For instance, if a piece begins with a "gapped" melody, then a *telos* for music is created by the gap, which might not be filled until the very end of the piece. This tension keeps the music in motion and produces the kinetic energy or catalysing impulse. An example is the opening of Sibelius's Fifth Symphony, where a motive sounds that is incomplete in three respects. Firstly, this motive is syncopated and in 12/8 meter. Secondly, its verse structure is irregular (Luyken 1995: 42–43). Thirdly, it is based on an open fifth-fourth intervallic shape, which causes the listener to remain waiting for these gaps to be filled (see Ex. 10).

Harmonically the music hovers around the six-four chord of E-flat major, similar to the beginning of Beethoven's Sonata Op. 31 No. 3. Beethoven lets the phrase cadence on the tonic rather soon, however, whereas Sibelius delays it until the very end of the symphony. There

*Ex. 10.*   Sibelius, Symphony No. 5, bars 1–3.

we also hear the fifths and fourths filled with a stepwise scale passage and leading tones. This is the great and relieving climax of the whole work, all the more since we have been oscillating between various tragic alternatives just before it arrives. The extremely restless and ambiguous theme on the Neapolitan chord ceases its wandering and is filled with an E flat minor scale (which the sketches show to be one of the symphony's founding ideas). But even the end of the symphony, where the tonic is confirmed with a cadence, does not attain rhythmic balance, since not all of the cadential chords occur on strong beats. There is a particular irony in this, a musical pun, the wish to show that this situation is not too serious (a rare moment in Sibelius). Rather, it recalls what happens in a play when the clown returns and addresses the audience directly to recite the final words, or as in the closing morality segment of Mozart's *Don Giovanni*.

Music thus has its own *telos,* which sets energies in motion. They emerge from musical designs which we expect to be completed. According to Jan LaRue (1992), music has a special dimension of *growth* – a rather organic term in itself – that binds all of the musical parameters together.

Can "organicism" arise from some other aspect of the music? For instance, Sibelius's music typically has fields that constitute the elements for the "space dramaturgy" analyzed by Luyken (1995). Sibelius's music often seems to be driven into a kind of fenced-in area, from which there is no exit. Such fields were already present in early Sibelius, for instance, in *En Saga*, realized by means of a simple repetitive form. That is to say, the same melody or theme recurs until, by repetition, it loses its character as a musical subject that distinguishes itself from its surroundings. The music itself becomes a subjectless environment. This is a particularly Sibelian way of deactorializing music, so as to make it an impersonal, natural process that involves no thinking or feeling subject. In the Fifth Symphony, such a field is formed by the chromatic lament motives in the first movement (score numbers J-M), which sound for a very long time. Such a situation is not far from Ligeti's field technique. But Sibelius's predominantly "static" field arises from a continuous, micro-organic process. How does one enter and exit such a field? In the Fifth Symphony, the field exhausts itself. It is not left by means of a musical "escape route", such as modulation.

The organic nature of music also depends on the method of analysis. Methods based on musical "functions" better account for organic qualities than do tectonic, segmentational, mechanistic models (such as distributional and paradigmatic procedures). The basic problem of organic music is not how the music can be divided into smaller parts but rather how those parts cohere.

As noted earlier (Ch. 2.3), Boris Asafiev viewed music as consisting of three main phases: *initium, motus*, and *terminus*. In Greimassian semiotics these correspond to the aspectual semes of inchoativity, durativity, and terminativity. In Claude Brémond's narratology, they parallel the three phases of storytelling: virtuality, passage/non-passage to action, achievement/inachievement. Similar theories have been developed elsewhere.

Music may become organic in other ways. Biologist Jakob von Uexküll's biosemiotics and doctrine of *Umwelt* have recently been provoking lively discussion among semioticians. His ideas might also apply to music. His theory is based on the idea that every organism functions according to a preestablished "score" which determines the nature of its *Umwelt*. The organism connects to that world by two processes, *Merken* and *Wirken*. Every organism has its particular *Ichton*, which determines its being and acting. We see in this concept an analogy to music, such that every theme, motive, and intonation lives in its own, characteristic musical *Umwelt*. An organic composer takes into account the relationship of a musical event to its musical environment. A good example of the relationship of a theme to its *Umwelt* would be the variations of the Andante theme in Beethoven's Fifth Symphony (Ex. 11). There the main motive continually shifts into new sound-milieus, and the listener pays more attention to these environments than to the theme itself.

In the classical tradition, melody and accompaniment are derived from the same material, as at the beginning of Schumann's *C major Fantasy*, where the accompaniment figure is the same as the descending theme in the upper register. In this case and others, the organic nature of music lies in the interaction of musical event and its environ-

*Ex. 11.* Beethoven, Symphony No. 5, bars 106–109.

ment. By contrast, the postmodern style – early examples of which are Poulenc's *Concerto for Two Pianos* and even Stravinsky's neoclassicism – uses quotation techniques and avoids organic unity. The environment of the theme must be alienating. That is to say, if the context is tonal, for example, then the citation has to distinguish itself as dissonant. Conversely, if the context is atonal, the citation has to be distinguished by its tonality. In Sibelius's Fifth Symphony, even in the earlier version of 1915, there is a strangely dissonant variant of the "Neapolitan" theme which is superimposed on the "Swan" theme – one of the rare futurist and fauvist moments in all of Sibelius's output. There the theme appears as if it were in a wrong isotopy or musical *Umwelt*.

Others have connected music with biology. Conductor Wilhelm Furtwängler wrote about the biological foundation of all music. However, his use of the term "biology" in music is metaphorical and thus as ambiguous as is the concept of "nature" when applied to any art form. To Furtwängler, the "absolute" music of the classical period was much more than functional or casual. Dahlhaus credits Vienna's musically rich and many-sided *Umwelt* for the emergence of the classical style. But Furtwängler believes that there was more to it than that:

> It is not only casual music bound with life ... it is not directly connected with the ballet, play or drama, but can also well be so. What it touches, it changes. It gathers into it the fullness of the entire organic life and reflects it there like in a mirror. It creates from itself the extremely broad world of independent musical forms – lied form, fugue, sonata form are only its basic types. It is able to do so because it is enough for itself. It naturally corresponds to man's biological presuppositions. (Furtwängler 1951: 27)

Furtwängler believes these presuppositions are based on the alternation of tension and relaxation: "The ascending and descending movement of tension and release reflects the rhythm of life: as long as we breathe, one activity is at rest, the other one in motion. The state of rest is more original and primal... One of the basic doctrines of modern biology is that in complicated bodily activities ... the relaxation of tension has a decisive meaning" (Furtwängler 1951: 27).

In my own theory of semiotics (Tarasti 1994), I address such tension and relaxation in terms of two basic modalities, "being" and "doing", derived from Greimas's model. These modalities also concern the organic in music. What brings about being and doing in music? What gives us the impression that we either simply "are" in music or that something is happening? These questions can be answered by observation of the temporal, spatial, and actorial articulations in music. These articulations belong to the music of all cultures, not just to Western art music.

Furtwängler, however, relates "being" (relaxation) and "doing" (tension) strictly with tonality: "The state of rest in music in its full cogency is only produced by tonality. Only it is able to create an objectively existing state of rest (subjectively we can of course consider any personal impression as rest)." Furtwängler is thus bound to a certain musical ontology. The deepest level of music for him is always tonal, since it is based on the Nature-given force of the triad.

Furtwängler's tonal ontology is a long-abandoned position, but in the context of our essay it has a certain pertinence. Even some semiotically oriented scholars base their theories on a "biological" ontology, though no longer joining it to tonality as a kind of ahistoric, universal principle. Ivanka Stoianova (1978), for instance, thinks that musical form has two aspects: processual and architectonic. The processual aspect refers to musical enunciation, and the architectonic aspect concerns the musical utterance as a ready-made text, as an art-work existing outside of time. Thus we get two musical counterforces: the kinetic, which is based on motion, change, process; and the static, which is based on immobility, stability, and architectonics. Musical form as a process, i.e., as sounding manifestation, and as aural architecture are two sides of the same artistic activity.

Architectonic form – the external mould as described by Réti and Kandinsky – seems to immobilize the stream of music. All musical style periods, from the classical to the romantic to the avant-garde, include such an immobilizing effect, which stems from architectonic form. The means of stopping the musical stream consist of hierarchical, historically determined formal schemes, whereas processuality appears in transformations and emergent contrasts, such as developing variation. For Stoianova, the "being" of music is the same as it is for Furtwängler. It is not an ontological or teleological end-state of music toward which everything strives, but is rather the stopping of "normal", and hence, "biological", musical time.

In this sense, generative models are epistemologically contradictory. The idea of a surface that is gradually generated from a deep structure is based on hierarchies, and thus on something static and architectonic, which stops musical movement. This has as its consequence the static, atemporal character and artificiality of generative analyses. They are mechanistic elucidations of musical grammars using hierarchical axiomatic rules. At the same time, the idea of a generative course contains the thought of a process, in which the immanent is in the end made manifest. The generative course thus refers to a basic semiotic force of the whole universe: the movement from content to expression. Greimas's generative course and other such models can clarify the "organic" course of processes of meaning. At the same time, however, they contain an inorganic and architectonic aspect, which is a strange principle when applied to phenomenal musical experience.

We can try to clarify further the "organic" in music by means of detailed formal and style analysis. A good example is Veijo Murtomäki's (1993) study of organic unity in Sibelius's symphonies. He confirms the importance of organic metaphors among all the proponents of "dynamic" form theory in German musicology. He mentions Kurth, Schenker, Halm, and the continuation of their thought in Schoenberg and Webern. The views of the latter are especially permeated by the metaphor of a biological organism that develops from a single, initial idea, from which emerges the music's inner unity (*zusammenhangen*). It is ironic that these reformers of musical grammars and pioneers of the "modernist" project used models of thought inherited from romanticism. In any case, Murtomäki lists five ways in which music can be organic, with special emphasis on how Stoianova's immobilizing forms – such as sonata, symphony, string quartet, and so on – become organic or processual by means of cyclic technique. For Murtomäki, organicity obtains when a composition with more than one movement is made to sound like a whole. This is accomplished by cyclic procedures, which can be either external or internal; that is, they can either unify the materials or join parts together: (1) Movements may be linked by similar thematic openings. (2) Either thematic "germs" or cells are moved almost imperceptibly from one movement to another, or themes appear in an easily recognizable guise in later movements. (3) A special motto or *idée fixe* may appear in every movement. (4) The principle may be one of family unity: the parts are connected by metamorphoses of the same theme. (5) The most sophisticated way is continuous variation, by which new ideas result from a process of transformation.

The last-mentioned case is the most intriguing one. When do we experience in music that some process "generates" or gives birth to another event? Put another way, When do we experience that some event T is the consequence of a former event P? Does event T serve as the *telos* of event P? If so, precisely what does this mean? The finale of Sibelius's Second Symphony is doubtless a good illustration of the

idea of a *telos*, given the way that it is attained only after much struggle. But we can also imagine a process during which the listener does
not know what will follow. Only when the result of T is heard after
the process of P does one realize that this is precisely what everything
prior to it was leading to. In such a case, one cannot say that T serves
as a teleological goal of P, since it is perceived as such only after the
fact.

How can we semiotically interpret such relationships? From a narratological perspective, we can consider some event a subject and its
goal to be the event, an object, that is searched for by the subject. In
Greimassian terms, at first the subject is disjuncted from the object,
then later attains or is conjuncted with it (cf. Ch. 1.3). For instance, a
theme in the dominant key "wants" to be united with the tonic. Yet this
does not quite correspond to the truth, since the result of the metamorphosis can in fact be something which its preceding event is not aware
of, so to say, or does not even "want". Only the musical superenuncia-
tor – the composer – knows that event T is a logical, organic result of
process P. Or rather, the subject S is transformed into another subject
S1 or Q or X, when the music steps, as it were, into "otherness", when
it shifts to a kind of non-being via the process of becoming. What is
involved, then, is an organic, abruptly contrasting shift from a subject
S to a subject Q. The subjects S and Q are felt to belong to the same
musical *Umwelt,* in which we move from the *Lebenswelt* of subject S
to that of subject Q.

To end our discussion on the metaphor of the "organic" as a music-
theoretical episteme, we can note that the same thing happens with it
as with the notion of "nature". As Lovejoy's analysis and our cases
show, "nature" can mean almost anything, both order and disorder. In
the same way, organic unity and growth can mean almost anything.
Why, then, do we examine a phenomenon which leads to such ambiva-
lence? It is because nature and organic growth have meant something
to philosophers and to musical scholars, especially to those studying
symphonic thought. They are notions loaded with powerful ideological concepts, whose precise meaning might be obscure, but which
have been and are still used when we speak about essential things in
music. We cannot ignore these terms just because their linguistic usage

is not always logical and coherent. Next I ponder their relevance to Sibelius, particularly regarding his Fifth Symphony.

## 4.2 Sibelius and the idea of the "organic"

One could turn Adorno's assessment around by claiming that *Sibelius's* music is "organic" whereas *Mahler's* music is "inorganic". In that case, the terms organic / inorganic would be primarily analytic concepts, such that "organic" music would be based on the following conditions: (1) All the musical actors inhabit their proper *Umwelt*; in semiotic terms, the themes move in their proper isotopies. (2) All the musical material stems from the same source; that is to say, thematicity, in semiotic terms, would be innerly iconic. (3) All the musical events follow each other coherently; this is LaRue's principle of growth, or the inner indexicality of music. (4) The music strives toward a goal; this has to do with temporality and the aspectual semes of beginning, continuing, and closing.

Sibelius's music can be experienced in many ways as "organic". First, many think that the category of Nature is present therein. As Lorenz Luyken has stated, Sibelius's music refers to the pastoral, in the manner of Beethoven, Mendelssohn, and Wagner. There is much evidence, on the part of both Finnish and non-Finnish scholars, that the *poiesis* (production) and *aisthesis* (reception) of his music is connected to Finland's natural geography. For example, when Leonard Bernstein introduced Sibelius's use of the mixolydian mode in the Sixth Symphony to an audience of young listeners in New York, he said that it evoked the lonely forests of Finland. But closeness to nature, as a category of reception, does not make music internally "organic".

What about the level of *poiesis?* Erik Tawaststjerna carefully studied the sketches of the Fifth Symphony, and related that work to Scriabin's ecstatic-mystical view of art and to his empathy with the cosmos. After quoting a poem by Scriabin, Tawaststjerna says, "But it is not erroneous to think what appealed to Sibelius in Scriabin was precisely the "cosmic" dimension of his music, which is related also to his efforts to break through the boundaries of tonality." This quotation has to be read in the light of the modernist project, insofar as it represents the detachment of man from "cosmos" and insofar as "organic" music means a return to this cosmic unity. For Scriabin it meant probing the extreme limits of tonality, but in Sibelius the "cosmic" style and rejection of the modernist project meant expressly the acceptance of tonality. The ecstatic E-flat major at the end of the Fifth Symphony is related to the finale of Musorgsky's *Pictures at an Exhibition*, which also cadences with a similar, pendulum-like motive. From this we might infer that the organic style and the return to cosmic unity, in the sense advanced by Charles Taylor (1989) in his *The Sources of the Self*, is not always the same as the return to tonality. This engagement, or *embrayage*, can also take place on levels of the musical text other than spatial ones.

Tawaststjerna's study seems to prove that Sibelius's organic symphonic logic is based on the composer's way of elaborating the material; it is clearly the category of *poiesis*. Tawaststjerna is moreover inclined to think that the organic quality of Sibelius's symphonies emerged as a result of a trance-like process guided by unconscious inspiration. When discussing the creation of the Fifth Symphony he deals with many of the musical ideas found in Sibelius's sketches of his Fifth and Sixth Symphonies. He compares this process to a puzzle whose pieces are fragments of a mosaic, like the "floor of the sky" (Tawaststjerna 1978: 61). In this phase the symphony still essentially appears as a paradigmatic table, and its elaboration is a completely rational, non-organic activity. But Tawaststjerna continues: "In the case of Sibelius I am inclined to consider his creative work an interaction of inspirational and intellectual components. Their relationship continuously varies. Basically he was dependent on his inspiration. He had his "wonderful" trances... The shaping of the themes seems to have happened intuitively" (Tawaststjerna 1978: 65).

Nevertheless, if we refer to our aforementioned criteria for organicity, then on a paradigmatic level organicism stems from the inner similarity of the musical substance. Tawaststjerna reduces all the motives of the Fifth Symphony to two: the "step motive" and the "swing motive". But even this is not enough, since the material has to be put into a syntagmatically coherent order. Only then can we experience music as organic.

Erkki Salmenhaara, another Sibelius specialist, takes a similar view of the composer's organic techniques. Like Tawaststjerna, he stresses that organicity emerges in the mind of the composer, who chooses from an infinite number of paradigms those which are relevant to the intended musical shape. In his study of the symphonic poem *Tapiola* Salmenhaara quotes the British scholar Cecil Gray: "The thematic materials in Sibelius ... seem to regenerate in a way which the biologists call cell division: they are split and broken into several theme units, [and] every bar of the original organism is subjected to development". Thus behind the conventional, formal outline of music there looms another shape, which is dynamic, processual, or, in our terminology, "organic" (1970: 37). Salmenhaara continues: "By organic development it must be understood that various results of the development – different themes and motives – are in an "organic" connection with each other" (1970: 37). What is interesting here is Salmenhaara's term "results". Themes in organic music can be experienced as results of a process – which is not the same as the *telos,* the Kantian *Zweck.* There are of course processes that from the start aim for a certain goal, but there are also processes whose result is not known in advance. For instance, the transition to the Finale of Beethoven's Fifth Symphony, the long pedal point on G, leads finally to the theme of victory, which is something like a product of this process: we know to expect something, but are not sure exactly what. The same thing occurs with the intermediate section of the *"Waldstein",* which leads to the sunrise theme of the last movement. Sometimes the result of the process is quite startling, as in Sibelius's *Karelia* music, where a long transition takes place before the theme bursts out into the national anthem of Finland. The result does not grow organically from the previous material but is a quotation justified by an extramusical program.

Salmenhaara also defines nonorganic music, one example being the variation sets of the classical style. In them the gestalt of the theme remains the same; it is just ornamented – think of Mozart's *Unser dummer Pöbel meint* or *Ah vous dirai-je Maman.* On the other hand, Salmenhaara emphasizes that, in organic variation, what is crucial is not the goal of the process but the metamorphosis itself. "It is like a self-reflecting process: the main thing is not that the development form bridges between architectonic climaxes, but the aim is for continuous transformation, the constant turning of the motives into new shapes." This latter comment is of great interest since it excludes *telos* from organicity: the organic transformation does not have a goal to strive for; rather, the variation becomes self-reflexive. What kind of phenomenal experience would this evoke? Doubtless a kind of static, slowly changing sound field. Has Salmenhaara unknowingly projected Ligetian field technique onto Sibelius in order to see the latter as a representative of a certain avant-garde movement? If organicity were the same as Ligeti's field technique, that would place Sibelius within the panorama of the new music of the twentieth century. The listener experiences such fields as stasis, a limbo from which there is no exit. This situation undeniably occurs in Sibelius's Fifth Symphony, especially at score letters J and K. The *Allegro moderato* section of K-P and the fluttering, Mendelssohnian string figurations in the last movement also contain such self-reflexive organic transformation.

It is essential to this line of reasoning to speak about music as *shapes* or *Gestalts* but not as grammar. Some composers, such as Arnold Schoenberg, have concentrated on reforming musical grammars. Other composers, by contrast, have made their main contributions at the level of gestalt, that is, made innovations even when the grammar remained the same. Debussy, Stravinsky, and Sibelius seem to belong to this line. Hence, Adorno could not appreciate them. His hyperrational music philosophy was bound with the modernist project, in the aforementioned philosophical sense. On this view, music is grammar, conventional, arbitrary, and must maintain this aura of artificiality in order to be progressive. Music that functions via iconic shapes would mean a rejection of such critical distance, by both composer and listener. Over the course of time humankind has become disconnected from nature and the cosmos; hence one must remain constantly aware of this primal negation and difference. The return to unity with the cosmos, with nature, would mean the return to a lawless and barbaric original state (the Germany of the 1930s is an example). It is always regression. The goal of organic music is precisely to return the listener to the cosmos, to natural principles which appear at the level of pre-linguistic gestalts. Organic music is pre-linguistic and non-verbal. It is impossible to reduce Sibelius's music to the language-likeness of tropes or rhetorical figures.

There is, however, one difficulty in defining the organic, which Salmenhaara clearly notices when he says, "... organic transforma-tion has one special feature which is difficult to analyze, namely, it is *musical* by nature. Precisely here we have the difference between the motivic techniques of Sibelius and Schoenberg. The music of the latter is theoretical and technical in nature rather than based on musi-cal gestalts." The twelve tones of a row can be manipulated in many ways that do not have a meaning-creating shape. Seen in this light, organic music is precisely music of *design*.

How can we prove that music based on a complicated motivic tech-nique is organic? For one thing, only a few of all the possible motivic transformations are used. Only those motives which are musically meaningful are taken into account, and that is why the listener notices their organic unity. The musical construction does not follow an exter-nal system – just purely musical logic.

Hence the term "organic" means the same as the "musically logi-cal", which in turn means the "musically meaningful". So we have fallen into a circle. What does it mean to be "very musical"? Some-times it means that the musical performance in some way touches or speaks to us. But just to say that a musical score is "musical" reveals very little. We cannot only look at the text, i.e., the score. We must consider the entire situation of musical communication, not only the utterance, but the utterer as well. Only the choices made by the human "brain" (or enunciator or composer) can make any music organic. This involves a quality made manifest by the musical enunciator, in the dialogue between the musical material and the person who deals with it. Insofar as the musical mind intuitively filters and shapes musi-cal materials into a certain gestalt, music becomes organic. Neither mere mathematical structure nor grammaticality suffice to make music organic. Although utterances may be "well-formed" or "grammatical", we do not necessarily experience them as organic. Principles said to stem from the brain of the enunciator have been studied by statistic-mathematical methods derived from the "law of Zipf". The latter says that, when all the notes or words of an art work are counted, they can be shown to follow a certain distribution along the "Zipf curve". Using this model, one can determine when a work is overwritten or under-written, that is, when it has too many or too few notes. Works written by a great master, in one breath, as it were, follow the Zipf law better than those written episodically. Here the question of the organic shifts from the textual to the cognitive level: How does the enunciator pick those elements which on the textual level will become organic?

To begin to answer this question, one might apply Uexküll's biosemiotic theory to music. As discussed above, each organism has its own *Ich-ton*, which determines the messages it receives from the *Umwelt* that surrounds it. Applied to music, this concept would mean that every composition is a kind of "model" of a living "organism". The life of such an organism, its "being" and "doing", is guided by its view of itself, which helps the organism to choose according to its "inner" score those signs which it sends and receives. If a musical organism consists of motives, those motives constitute kinds of "cells" that communicate with each other, as happens in living organisms. This communication is completely determined by the inner organisa-tion of the organism, its *Ich-ton*.

Music is a symbolic depiction of this process. The musical organ-ism that emerges from the brain of the composer takes shape from a certain basic idea or isotopy, what Sibelius called an "atmosphere", which determines which motives are accepted into this inner process and which ones are rejected. By observing this microlevel of musical "cells" in the life of the musical organism, we can follow what some motivic cell or "actor" is doing and how it influences the other cells. Sometimes the "act" of a motive at first goes unnoticed, becoming influential only later. Sometimes the composer decides upon the *Ich-ton* of the work as early as in the opening bars. For instance, the core motive of Sibelius's Fourth Symphony sounds at the very start of the work. In the same way, the "bucolic" horn signal at the opening of the Fifth Symphony is a "cell" that, in order to become a complete gestalt, needs to have its interval filled, which does not happen until the end of the symphony. Hence, in music as in living organisms, one cell "calls out" for another. Precisely this type of inner process makes a work organic.

Organicity therefore depends on the enunciator's (composer"s) consciousness. In organic music, this consciousness in turn follows the biosemiotic principle by which motives communicate with each other according to a certain "inner" score. One may presume that the inner score is different in each work. But one may also claim that in certain respects it is always the same, as Schenker, Kurth, and Asafiev have done. Nevertheless, the idea of an organic composition cannot be limited to a single, universal principle. For nature's scope of variation is unlimited, and thus always capable of producing new types of organisms. Basically, the organism always decides upon its own *Umwelt* or relationship to external reality. It is the organism that determines which signals, style influences, motivic borrowings, and so on that it accepts from the style of the time, from other composers, and even from itself. An instance of the latter occurs in Sibelius's moving materials from the Sixth Symphony to the Fifth. That is to say, the *Ich-ton* of the Fifth Symphony, its "inner score", allowed certain signs to be shifted into its own "cells", while rejecting others.

We can now return to the thesis presented above, namely, that Sibelius's music is organic and Mahler's is not. The *Ich-ton* of Sibelius's symphonies determines precisely which musical cells are accepted into the inner network of musical communication, that is to say, into the "community" of its musical actors. In contrast, Mahler chooses heterogeneous elements; his music's *Ich-ton* is far more fragmentary than that of Sibelius – it is contradictory and "modern". Mahler's symphonies encompass everything, but do so without the aforementioned selection criteria of the *Umwelt*. His musical actors do not communicate with each other as intensely or as intimately as do those of Sibelius. Rather, Mahler's work is ruled by "unit forms", by topics and musical cells articulated by social conventions. His music adapts itself more to structures of communication than to those of signification.

One of the best-known recent interpretations of Sibelius's Fifth Symphony is that by James Hepokoski (1993). His central concept for explaining Sibelian formal processes is the "rotation principle". Hepokoski denies the relevance of traditional *Formenlehre* for Sibelius, since his musical form grew from the inside out, as the composer himself often said (Hepokoski 1993: 22). Hepokoski claims that Sibelius typically uses repetition to "erase" the linear time of a work, by letting certain elements, motives, and entire sections recur cyclically again and again. Hepokoski thinks this phenomenon stems from the Finnish *Kalevala* recitation, as shown in the song *Illalle* (Op. 17 No. 6), in which a figure of 11 notes is repeated 16 times. Hepokoski observes that the rotation idea occurs not only in Russian but also in Austrian-German music, such as that of Schubert and Bruckner. In Sibelius, however, the rotation is a process rather than an architectonic scheme or mould. In this sense, such rotation serves well as an example of organic music. In Hepokoski's view, the rotational process starts with a musical statement that serves as the point of reference for later statements. The statement can be extensive at first hearing, containing various themes, motives, and figures which can even differ one from the other. It returns later, transformed a little, and can recur many times, such that it is heard each time as being more intensified.

In Hepokoski's theory the rotation principle in Sibelius is connected with the idea of a *telos*, that is, with the final climax of a piece as the goal of the musical process. Together, these two principles – rotation and *telos* – help explain the form of entire works, such as the Fifth Symphony. From the perspective of organicism, Hepokoski's notion of rotation provides the inner iconicity of a work, and *telos* serves as the extreme point of maturation of the work, which, so to say, pulls earlier rotations toward itself, causing them to grow and transform. From the beginning, inner processes among musical signs aim for the climax. This view differs from Salmenhaara's, which stresses the self-reflexivity of the transformation process. Hepokoski emphasizes more the syntagmatic aspect of music, whereas Salmenhaara focuses on the paradigmatic one. From a biosemiotic perspective, we can consider the *telos* of a symphony to be the same as its *Ich-ton,* which is revealed only at the end. On this view, Sibelius's symphonies constitute symbolic portrayals of his "wonderful ego".

## 4.3 Organic narrativity

This chapter would be incomplete without our relating the organic principle to an important kind of musical semiosis: narrativity. Narratologists demonstrated that texts extremely varied as to their material and their external shapes can be based on just a few narrative categories. Here we speak of the narrativity of a symphony on the level of form, not of aesthetic style. If Richard Strauss's *Alpine Symphony* and *Heldenleben* are narrative on the level of verbal reception, in Sibelius narrativity should be understood in a deeper sense, as a property of dynamic formal processes.

If music is organic, can it also be narrative? Is narrativity like language, rhetoric, grammar and other categories that separate the listener from the world of musical gestalts? Not at all, if narrativity is understood in a broader sense, as conceptualized by Greimas. Narrativity is a way of shaping the world in its temporal, spatial, and actorial course. Does "organic" narrativity thus mean that the text is articulated according to some primal narration? that it is a story of man's conjunction with or disjunction from nature and cosmos? Narrativity covers many of the sign processes discussed above. Further, one might assume that, in certain forms, it is precisely the way in which man's *Dasein* imitates the cosmic principles of nature. Narration can of course merely describe and classify the inner events of *Dasein*, but it can also be the way in which transcendental ideas are concretized in temporality. As a temporal art, music is thus one of the best means of narrativizing transcendental ideas.

I return again to Sibelius's Fifth Symphony, in order to make a narratological interpretation that relates to the aforementioned ideas of nature, the project of the "modern", and metaphors of organism. My interpretation derives from two listenings during which this narrative program was revealed to me. The first listening occurred in the early 1960s, at a performance by the Radio Symphony Orchestra at the University of Helsinki, under the direction of Jussi Jalas. I was seated quite near the front of the hall, on the right side, from which one could clearly see the conductor. Nothing remains in my mind from that performance except the climax: the *Largamente assai* at the end of the finale, the unison orchestral tutti on the note C. There the dissonance is at its sharpest, and the listener does not know where this tragic development might lead – until soon after it the whole symphony cadences and turns toward the tonic E-flat major as its final *telos* (compared to which the E-flat tonic at the end of the first movement was not a real return to home). At this crucial juncture, on the C and its leading tone, the conductor raised himself to full height and trembled all over (as Sibelius is also said to have done; see Tawaststjerna 1978: 147). This corporeal sign has remained in my memory.

The second listening took place in the summer of 1998 when Esapekka Salonen, visiting conductor of the Marinsky Theater in Mikkeli, included Sibelius's Fifth Symphony on the program. By then I was already familiar with the piano score, which naturally deepened the experience of hearing the work. At that performance, the true climax and solution of the work revealed itself as the events in score letter N, *Un pochettino largamento*, the E-flat minor section. The melody of that section is the first full theme-actor in the entire symphony, which is articulated in periodic form ending with a "normal" cadence. This theme is thus experienced as representing a kind of human subject that shows itself against the backdrop of the "cosmos". As noted earlier, Sibelius's music often gives the impression of a landscape without any human protagonist. Here the subject enters the stage, and it is the suffering, sentimental subject of Schiller (1978), a subject disjuncted from its object and given to resignation. It is a Tchaikovskian, resigned self, whose story has come to an end and whose speech is finally cut off (N: 16), as if by the dysphoric weight of its emotion. It is a subject who is detached from the cosmos, and yet it is basically the same subject which we heard in the previous movement, where it hovered restlessly, not yet knowing its fate. Tawaststjerna reduces it to another important theme of the Fifth Symphony, the step-motive, which is one of the very first ideas in the work. Certainly these motives were earlier fragments of a subject, but here in the *Un pochettino largamento* section the subject steps into the foreground, as a complete "person" who has suffered a catastrophe. At the end of the theme, the E-flat minor turns into major, which is like a *deus ex machina* solution to the threat of impending tragedy. The subject is rescued, so to speak, by being transported to another, cosmic level of nature, the latter represented by the well-known swing-motive. The association of this motive with nature is obvious already from the viewpoint of *poiesis*, as evidenced by Sibelius's diaries, in which he mentions swans in reference to this theme.

This theme thus symbolizes nature and cosmos for the whole symphony. But just when we have reached it, as a safe haven and salvation of the individual from tragedy, even this level falls into a crisis. The swing-motive is led into deeper and deeper dissonance via modulations that move still further away from the tonic. The theme-actor whose fate we were following was thus not safe, as we had thought. What is now involved is nature's crisis, Sibelius's *Götterdämmerung*. The crisis culminates in the above-mentioned C, after which the music leads to a cadence on the tonic E-flat major, with many ensuing chromatic tones – an answer to the gap opened by the "bucolic" motive of the first movement. Therefore the answer, which has been kept secret, finally comes to light. Perhaps because it represents a kind of rescue on the cosmic level, it is impossible to describe this moment verbally. In any case, there remains yet one more surprise: six *sforzando* chords punctuate the ending, played by tutti orchestra. These resume the problem of the horn signal and its solution, but the effect is very surprising, lightening, consciously alienating – all is only play; we can sigh in relief.

The above description holds true only for the final version of the symphony. In the earlier version, of 1915, the subject-theme appears to the very end as detached, disjuncted from the cosmos, as an individual and alienated theme-actor who does not unite with the cosmic order. As a symbol of the modernist project, it constantly evokes its existence by means of dissonances. Its relation to the ambiguous Neapolitan motive is quite clear as early as in section D of the Finale, when the swing-theme bursts out and the subject-theme sounds as a savage, illogical, and dissonant counterpart, such as one hears in the riotous simultaneities of Charles Ives. There the subject-theme obviously belongs to the same family as the descending and ascending leaps of fourths in the Neapolitan motive of the first movement (score letter B: 5–6). The impression is even one of bitonality, as was noticed at the first performance of the work. Otto Kotilainen spoke of a "strange, piercing signal which … gives an upsetting impression." The effect is completely modernistic, and it represents, in the philosophical sense, the "modern" subject, alienated by its separation from the cosmos.

The gradual unfolding of the subject-theme in its various "rotations" is is the central narrative moment of the whole symphony. In the 1915 version, the theme never seems to find its proper isotopy, its own *Umwelt*. Its difference remains until the end, when it returns in the *Un pochettino largamente*, and even there it is still the tragic and isolated theme actor, who is destined for destruction. But in the *Un pochettino largamente* section it takes on an extremely appealing sensual shape, as if a last gesture to serve as the counterpart of the swing-theme. This is related to the idea of the return to the cosmos. In the 1915 version, this subject-theme does not merge with nature in the end, as it does in the final version of symphony. It remains as the pedal point of the strings, to remind one of its existence – even the six chords at the end are heard against this pedal. In the philosophical-semiotic sense, the 1915 version keeps to the modernist project in its narrative program. To the very end, the subject remains separated from the cosmos. By contrast, in the version of 1919 the subject fuses with the cosmic level. Thus, even in the narrative sense, this symphony represents the "organic" in music.

# Chapter 5
# The emancipation of the sign: On corporeal and gestural meanings in music

Anglo-American musicology is now embracing the semiotic point of view. The fact that so many scholars are now writing about Otherness in music, about difference, and about the construction of social reality, as well as about implicit meanings hidden in musical institutions, about the body as a social and ideological product, gendering, and much more – all this is a consequence not only of the acceptance of post-structuralist, sociological, post-modern and feminist premises, but of something without which none of these approaches would have been possible. This phenomenon could be called the "emancipation of the sign".

Scholars have suddenly recognised that music always has a content, and that this content has a conventional, arbitrary relationship to its signifier, i.e., the aural and physical embodiment of the musical sign. Since this relationship is arbitrary, one might exclaim: "Let us find other kinds of agreement – *un nouveau contrat sémio-social!* Away with traditions!" We want to make a new start, one that is no longer ideological, essentialist, racist or secretly nationalistic – a new beginning which neither consciously nor unconsciously creates differences or makes value judgments. As extreme examples we may consider certain feminist analyses, such as Susan McClary's famous image of Beethoven as a rapist in the recapitulation of the finale in the Ninth Symphony. In such analyses, the musicological cards have been reshuffled, as it were, and the game is played from new starting-points – but whether it is also played according to new rules is not so certain.

True, feminist scholars have revealed the centuries-long oppression of women in our music culture, as well as the immanent patriarchal systems of signification in musical discourse itself. But when one attempts to disclose the concealed and rejected "feminine" in musical traits, one has to ask, What is their origin? Are they only Hegelian negations of the dominant masculine culture, negations which now have their turn at participating in the dialectics of becoming? If so, one has to ask, From where did the categories of masculine culture or "being" originate? From corporeal qualities? Is, as Freud said, anatomy destiny? If this is true, then such a negation is itself bound to essentialist assumptions about the corporeality of masculine culture. From a man's body one can iconically infer, if you will, all the symbolic forms in Western culture. To proceed in this way, however, we can never get beyond the corporeality thesis. Consequently, feminine culture would always carry within itself the negation of men's culture, and would thus remain altogether dependent on the latter (at least, until genetic engineering produces new types of men). Let us suppose that the features of feminine culture are the result of woman's corporeality, and that to recognize feminine autonomy is to become aware of that which has been suppressed by the patriarchal order. Seen in this light, "progress" would be the valorization of signs of feminine corporeality. And yet, this is very far from another key notion promoted by feminists, namely, that of the "constructedness" of social reality, which asserts that the latter is artificial and deliberately made rather than "naturally" given. If women have been oppressed, then now it is their turn to oppress men and to banish all the quasi-universal masterworks of patriarchal culture (such as Beethoven's Ninth). This idea resonates with Marxism: since the bourgeois class has always subordinated the workers, it is now time for the latter to transform themselves into a "dictatorship of the proletariat".

Therefore, such a feminist thesis is founded on a deterministic and in some ways fanatical way of thinking, a thesis according to which gender absolutely determines the whole human being. This possibility cannot be dismissed out of hand, but at the same time one should recall what Merleau-Ponty writes in his *Phenomenology of Perception*:

> [La vie sexuelle] est ce qui fait qu'un homme a une histoire. Si l'histoire sexuelle d'un homme donne la clef de sa vie, c'est parce que dans la sexualité l'homme projette sa manière d'être au regard du monde, c'est-à-dire à l'égard du temps et à l'égard des autres hommes. Il y a des symptomes sexuels à l'origine de toutes les névroses, mais ces symptomes, si on les lit bien, symbolisent toute une attitude, soit par exemple une attitude de conquête, soit une attitude de fuite ... et la question n'est pas tant de savoir si la vie humaine repose ou non sur la sexualité que de savoir ce qu''on entend par sexualité... Quand on généralise la notion de sexualité et qu''on fait d'elle une manière

d'être au monde physique et interhumain, veut-on dire qu'"en dernière analyse toute existence a une signification sexuelle ou bien que toute existence a
une signification existentielle? Dans la première hypothèse l'existence serait
une abstraction, un autre nom pour designer la vie sexuelle ... mais comme la
vie sexuelle ne peut plus être circonscrite, comme elle n'est plus une fonction
separée et définissable par la causalité propre d'un appareil organique, il n'y
a plus aucun sens à dire que toute l'existence se comprend par la vie sexuelle,
ou plutôt, cette proposition devient une tautologie. Faut-il donc dire, inversé-
ment, que le phénomène sexuel n'est qu'une expression de notre manière
générale de projeter notre milieu? (Merleau-Ponty 1945: 185)

[(Sexual life) is what makes a man have a history. If the sexual history of a
man provides the key to his life, it is because in his sexuality man projects
his way of being to the world, that is to say, concerning time and concerning
other men. There are sexual symptoms at the origin of all neuroses, but these
symptoms, if one reads them properly, all symbolise an attitude, be it, for
example, an attitude of conquest or an attitude of escape ... and the question
is not so much to know whether or not human life is based on sexuality, but
to know what is understood by the term "sexuality". When we generalise the
notion of sexuality, and when one thinks of it as a way of being in the physical and interpersonal world, can we say that in the final analysis all existence
has existential significance? In the first hypothesis, existence would be an
abstraction, another name for designating sexual life ...but since sexual life
is no longer to be circumscribed, since it is no longer a detached function and
definable by the causality proper only to an organic apparatus, it no longer
makes any sense to say that all existence is to be understood by sexual life;
or rather, this proposition becomes a tautology. Should it be said, conversely,
that the sexual phenomenon is only an expression of our general way of pro-
jecting our situation?]

The causality mentioned by Merleau-Ponty – between the human
body and its symbolic manifestations – is precisely that of "iconicity". Merleau-Ponty's warning is quite reasonable. For one may jus-
tifiably assume that "gendered" meanings reflect some more general
form of human existence, that such meanings are themselves signifiers
of something else, and not definitive signifieds.
   The problem is that, once the emancipation of the sign has taken
place, semiotics can be used to "prove" almost any thesis whatsoever,
so long as one's reasoning gives the overall impression of a cogent
and scholarly discourse, and provided some social motivation makes

people pay attention to this so-called "semiotician". The danger of semiotics is that its tools are neutral; they can serve virtually any ethics and any ideology. What constitutes a "good" or "bad" ideology lies outside the scope of semiotics. Thus, if semiotics wants to attain the status of a universal method, then it cannot exclude ethics. This fact was realized quite early by great nineteenth-century semioticians such as Charles Peirce as well as by pre- or would-be-semioticians like Vladimir Soloviev. A good illustration of the combination of semiology and "new" musicology is Marc A. Weiner's study, *Richard Wagner and the Anti-Semitic Imagination* (1997). The author scours Wagner's operas for various signs, for semiological qualities and their "concrete logic", and does so with undeniable success. His book has opened a new chapter in the semiotics of Wagner by scrutinizing Wagnerian smells, colours, gestures, sounds and other signs. He even deals in passing with Musorgsky, referring to the composer's "Nibelungen" in the form of Goldenberg and Schmuyle in *Pictures at an Exhibition*. This involves "sonic signs" (Weiner 1997: 144) or "speech patterns" (Weiner 1997: 146). In *Parsifal*, though, the olfactory signs play a significant role, evoking compulsion, entrapment and sexual urgency (Weiner 1997: 229). In Weiner's reasoning the German body does not appear as iconic-indexical signs, but as pure metaphor. Moreover, he claims that "the foot has an iconic function in Wagner's works for the stage" (Weiner 1997: 264). But when he seeks the signifieds of these signs he can find only one: anti-semitism. Hence, all the negative and dysphoric types on stage come to represent Wagner's hatred for Jews and concretizations of his racism. The author claims that these signs were apparent, although implicit, to nineteenth-century audiences. At the end of the twentieth century, however, we have lost our ability to decode these signs, because we are blinded by the musical genius of Wagner. Yet one must pose this question: If Wagner intended all his major operas to project or promote racist and anti-semitic distinctions and differences, why did he not express such things overtly in his operas, but restrict these views to his pamphlets? Why were these "immanent", but according to Weiner vital, significations concealed? Couldn"t Wagner, the consummate theatre professional, have exposed his ideology even more efficiently by using artistic signs?

To return to gender: if gendering ultimately means the creation of differences, as Ruth Solie argues in her preface to *Musicology and Difference* (1993), then we should expect to find corporeal messages in music itself, messages which could be studied and further analyzed. Weiner's theses are based on the idea that the bodies Wagner created on stage represented, to his contemporaries, an immediate ideological reality which brought these bodies to life. If that is true, then how do they still spring to life in our time? They are still fascinating characters. Is it simply that all admirers of Wagner's operas are implicit anti-semites? Or is there a level of corporeality in music which is deeper than and determines other musical signs? American musicology frequently identifies semiotics in this Kristevan way, i.e., with the bodily level of music.

Let us take another, less extreme example, namely, Richard Taruskin's book *Defining Russia Musically* (1997). It is noteworthy that whenever he uses the term "semiotics" it occurs in the context of body in music. Particularly when dealing with orientalism as a manifestation of the Russian school in music history, he foregrounds the role of semiotics. He juxtaposes the "Eastern theme", which is neutral, to "Orientalism", which is "charged" and in which one can perceive "semiotics, ideological critique, polemic, perhaps indictment" (Taruskin 1997: 152). "If one is going to talk about oriental style as a sign, one must specify its referents" and thereby "let the music speak [for] itself ... so as to let a certain semiotic point emerge". To illustrate, Taruskin looks at some compositions having a certain "oriental flavour", ranging from Glinka to Rachmaninov, all of them based on a poem by Pushkin (*Ne poy krasavitsa*). In the piano accompaniment he picks up "a characteristic semiotic cluster: a drone (drum) bass ... and a chromatic accompanying line that in this case steadily descends along with the sequences of undulating melismas". This cluster of signs, for Taruskin, evokes not just the East, but the seductive East that emasculates, enslaves, renders passive. He states that the "syncopated undulation itself is iconically erotic, evoking languid limbs, writhing torsos, arching necks". All these signs he designates by a term from old Russian literary style – "nega". The network of such signs can be easily discerned in Tchaikovsky as well, whose overture to *Romeo and*

*Juliet*, which Taruskin says displays "frank sensual iconicity" particularly in the "strongly marked chromatic passing between the fifth and sixth degrees". Of course, many classic works of the Russian repertory have similar features, from Rimsky-Korsakov's *Scheherazade* to Borodin's *Prince Igor* – it is certainly no accident that the dance of the Polovetsian slave girls has the same undulating motive as the one Wagner used in his "oriental" second act of *Parsifal*, to depict the gestures of the *Blumenmädchen*. What interests us, however, is how the semiotic moment in music is so strongly interwoven in these studies with the human body, not expressly those of men or women, but the body in general. Intuitively this seems to be justified, but can we formulate an analytic method on the basis of such an intuition?

How can the body in music be studied semiotically in the proper sense? A traditional way to approach this issue would be to study gestures. Adorno attempted to do so in his study on Wagner, but reached the disappointing conclusion that gestures cannot be developed, only repeated. Some recent music semioticians have paid much attention to gestures of various kinds, from Gino Stefani's study of accents to Robert Hatten's explorations in the Classical and pre-romantic styles, in which as Adorno said, gesture is sublimated into expression. Some hints at how corporeality might be construed according to a new musical semiology can be found in Merleau-Ponty's work on *signification gestuelle*. For him, the latter is something like a preliminary sketch, drawn before the receiver has apprehended the semantics of a message: "Une musique ou une peinture qui n'est d'abord pas comprise finit par se créer elle-même son public, si vraiment elle dit quelque chose, c'est-à-dire par sécréter elle-même sa signification" ["A piece of music or a painting that is not complete becomes so by creating a public for itself, that is to say, by securing signification for itself."] (Merleau-Ponty 1945: 209). On this view, one might think that a musical work yields a certain implicit meaning, before the latter is connected with any ideological, aesthetic or other significations determined by its historical situation. Should we not first examine this level – both feminists and traditionalists together – so as perhaps to reach some agreement on what constitutes corporeality in music? Most probably, gender analysts would refuse this offer of reconciliation, since their thesis is that, from the beginning, everything is gendered, there being no previous, "lower" level to which things could be reduced. Such a response falls into and remains in the trap of the difference-ideology, and fails to see how one could get out by developing a solid semiotic basis for what body is – whether feminine or masculine – in music. On this "road less travelled", one can find guideposts in the theories of George Herbert Mead (1967), who studied "I" as both subject and object, that is, as both "I" and "me". An important achievement of phenomenologists like Merleau-Ponty, and before him Husserl, was to determine that the body can never appear as mere object to a subject. Even some feminists, such as Teresa de Lauretis (1990), distinguish between the "experiencing body" and the body experienced by others. Subjects' relationships to their body change essentially when they notice that their body is perceived by someone else. It is an everyday experience of any musician that the same piece played alone for oneself becomes a greatly different experience when it is performed for even a small audience. When below I speak about the corporeality of music, I shall not be so interested in the "body" as experienced by others (i.e., the "me"). For in that case, its corporeality would be determined from the outside, and hence connected with surrounding ideologies. We can argue that a musical piece is in a metaphorical sense like a "living organism", a kind of "body". The only way to get under the skin of this "body" is of course to perform it. The question is, Can this kind of "musical body" be studied from the inside?

George Herbert Mead sees symbols as emerging from a continuous interplay between inner impulses and outer responses. He speaks of gestures in conversation as vocal gestures, and calls them "significant symbols". He does not intend "symbol" in the abstract sense, as something apart from conduct. Rather, a symbol is a stimulus whose response is given in advance. Assume there is a word and a blow, and that the latter precedes the word. But if the word, as stimulus, conveys an insult, then the response is now involved in the word; it is given in the very stimulus itself. If that response can be given in terms of an attitude utilized for the further control of action, then the relation of that stimulus and attitude is what Mead means by a "significant symbol" (Mead 1967: 181). Mead argues that our thinking proceeds along these lines, inside us, one might say, and this to him is a "play of symbols" (Mead 1967: 181), through which gestural responses are summoned by our attitudes. What was meaning becomes a symbol, which in turn has another meaning. The meaning itself has become a stimulus to another response. In this way, Mead reasons, conversation continually goes on. What was response becomes, in the field of gesture, a stimulus; and the response to the latter is the "meaning". The great advantage of Mead's approach to meaning is that he does not see it as static, but as a continual process. I have taken this notion further, and distinguished between three stages of signs in such a "conversational" process between inside and outside: (1) stimulus and response, which are pre-signs; (2) act-signs; (3) and post-signs. The pre-signs are "stimuli" or gestures used to produce secondary signs (act-signs), which are "responses" to these initial gestures (it is irrelevant whether or not they really exist). Furthermore, they become "stimuli" to signs which they in turn evoke. The post-signs which follow may also exist virtually, in the minds of receivers, or they may be concrete, material new signs. The latter are traditionally called "interpretants"; the pre-signs may be termed "enunciants". In pieces of music, gestures of affirmation and negation alternate in this type of "inner dialogue". In music, gestures have their "home".

I shall apply this simple model to the analysis of a piece whose highly organic and lively gestural level ceaselessly puts in question any kind of pre-established musical form. It is the piano quartet by Ernest Chausson, a composer whose music, on the corporeal level of its signs, overturns the Germanic formal hegemony, or "patriarchal" order. To realize that such is the case, one only needs to compare Chausson's music to, say, Gabriel Fauré's piano quartets, whose texture is congenially idiomatic but whose formal outline is not as radically individualistic, as anti-Germanic, so to speak, as is Chausson's. Consider just the opening gesture of the quartet (Ex. 12). Full of Mediterranean energy and featuring clear rhythms, it is quite suitable to begin a "masculine", first movement of a sonata.

The four-/eight-bar periodic form is immediately questioned, however, by a rhythmic asymmetry, and by the time we reach bar 27 we

*Ex. 12.* Opening to Chausson's Piano Quartet in A major, op. 30.

realize in what country and century we are, i.e., what the real musical situation of this message is. This realization occurs when the dominant ninth chord sounds, with all its Impressionistic flavour (Ex. 13).

This opening seems so innocently positive in its clear-cut form, that one only notices later that this sign, felt as a real First in the Peircean

*Ex. 13.* Chausson, Piano Quartet in A major, op. 30. bars 27–30.

sense, has at least one pre-sign in French music: It is the same motive as that of the Chorale in César Franck's *Prélude, chorale et fugue*. But this pre-sign has an even earlier pre-sign: the bell motive from the Grail scene in Wagner's *Parsifal*. In the Chausson quartet, what at the outset seemed to be a purely masculine, naively corporeal sign of a vital musical body now seems to be a parody of a much more profound, internal, and psychologically complex chorale-motive. Hence, Otherness was animating what seemed to be a purely corporeal gesture. Viewed in this reversed direction, this sign leads us to another sphere of Otherness, from the Gallic spirit to the Germanic one, with its evocation of *Parsifal*. The process also goes on in other directions. Later this main motive is not only formally repeated in the recapitulation but returns at the end of the piece. Initially he seems to let the main theme from the first movement return, fragmented in a long development. Then as a surprise, at the psychological and tensional climax of the whole piece, it gives place to the main theme of the second movement, in a move which may be described as trans-descendence and trans-ascendence (philosopher Jean Wahl's terms). But this theme of redemption does not remain the last word. The bold gesture of the beginning also recurs, now united in stretto in the bass with the cantabile theme, in an overwhelming reconciliation and closure of all previous gestures in this piece. The conversation can continue no longer. The music has stopped time. What has been Other has become Same. This narrative technique is quite far from the Germanic type of thematic construction that produced "Greatness" in music. Chausson frequently stops the flow of gestures, producing a timeless feeling of "*verweile doch Du bist so schön*" by means of a series of dominant-seventh and ninth chords which do not set up structural tension but which merely foreground the colour of the harmonies – a process often considered very "French".

My deeper project is to present a kind of "semiotics without semiotics", in answer to the question, What can remain of semiotics when all previously-articulated semiotic theories have been forgotten? I have classified all musical semiotic theories – in the epistemic sense – into two groups. The first of these starts with rules and grammars belonging to all music, hence emphasizing the musical surface. This view supposes that before the rules formulated by theoretician, nothing exists; and consequently, when the rules stop functioning, nothing remains. This type of semiotics, as a philosophical "style" rather than a systematic classification, is what I call "classical" semiotics. Here I am inspired by Taruskin's wonderful distinction between civilisation and culture, beauty and profundity (Taruskin 1997: 257). These dichotomies seem to fit amazingly well even in the area of science, and my own theory of "existential semiotics" (2001), could, *mutatis mutandis*, be defined in quite similar terms. Says Taruskin:

"The other main idea... consists in the radical dichotomization of beauty on the one hand, and a whole discourse of profundity/strength, loftiness/ seriousness/power – in a word – greatness, on the other. The distinction was perceived, at the time, in national terms, and so we had best translate our operative term into German: *das Erhabene*.... These transgressions arose out of a stubborn adherence – from the German national perspective an outmoded and treasonable adherence – to the ideology of the Enlightenment which is to say the ideology of civilisation, which is really to say the ideology of the hated French..." (Taruskin 1997: 261).

He continues:

As the discourse of romanticism achieved its maximized expression in what we now look back on as the modernist period, the dichotomies we have so far encountered ... took on an even more radical aspect. What had formerly been expressible as a cleavage between national schools or between the cultivation of the beautiful and the cultivation of the sublime, or between the aesthetic of enjoyment and that of contemplation, or between the aesthetic of pleasure and that of disinterestedness, or between the discourse of enlightenment and that of transcendence, or of utility vs autonomy, or of convention vs originality, social accommodation vs social alienation, opera vs symphony, motley vs wholeness, melody vs motive – all this eventually came down to a gross discrimination between the serious and the popular, or even more grossly and peremptorily, into that between art and entertainment (Taruskin 1997: 265).

What Taruskin says also applies to semiotic theories that in the twentieth century inherited much from the classicist / romantic dichotomy. By the end of the twentieth century, this dichotomy had become trivialized, banal, and embodied in forms of semiotics that qualify only as postmodern entertainment. The romantic tradition, too, had its moment of decline in semiotics, leading to exaggeratedly introverted, solipsistic approaches that became detached from social context and ethical values. We can trace this romantic line from Hegel via Kierke-gaard to Peirce, and on to Soloviev, Bakhtin, Lotman, Lévi-Strauss, and Greimas. By contrast, the "classicist" line follows the logical empiricism of Anglo-Saxon analytic philosophy

In contrast to the view that nothing exists until it is formulated by theoretical rules, is the concept that all signs exist only on the basis of an order that is in place before the scholar starts his/her work and which remains after he/she has finished. This semiotic philosophy approaches meaning in three ways: (1) as a process, i.e., on the sup-position that signs cannot be defined without taking into account time, place and subject (actor). (2) It also views meaning as immanent, as do Mead and Merleau-Ponty; i.e., that meaning is produced mainly within a given system or organism; it does not come from outside, as a *deus ex machina* (as at the end of the Chausson quartet, the rec-onciling themes do not stem from outside but from materials within the piece). (3) The view that meaning pre-exists theoretical formula-tion also emphasises the content, the signified, which, however, can be non-verbal, "ineffable", expressible only in terms of a quasi-corporeal experience. It is this latter type of musical semiotics that I have addressed in my arguments, both for and against, concerning certain current theories and achievements of the so-called "new musicology".

# Chapter 6
# Body and transcendence in Chopin

Continuing our theme of corporeality, this chapter presents a two-dimensional view of Chopin. His music is examined both in terms of its bodily connections, and also as a more spiritual and philosophical, in a word, transcendental phenomenon. The word "corporeal" might call to mind gender studies, though one hastens to add that the gendered body is not the only channel for expressing corporeal meanings of music. The transcendental aspect is something that, if not directly Kantian, at least approaches the "existential". My aim here is to show that both corporeality and transcendence are semiotical in nature, and that semiotics can provide answers to the interpretive challenges presented by those phenomena.

Musical aestheticians have traditionally been divided into those who believe that music can "represent" something in the external world, and those who deny its ability to do so (from Eduard Hanslick to, say, Roger Scruton). According to this division, Chopin is seldom considered a "representational" composer. He is most often taken to be a non-programmatic composer, with Liszt as the most obvious counter-example. Some even say that Chopin is stylistically a classicist and not a romantic composer at all.

Contrasting voices are also heard. Is not the *barcarolle*, for instance, related to water images in music, as Gunnar Larsson (1986) has asked? Are not Chopin's Ballades musical metaphors of Mickiewicz's poems? Do not march and galloping rhythms, nocturnes, chorales, military signals (as in polonaises), and so on all have extramusical connections to social conventions of nineteenth-century life, or to oneiric and subconscious impulses, and the like? Moreover, these connotations often have a corporeal origin: the *barcarolle* is based on the ostinato rhythms of rowing a gondola (see Bücher 1909, on the rhythms of manual labor). The languid style of the nocturne is related to the dream state of the relaxed body, almost a musical illustration of the free play among khoratic-kinetic elements, as Julia Kristeva proposes (more on this, below). Polonaises may in turn reflect extreme masculine virility. Listen, for instance, to the *Polonaise in F sharp minor*, with its drumming pulsations and frenetic melody; the extremely marked rhythms typical of the genre are so accentuated here that they transgress the limits of social conventions. As to transcendental meanings, Chopin is often said to represent romantic melancholy. But let us remember that Friedrich Nietzsche, in his anti-Wagner period, considered Chopin both "heiter und tief". Thus, under closer scrutiny the stereotypes shatter.

It is trivial to consider Chopin as a model of an effeminate composer. Yet Marcia Citron relates Chopin to stereotypes of feminine musicality in her *Gender and the Musical Canon*: "The early nineteenth century, for example, might be considered a period of varying musical gender: the masculine vigour of Beethoven's music and the feminine, or perhaps effeminate grace of Chopin's compositions. We

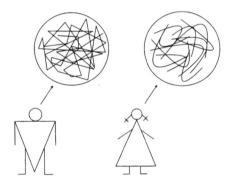

*Figure 9a.*    Male and female bodies producing iconic signs.

*Figure 9b.*    Chopin and Georges Sand producing their iconic signs.

could consider the Italian lyricism of Mozart in the late eighteenth century a feminine trait, to be quashed by the masculine energy in Beethoven. In the 1830s and 1840s the feminine elegance of French culture takes hold in much of the music of Chopin" (Citron 1993: 163). Citron lists more qualities of a feminine aesthetics, one of which is a

*Figure 9c.* Chopin and George Sand producing indexical signs, i.e. about Sand and Chopin respectively.

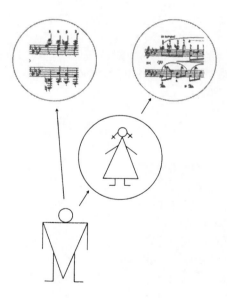

*Figure 9d.* Chopin and G. Sand represented as symbolic signs in Chopin's *Fantasy in F minor.*

fascination with process: an intuitive, whimsical approach that values fantasy and experimentation above received structures and techniques. Another "feminine" quality is a lyricism that recalls styles practiced in such female spheres as the salon, and that is marked by long melodic lines and horizontal connectedness. Citron tries to prove how arbitrary such categories are; but it is undeniable that they are often echoed in writings about Chopin. For instance, the fascination with process – certainly a characteristic of Chopin, but also of his "masculine" counterpart, Beethoven – relies on a general episteme of romantic culture; namely, the Goethean idea of art imitating the growth processes of a living organism, and thereby providing the ultimate category of aesthetic enjoyment and value. The way musical narration unfolds in the Ballades, for example, has something unquestionably "organic" about it – and not necessarily anything that genders the pieces in an effeminate way. Far from being strictly feminine, "organicism" is an episteme of all Western culture, and a shared value in most nineteenth-century thought.

As pointed out in the previous chapter, the gender-relatedness of corporeal meanings in symbolic representations such as music rests on theoretically shaky ground, to say the least. No theory exists of how the body is reflected in the signs it creates. To put it simply, if the male and female bodies create, represent, and express themselves via certain kinds of *signs*, then what is the nature of that sign-relationship? In Peircean terms, is it iconic, indexical, or symbolic?

## 6.1 Are corporeal signs iconic?

Are certain qualities of the male or female body iconically represented more or less directly by their appropriate signs? For instance, are military rhythms and signals, galloping horses, and the like conventionally masculine? When Chopin exploits such musical devices, is that when his male body is "speaking" to us? Roland Barthes (1986), in his famous essay on Schumann, speculated similarly, that in the rhythmic quality of *Rasch* the Schumannian body starts to speak to us via its particular *somathemes*. Here, as with Barthes, this issue raises many questions. Is it certain that in such cases only Chopin is speaking, rather than the social conventions and topics of military and other types of music? And are such signals always masculine? Let us recall that, in Wagner's *Walkürenritt*, female bodies are portrayed by precisely such rhythms. Thus the idea of iconic signs of the gendered body seems to fail, and even more so when we remember that every woman has some male characteristics, as every man has female ones.

Very often in Chopin, such corporeal signs as dancing and rowing rhythms reflect the social sphere of musical topics. Chopin was no doubt fully aware of the topics of the Classical style such as military calls, hunting signals, dances, Storm and Stress, *galant*, learned, *Empfindsamkeit* and so on, and he richly exploited them in his music (see Ratner 1980). In this sense, the body in his music is often the socialized "body" of norms and stylistic constraints – which he just as often tries to transgress. This is one way that his music reaches the other category of our study – the transcendental realm. Chopin often wants to go beyond such conventional signs, sometimes taking a radical distance from them, as in the Polonaise-Fantasy, where the polonaise is but vaguely evoked by its traditional markers. At other times Chopin expands or exaggerates conventional signs in a way that transforms them into something else. Dialectically, a new quality emerges from the endless repetition of such conventional corporeal signs. This occurs, for example, in the triple, "balladic" rhythm in the last movement of the B minor Sonata. There the dance-like figure, which as such has an almost pastoral quality, turns into a fanatic, frightening, and obsessive process which takes the subject of enunciate, and often of enunciation as well, under its power, bringing both to a state of ecstasy. Another case would be the repetitive, didactic figures in the Etudes. In Chopin these become more than mere exercises in idiomatic figures; they surpass the quality of etude-likeness and gain a new, emergent meaning that attains the sphere of the transcendental.

## 6.2 Are corporeal signs indexical?

Indexes are signs based on continuity (smoke as an index of fire, e.g.). Musically, they stem directly from the composer or performer as emanations of his/her bodily or emotional state. In the same manner, they directly influence the receivers of the musical message, to the point of impacting them in what Roman Jakobson described as the conative function of communication. This category of possible corporeality leads us to consider not only the utterance itself but the whole process of uttering. This is something to be taken seriously, for when interpreting corporeal signs in this manner we should engage the act of musical performance as well as that of reception. Is it here that the Chopinian body is manifested?

Let us first make an important theoretical distinction: when speaking about the "Chopinian body", what do we mean? Is it Chopin as a physical, biographical person, or is it Chopin as the subject of enunciation? Chopin as the subject of enunciation can mean two further things: Chopin as the composer and Chopin as the pianist. We should not underestimate the latter, since there is abundant evidence, in Eigeldinger's studies among others, of Chopin as a pianist and piano teacher, which certainly represents an "act of uttering" or "enunciating" music. In addition to the "Chopinian body" understood as either the flesh-and-blood Chopin or as Chopin the composer/pianist, we have a third category: namely, the bodily signs of the aforementioned two or three species *within* the utterance. Chopin has left signs of his body in the music itself, as the analyses below will elucidate. Thus, Chopin's body is represented in the musical text. For instance, he writes passages which we know were easy for him to play, those which best suited his abilities as a pianist. But even here the indexical signs of him as a performer do not necessarily always reflect just his individual body. What about such intertexts as the vocal gestures in his melodies? And there is also the well-known passage in the Polonaise-Fantasy where a cryptic crescendo appears between two notes an octave apart, a crescendo which only could be rendered by a singing voice.

Such bodily meanings are thus not only a reflection of Chopin as an instrumentalist, but also of what he imagined to be the ideal *bel canto* of his time. This third category of corporeal signs would be the *symbols* of the body, that is to say, the body as a completely cultural entity, like the body of the speaker in rhetoric, for instance, or the bodily expressions of social spheres such as balls and other festivities of nineteenth-century life as found in his mazurkas and polonaises. When encountering such signs in Chopin's music, we do not connect with his individual, physical existence at all, since the body appears there as a certain corporeal technique. We may conclude that the body is something extremely complicated, not only in Chopin but in music altogether. Concerning the body, Kristeva speaks of the "semiotic sphere" of prelinguistic kinetic rhythms, gestures, expressions, and fluctuating pulsations, which for her constitute the field of "significance", a feminine space which she calls, following Plato, the *khora*. The latter represents the archaic level of consciousness, which is our prevailing state in early childhood but which is present even in later developments of our psyche, after we have entered the social sphere of the *symbolic order*. This order represents the penetration of language and all its social norms into our existence. In gendered terms, it is also the patriarchal moment, since, according to Kristeva, it is through the father that this symbolic order is attained in a child's development. In this scheme, the "semiotic" is the vast area of indefinite, non-verbal meanings in their purely kinetic form. The musical counterpart would be what Ernst Kurth, in his *Musikpsychologie* (1947), called the energetic-kinetic impulses of music. As noted before, these inner tensions, not the sounding manifestations, were for Kurth the authentic moments of music. That is certainly also the sphere of the body in the process of signification. The superimposition of the symbolic order thus represents a denial of pure corporeal reality, by the social norms and constraints set upon it. For Kristeva, the khoratic realm, not the symbolic order, is the essential one. The symbolic order is merely the tip of the iceberg. "Real" meaning emerges only when the khoratic, unsocialized body breaks with social conventions.

Whatever we mean by "body" in music, in Chopin it always appears via the piano and its idioms. The passages in which we feel the pres-

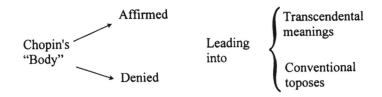

*Figure 10.*

ence of the body in Chopin resemble what Heinrich Besseler called playing-figures (*Spielfiguren*). These are figures that, in clear contrast to vocal style, are purely instrumental and even idiomatic to certain instruments, especially piano and violin. For instance, those played on the piano are easily repeated, and their unified rhythms often lead to sequences. Such playing-figures often show up in the Preludes of the *Well-Tempered Clavier,* where their musical logic is more improvisational than that of the fugues which follow. In romantic music they appear often in the accompaniment to a melody. (Besseler gives an example from Chopin, the Prelude Number 8 in F sharp minor.) In many of Chopin's Etudes, merely passing through a *Spielfigur* constitutes the main idea of the piece. The level of *Spielfiguren* represents the presence of the body amidst an otherwise esoteric, spiritual, and transcendent musical expression.

All the theories mentioned thus far might prove relevant to a study of the body in Chopin. The body in his music, as said above, often appears as a "socialized" and conventional body, a tamed entity. Conversely, in Chopin it can also mean the appearance or breakthrough of the khoratic body, which occurs when socialized bodily conventions are rejected. In music this would signify moments when the topical logic of the surface levels collapses, as well as the syntax of other musical parameters, and normal tonal logic gives way to something else.

Here we also encounter in musical terms the problem of the classical and the romantic in Chopin. Following the definitions by Guido Adler (see Ch. 2.1), we could say that the classical style appears as a congruence of parts and subparts, in balanced formations such as periodic phrasing, in the mastery and economy of the devices, and in a certain reserved way of expression, a kind of aversion to excess or to transgressing certain limits of beauty. The classical style was for Adler the "perfect style", in which all the parts manifested the purity, equality, and congruence between content and form.

There is obviously much of the classical in Chopin. But just as obviously his music displays the romantic style, of which Adler says: "it aims for blending of all the forms, rejection of all strict norms of classical art forms, irregularity and devoid of rules, the favouring of colorism and tone painting ... and inclination to programs". By these criteria, we could easily classify Chopin as "romantic", though the programmatic aspect might be more questionable, and should perhaps be replaced with the idea of narrativity.

Adler's theory becomes interesting in the present context if we link it to Julia Kristeva's notions of *khora* and symbolic order. For our purposes, the *khora* in music is the sphere of the body, and the symbolic order is the realm of stylistic norms and constraints. The *khora* would represent the acceptance and affirmation of the body, in a certain sense, and symbolic order the repression of the body in favour of the patriarchal order, which feminists identify with the musical canon. Yet we must always remember that in music the body can also appear in a tamed form, as conventionalised mannerisms or topics. To say that Chopin accepts these norms means that he also accepts the symbolic order in the guise of corporeal schemes in his music. But if we consider the most important moment in music to be its unique message, which transgresses the norms of *langue*, then those moments in which the Kristevan khoratic body is affirmed are also those moments in which the logic of the symbolic body disappears and is replaced by the logic of kinetic energy and tension. Perhaps this might be the "true Chopin". Of course, one would hardly claim to have found the "true Chopin". But to paraphrase Carl Dahlhaus, no one attends a concert to listen to documents of nineteenth-century life, but rather to experience the *ästhetische Gegenwärtigkeit*, the aesthetic now-moment of music. Music provides such moments by speaking to us directly. I believe that it is the Chopinian "khoratic" body that makes his music still so impressive to listen to. As Marcel Proust put it, "Every musician is in search of a lost fatherland; sometimes they find it, sometimes they only approach it, and sometimes they do not reach it. The music really moves us only when we have that feeling of being united with this lost "fatherland" – And how well this fits Chopin, quite literally, who could sigh in the most beautiful moment of his Etudes, E major op 10: O ma patrie!" (Eigeldinger 1979: 105). Composers can either accept or reject their body in the music.

In searching for the counterpart of body – namely, the moments of transcendental, or *existential*, meaning – in Chopin's music, we could apply one of my models of existential semiotics. The Chopinian body is something that appears philosophically as the musical *Dasein* of his subjectivity. In logical terms, this body can be either denied (negated) or affirmed (accepted). Much recent feminist writing has cantered on how women composers have been forced to deny their body and its particular signs, because they have been silenced by the dominant musical canon. Such a thesis presupposes that, if these women composers had been able to create freely, following their own bodily inspiration, then they would have created different musical signs from those that eventually emanated from their pens. The same could be said of Chopin, if only hypothetically. We could say that, by accepting certain stylistic constraints of genre, he allowed the patriarchal order, the musical canon, to force him to deny his real musical "body". At other times, and in fact rather often, he affirmed his real body in his music and by doing so reached a transcendental moment that takes us beyond the surface of topics, genres, and traditional forms. Much has been written, for instance, about Chopin's transgressing the norms of genre. This could be portrayed as follows:

To affirm or to negate the khoratic, primary body is to commit a transcendental act. The affirmation of the body, in this sense, signifies implicitly the rejection of the "social body"; the denial of the khoratic body means subjection to the rules of the social body. Thus, when the primary, archaic body – that which is *sans sexe* (Kallberg 1996) – is affirmed, the normal syntactic-logical discursive order of the music is disrupted and an individual moment of creation enters, transcending the social norms. When this body is denied then music remains on the level of *langue*, genre and style norms. Still, these acts are in mutual need of each other in the dialectics of enunciation.

What does this mean concretely, at the textual level, in the music itself? Ruptures in discursive logic also appear as moments of *estrangement*, or what the Russian formalists called "making strange" (*ostranenie*). Such moments contradict our expectations of a given code. Nothing is more common in Chopin, for instance, than for something in the music to go against the very title of the piece. Suddenly amidst a polonaise we lapse into a nocturne or mazurka – not a literal nocturne or mazurka, but merely a faint evocation of those genres. Or amidst a ballade there intrudes a development in the polyphonic, learned style. A chorale might show up in a scherzo, and in a nocturne a Storm and Stress passage, and so on. Such estrangements, which go against our expectations of a genre, characterize not only the late Chopin but are present in his music from the very beginning. In bodily terms, the social-corporeal meanings are negated and replaced by individualized, khoratic entities.

Estrangement is related to another interesting aspect of nineteenth-century culture, though one not often related to Chopin, namely, the idea of romantic irony. By this, we do not necessarily mean humorous, parodistic, or grotesque devices – Chopin remained too "classical" a composer to use such a vocabulary. Still, the philosophical principle of romantic irony is applicable here. After the transcendental act, the moment when artists sink into the eternal, ahistorical time of their creation, they return to their respective worlds of *Dasein*. But now that world looks quite different. What used to be meaningful is now viewed as completely unnecessary, indifferent, valueless, and relative. Søren Kierkegaard spoke about romantic irony as an attitude toward life, stemming from the transcendental act. Man is always aspiring towards transcendence, and when everyday life is suddenly illuminated by the feeling of the transcendental, it may even appear ridiculous. For Kierkegaard, "to exist" is not easy, as one might think, but is in fact our most difficult task. In the Kierkegaardian manner, Chopin aimed for "existentiality" in his music. At every moment he struggled to transcend the social body of musical topics so as to reach the individual khoratic body. In her preface to Sénancour's *Obermann*, George Sand gave a sociological interpretation of romantic irony in her discussion of typical romantic heroes, from Werther to René and Obermann. According to Sand, these heroes, abandoned to their individual sufferings, were powerless to act, to make choices, to live in society: "There is one disaster which has not yet been officially noticed. It is enjoyment without power, it is the exhaustion of failed passion." Sand thought that civilisation and society were to blame for this disaster. In modern terms, such heroes were left in their primary, khoratic bodily sphere, and rejected by the symbolic order. They were unable to transform their individual, kinetic bodies into conventional, socialized bodily expressions, and this was due to the "canons" established by the patriarchal order. Chopin's romantic irony includes both the Kierkegaardian notion of looking down at the social world from transcendental heights, as well as Sand's idea of the powerlessness of being accepted by the social-corporeal sphere.

These reflections bring me to the idea of a *transcendental subject*. By this I mean that, behind the various types of "Chopinian bodies" mentioned above, stands a transcendental subject which makes it possible for the same subject to express him- or herself in what may sometimes be contradictory ways, both with the estrangements of romantic irony, and as a positive agent expressing his or her own message. This complicated play among various "bodies" in Chopin's music, as well as their metamorphoses and in some cases genuinely romantic journey, from the material world to the spiritual sphere, almost forces us to hypothesize the existence of a Chopinian transcendental subject. The latter is the methodological construct that is needed to make all the utterances of this subject cohere.

Various kinds of music can have various types of subject. Viatcheslaw Medushewski (1989) has identified at least seven categories of musical subject: (1) the spiritual "I" (or "We"), as the hidden subject of polyphonic music; (2) the meditative subject of inner monologue; for instance, in recitative-like passages in Beethoven; (3) the ecstatic-motoric "I", as in the strikingly kinetic music of dance; (4) the lyrical hero, found in romances such as Bizet's *Pêcheurs de perles*; (5) the reader, as at the beginning of Bach's C minor Partita; (6) the narrator, as in Chopin's Ballades; and (7) the personage "he", as projected in clearly programmatic narrative situations. All of these "subjects" appear in Chopin's music as well, each with its own way of speaking and of calling attention to its own utterances.

## 6.3 Analysis

Let us now look at the different ways this transcendental subject "speaks". My method here approaches that used by Roland Barthes in *S/Z* (1980), his study of a Balzac novella.[7] Much like Barthes parsed Balzac's text into "lexemes," I shall examine Chopin's music through its various *utterances*. "Utterance" designates a unit whose length can vary from one bar to whole phrases, sections and even whole pieces. The length of a musical utterance is unimportant. Sometimes the composer may require extensive passages to utter something; at other times it is said at once, in a moment.

Nor are utterances connected to specific musical parameters. Utterances may involve only one parameter, say, melody alone; or they may include several or all musical elements: melody, rhythm, timbre, and so on. The levels of pertinence are determined by what our "transcendental subject" wants to utter. At the same time, utterances are meeting-points of all that has been "spoken" by the body, the genre, the stylistic norms, the topics, and also the acts of enunciation.

What is important here is not so much the syntagm and its "horizontal" workings, but rather the dimension of depth. In other words, the goal is to construct the transcendental significations indicated by the surface of the music, by its physical signifiers. If the "surface" of the work is something physical, or corporeal, then every piece constructs, so to speak, its own subject. Here we shift from the apparent modalities of the surface – whose grammar can be formulated – to the *metamodalities,* which pertain to the transcendence of the work.[8] This may sound overly "metaphysical", but in every composition a kind of atmosphere, aura, or poetics characteristic of the piece emanates from its concrete signs, from the traces of its creation, in a word, from the enunciation.

Transcendence is not bound to the isotopies of a work, since the transcendental is a living, organic, continuously changing semiosis, which has its own micro- and macroprocesses. Isotopies, on the other hand, are historically determined, recurrent classemes of meaning (see Tarasti 1994; Grabócz 1996).

Our analytic procedure can be sketched as in Figure 11. A crucial question remains: by what metalanguage can we describe the emergent, transcendental qualities that emanate from the musical surface? Can they be grasped by verbal discourse? In general, they can be described by intertextual analogies such as colour, movement, light, and so on. These intertextual fields are opened in certain situations of de-enunciation. This "atmospheric" level is also the Other, the Double of the work in question, that which we remember, and because of which we want to hear the piece again and again. It is like a domain of energy that we wish to enter, similar to what Umberto Eco calls a "semantic field", yet one in which nothing is fixed or definite.

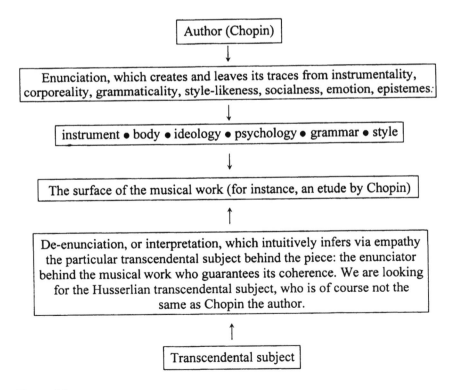

*Figure 11.*

The following statements summarize some theses of the method followed here: (1) Chopin's music consists of utterances. (2) Utterances are meeting places of corporeal (social and "khoratic") and stylistic (topical) meanings. (3) Utterances are kinds of lexemes. (4) Utterances constitute musical situations (cf. Ch. 3). For instance, the syncretism of Chopin's style consists in an utterance no longer occurring in its original situation, but being shifted to a new one: a nocturne or mazurka topic amidst a polonaise, and so forth. (5) One can study utterances by reducing them to semes. (6) Utterances have a subject, ultimately a transcendental subject, which is construed to explain situations in which various subjects seem to have enunciated the text. For instance, a subject can utter something contrary to expectations, such that the aural realization differs from the pathemic state of the enunciator. (7) Chopin's utterances share the following aspects: (a) the utterance as such, with its stylistic and normative background topic (genre) as its legisign; (b) pianistic corporeality; (c) other types of corporeality serving as presign(s) of an utterance; for instance, dance-likeness alluding to a polonaise, or nocturne-likeness as reference to dream states; (d) each utterance has a pathemic content: sublime, gracious, dignified, tragic, and so on; (e) each utterance has a transcendental dimension, a reference to the fact that there are no utterances without a subject. (8) When an utterance goes beyond its proper musical *Dasein* it always evokes transcendence; any deviation from the commonplace stylistic or the generic represents the voice of a transcendental subject in Chopinian discourse. (9) A work may consist of only one utterance (as do some of the Preludes); larger pieces are series of utterances. (10) Sometimes utterances overlap and coincide: our transcendental subject speaks polyphonically, with several voices. (11) Ultimately, utterances are organic, "self-organizing" entities.

For a practical analysis, we take a piece from late Chopin, his Fantasy in F minor. Here again, Chopin is playing with the title. "Fantasy" leads one to expect something rather free, but in fact this piece follows a clearly defined sonata design. So at least the formal outline is not at all like that of a fantasy.

The Introduction is a dirge, "Polishmen as prisoners in Siberia", as described by Jules Gentil. (1) The *funeral march*, with its clear-cut, periodic phrases, is a recurring utterance in Chopin, from the B flat minor sonata to such vaguely funereal marches as in the Nocturne Op. 48 No. 1 or in the C minor Prelude. Chopin never repeated himself exactly, but always provided something new upon repetition. This principle of enunciation is seen in the enunciate here, where it is realized as early as bars 7–8. There the "response" to the heavy and sinking, unison march motive rises from F minor to A flat major. At the same time, this response serves as an (2) *affirmative* utterance in relation to the foregoing musical "question".

Within this funeral march, a (3) *colourful change* takes place in bar 17, accomplished by the enharmonic transformation of C flat into B. This highlights Chopin as a synaesthetic, "colouristic" composer. According to Olivier Messiaen, Chopin writes many modulations whose purpose is not functional but colourful (as in the transitions to B-sections in the Scherzos). The latter half of the funeral march constitutes a special (4) *understatement*. It is like a brief aside that comments on the main phrase, but in a negative or tentative way, like a sentence that starts with "but" or "however". Chopin often emphasized the language-likeness of music. The following statement by Kleczynski says a lot about this type of utterance: "The entire theory of style Chopin taught to his pupils was based upon the analogy between music and language, on the necessity to separate different phrases, punctuate and render in a nuanced manner the voice ... they were the main principles of musical punctuation and declamation" (cited in Eigeldinger 1979: 70).

After the funeral march comes a transition (bars 43–67) in which something begins gradually. Such a "beginning" section could be called an (5) *inchoative* utterance. These bars show Chopin as a composer of (6) *linear* expression, as opposed to strictly periodic *Lied-* and march-phrases. Essential here is the linear impulse stemming from the polyphonic structures reminiscent of Palestrina (cf. Kurth 1922). But the linear impetus is abruptly interrupted by the falling, *sforzato* octaves. Only on the repeat does the linear impulse grow so strong as to become the real *passage à l'acte* in this musical narration (Claude Brémond's term) .

The main part starts with a motive that unites two ancient topics: (7) the *learned style* in the contrapuntal motion and suspended notes between the melody and bass lines, and the (8) *Storm and Stress style* manifested in the syncopated melody, its agitation, and its passionate, upward, octave leaps. Compared with this one, the second motive is more "feminine", an example of a (9) *bel canto* utterance in the glimmering upper register, a melody phrased and punctuated like that of an Italian soprano singing an aria. The descending movement especially, with its lingering stops, triplets and hemiolas, attempts to restrain and counterbalance the eagerness of the enthusiastic rising gesture. This is a special instance of Chopinian (10) *rhythmic ornamentation*, as one finds in the first movement of the B minor Sonata (bars 63–64). But here it also has a centrifugal nature due to the pianistic holds of consecutive intervals in the right hand. There is also a feeling of (11) *rubato*, which is written into the time values. This is certainly a passage of which Chopin would have said, "One has to sing with the fingers!" (Eigeldinger 1979: 73). What Chopin supposedly said to Mathias might elucidate this musical utterance: "Rubato is a nuance of movement. It has anticipation and delay, disquietude and relaxation, agitation and calmness... Chopin often demanded that when the left hand rigorously maintained the rhythm, the singing upper part had liberty to alter the time values" (Eigeldinger 1979: 78).

The arpeggiated diminished seventh chords in bar 85 are something that Chopin also uses in transitions. It is transition as a marked gesture, and it sometimes appears together with the learned style, as in the Ballade in F minor. This passage also exhibits a virtuoso playing figure, one of the rare moments in Chopin where (11) *virtuosity* is foregrounded as such. This transition leads effortlessly to the passionate, almost Wagnerian (12) *chromatically falling melody*. (Chopin also exploits the power of this "Wagnerian" figure in other contexts. For example, it can refer to falling asleep or to another state of relaxation, as at the end of the C sharp Nocturne Op. 48 No. 2 in bars 119–126, where it evokes Wagner's Wanderer and the chromatically descending sleep motive.) If the first two themes portray "Chopin" and "George Sand", the masculine and the feminine, then this chromatically descending melody may show their relationship as a representation of musical desire. This utterance means (13) *abandonment to desire*. Psychoanalytically this would signify a paroxysmal impulse (see Szondi 1986, on *Schicksalsanalyse*). If the music in bars 93–98 still shows some hesitation, in its movement towards and withdrawal from something, from bar 99 we are thrown headlong into the paroxysmal and manic fulfilment of desire. This culminates in the *fortissimo* octaves in bars 109, 111, 113 and 115, where the excitement reaches its peak, and the *khora* breaks the chains of the symbolic order. But what follows is the negation of desire in the catatonic stasis of the repeated chords in bars 116–123. However, there is a means of escaping this catatonic state, namely, the strong (14) *cadence utterance* in bars 124–125. (Such a cadence utterance becomes a common device in Chopin's Preludes, which often start totally "disengaged" and at the end require a moment of stabilization.) This leads to the positive transformation of the funeral march into its counterpart, the (15) *triumphant march*. At the same time, the main theme of this passage is a major-mode version of the syncopated, very actorial main theme from the beginning of the principal section, our "Chopin" theme. Here, in a Lisztian manner, the hero reveals a new side of himself – certainly *himself*, since there is no doubt about the masculinity of this utterance. The following idiomatic figure (bars 143–147) is one of the *Spielfiguren* utterances in Chopin, in which the hand assumes its most comfortable position on the keyboard, with long fingers on the black keys and short fingers on the white keys.

The whole exposition is repeated, and then comes the "slow" movement nested within this one-movement piece. The slow section is a kind of (16) *lullaby* that enharmonically shifts from a flatted to a sharpened key.

The rest of the piece provides no new types of utterance. It is in fact redundant to the point of belying the "fantastic" aspect announced by the title of the piece (Chopin's romantic irony?). Only in the *adagio sostenuto* of the coda, in bar 321, do we find a (17) *recitativo* utterance, in which the musical declamation is completely language-based, on the order of the famous recitative passage in Beethoven's "Storm" Sonata in D minor. Here the melodic formation is clearly *logogenic*.

Within this single late piece by Chopin we have found 17 different types of utterance. When we scrutinize other pieces where they recur, a new question arises: Are these utterances *commutable*? That is to say, could we exchange an utterance from one piece for that of another in the same category? For instance, could *virtuoso, lullaby, Storm and Stress, linear, funeral march, cadence* and so on perform *functions* independent of their musical substances, so that such interchange or substitution among them would be possible? Naturally music is made up not only of functions but also of thematic materials, which help form the coherence of each piece's musical narration. Nevertheless, these utterances are clearly determinable beyond the boundaries of normal musical parameters.

Let us now turn to another late piece by Chopin, the F minor Ballade, the beginning of which forms the "key" to all that follows. This work appears to be more on the side of linear, polyphonic art than are the *Lied* and march articulated by the Fantasy in F minor. Ernst Kurth neatly clarified the world-views of this artistic dichotomy. The classical periodic style emphasizes joy of life, mere being in *Dasein.* amidst its desires, worries and victories. In contrast, the linear art of the polyphonic masters evokes a world-view that strives for eternity and transcendence, with the Gothic cathedral as its arche-symbol.

Even the title "Ballade" can be understood as a gesture to the world of the past. Permeating this polyphonic texture is the romantic search for the "blue note" on the repeated G in the soprano and its counterpart in the tenor. At the same time, the unit as a whole resembles a homophonic *bel canto* utterance, in which the melody is supported by bass arpeggiations. Thus, this passage belongs to the category of (18) *mixed, syncretic* utterances, just as it is also *inchoative*.

The main theme, too, is complex. A slow dance in triple meter, it is waltz-like, but not a true waltz (like the main theme of the G minor Ballade). It moves in the walking rhythm typical of some dirge topics, but it is not a pure funeral march. Hints of learned-style utterances can be heard in the suspended notes (in bar 8, the melodic B against the F in the bass). This "axial" melody (in Leonard Meyer's sense) hovers around the diminished-seventh chord tones of E, B flat, and D flat, a chord which resolves to A flat at the end. This basic motive thus has the kinetic energy that arises from a search for something. It is unstable as such, and this inner disquietude provides forward momentum. The utterance lasts so long (until bar 37) that it gives the overall impression of a pacing lion imprisoned in a cage.

Then comes a mystical, *pianissimo* transition on the black keys. It seems to prophecy something to come, as soon happens with the entrance of the lullaby theme in bar 81. That utterance could be heard as a special *understatement*, but in the corporeal sense it is like a brief (19) *oneiric* state, in which the body is completely freed from desire and the musical subject has sunken into something like a Bergsonian *memoire involontaire*, a state in which all kinds of surprising ideas circulate in one's mind. It is at once a remembrance and an anticipation, during which time seems to stand still.

The following section starts to ornament the simple melody, while keeping its structure unchanged. Bars 46–54 and 58–72 constitute an (20) *unfolding* or *organic growth* utterance. After the second theme comes a lullaby section in triple meter, which also has a tinge of the pastoral. It exhibits typically Chopinian rhythmic ornamentations, such as those in the "George Sand" theme of the F minor Fantasy.

In bar 134, with the metrically free small notes, we encounter a new type of utterance, an imitation of (21) *coloratura* singing style, here beautifully transformed into a pianistic texture. Bars 135–144 display a polyphonic development, in which Chopin employs the German (22) *Durchführung* idea with a reference to the fugue-like, or at least imitative, learned style. We catch only a glimpse of this style, however, for the music soon shifts to a homophonic texture (bar 145).

Bars 152–167 constitute an interesting mixture of (23) *logogenic, bel canto, coloratura* and *improvised* utterances. In what follows the second actor seems to "win" the narrative struggle between protagonists. It is glorified by all kinds of congenially pianistic devices, such as the ascending scale passages in the bass (bars 169–171), arpeggiations, hemiola rhythms, and centrifugal, syncopated melodic articulations (bars 175–176). (The same idea occurs in the subordinate section of the *Fantaisie impromptu* and in the A flat major Etude Op. 10.) This represents an utterance of (24) *song amidst sound*.

The essentially vocal impulse of this Ballade is overtaken by the instrumental figuration in bars 191–194. Here again the body abandons itself to *Thanatos*, to the paroxysmal, manic desire for destruction. The chords in bars 203–210 do not restore complete calm after this extremely violent activity. They represent a *cadence* utterance, but their position in the narrative process is (25) *non-terminative*. Thus we have the paradox of something that serves as closure but that is not performing as such.

The long coda constitutes what we might call a (26) *destruction* utterance, in which the musical substance dissolves into its smallest atoms. It is thus a kind of symbolic representation of death. In corporeal terms, here the body undergoes aggressive, destructive forces. But at the same time, the instrumental utterances are extremely rich and full of new innovations. In narrative terms, neither of the two actorial protagonists survive: not the first theme (axis-melody), with its archaic, polyphonic style, nor the second theme (the pastoral lullaby). They both come apart under this process of total dissolution. Metaphysically, this signifies what we have called the first transcendental act: negation, or the encounter with Nothingness.

The foregoing analysis shows how relatively new types of utterance can arise. Chopin combines utterances in new ways, thereby creating an aesthetics of ambiguity, which is also a characteristic of his "romantic irony". Now we shall look at some less complicated pieces and at other genres. Chopin's Preludes, for example, often consist of only one utterance. Before composing, Chopin played music by other composers, particularly J. S. Bach, and one can easily see the preludes from the *Well-Tempered Clavier* as the "legisign" or "type", of which Chopin's own Preludes are "tokens". Strengthening this view is the fact that all the keys are represented in Chopin's Preludes. Vladimir Jankélévitch says the following about Chopin's Preludes:

Le Prélude ne cesse de préluder... Le préambule est devenu la pièce elle-même. La concision, l'improvisation, c'est-à-dire l'état inspiré durant lequel la phrase en travail germe et tatônne et subit d'incessantes retouches. – telles seront les seules règles du Prélude. Cette forme n"a aucune forme. (Jankélévitch 1957: 90)

[The Prelude never stops warming up... The preamble has become the piece itself. The concision, the improvisation, that is to say, the inspired state during which the phrase slowly germinates and feels its way around, going through incessant alterations – such are the only rules of the Prelude. This form has no form.]

Jankélévitch lists some examples, indicating how chaotic the Preludes are in their mixing of genres. Numbers 2, 4, 9, and 13 are nocturnes; 7 is a mazurka; 23 an impromptu; 20 a funeral march; 10, 18 and 24 are scherzos; 1, 5, 8, 12 and 19 are etudes. Perhaps our analyses of Chopinian utterances can add something new to Jankélévitch's classifications.

Prelude 1 is an example of *bel canto*, played with the thumb of the right hand, of which there are many instances in Chopin, ranging from the middle section of the *Fantaisie impromptu* to the middle section of the B minor Scherzo. The texture is very "Bachian" in its counterpoint, but the overall impression is of a painting on canvas, inasmuch as the layers of texture form a unified (26) *sound field*, which itself forms a pre-sign for subsequent impressionistic devices.

Prelude 2 exemplifies what Jankélévitch calls improvisation, but may be better described as *in medias res*: the piece starts in the middle of the action, without any kind of preparation. In Greimassian terms, it starts with "disengagement". There is no "inchoative" section, or what Asafiev would call "initium"; rather, we start in the middle of "durativity" or "motus". At the end such preludes have a strong "engagement" in the form of a cadence consisting of a simple chord progression that reinforces closure. A similar narrative program is found in Preludes 4, 8, and 11. But some preludes do not have even that; for example, Prelude 14 in E flat minor has only durativity, without beginning or end. Such utterances could be called (27) *durational* or *disengaging*, and the former kinds viewed as (28) *terminative* or *engaging*.

Prelude 3 represents a special *Spielfigur* employing the "jeu perlé" technique, such as one finds in the first movement of Bach's G major Partita and in the Preludes in his *Well-Tempered Clavier*. This is Chopin's "Forellen" style, which calls to mind the Rhine Daughters swimming. Preludes 4 and 6 are very *cantabile*, their songs not evoking *bel canto* voices, however, but rather a stringed instrument. Thus they are a kind of (29) *intertext*. Prelude 5, with its centrifugal and disengaged texture, has an etude-like quality. Prelude 7 is a "mazurka oubliée". Number 8 is an example of the "singing-thumb" voice in the middle, surrounded by a particular *Spielfigur* texture. Prelude 9 illustrates a simple (29) *crescendo* narrative program. Prelude 10 is an ornamented mazurka, in which the embellished figure is more important than the main topic itself. Prelude 11 vaguely evokes the delicate pastorale of Bach's F sharp major Prelude and Fugue from Book I of the *Well-Tempered Clavier*. This Prelude is an etude for the fourth and fifth fingers of the right hand (like the Etude in A minor Op. 10), while at the same time "balladic" in narrative content.

Because we are encountering few new types of utterance in the Preludes, let us skip to some more interesting moments. Number 17, towards the end, with the pedal point on A flat, represents the afore-mentioned case of a pre-sign for impressionist painting. Prelude 18 is a declamatory recitative, recalling such moments as the dialogue between piano and orchestra in the slow movement of Beethoven's Fourth Piano Concerto – here, in a much accelerated guise. A kind of post-sign for this prelude might be the portrayals of the rich and poor Jews in Musorgsky's *Pictures at an Exhibition*.

Prelude 23, with its "jeu perlé" techniques, refers to the previous G major Prelude (no. 3), but it has one more utterance, which is very short – only a single note. This is the famous E flat at the end, which does not resolved, but vibrates freely as a special tone colour – a splen-did example of how a colourful utterance can create an entire sound field.

The theme of the last prelude, number 24, has a clear pre-sign – the opening motive of Beethoven's "*Appassionata*" Sonata – which almost makes the piece *Musik über Musik*. Here the performer should remember that Chopin always viewed *forte* as a relative dynamic, to be determined by context. The balladic ostinato in the left hand evokes the F minor Etude Op. 10 as its *Spielfigur*, but its almost demoniacal dramatic effect approaches that of the Finale of the B minor Sonata (notice also that the key is D minor, the same as Mozart's *Don Giovanni*). But the ending is very sinister, like that of a saga. In terms of corporeality, a very violent, eruptive body is "speaking" here.

Some of the preludes prove conclusively that Chopin's narrative programs do not necessarily follow the scheme of an initial problem followed by its eventual resolution. Sometimes the narrative program does not move linearly, along the syntagmatic chain of the piece, but vertically, in the dimension of depth. It may proceed from surface to deep structures, as in those short "improvisatory" and "disengaged" preludes which at the end find stability in a clear-cut tonal cadence. Or the narrative may run from surface to "super-structure", that is to say, into the transcendental sphere. At such moments, corporeality is sublimated into expression (as Adorno used to say about Wagner). As the musical material thins out, the body is transfigured, so to speak, into spirit. This is the case, for instance, in the F minor Fantasy. The body also can be transcendentalised to the point of reaching its utmost expression, after which the corporeal process can no longer continue, but something new must emerge from it. This seems to occur in many of the Etudes as well, which by their very title evoke corporeality in the form of pianistic devices, but at the end transcend such materiality. This phenomenon happens in some of the Ballades, too, and very clearly in the Sonatas.

For instance, the Etude in A flat major Op. 25 is an example of *bel canto*, in spite of its heavy texture. Essential to the piece is the overall aesthetic quality of *Schönheit und Poesie*, as the Polish master Jan Hoffman used to describe it. In some cases, the *bel canto* expression and the tonally stable pastoral field shift to a search for the first minor harmony in a piece, which after a long time spent in the major mode comes to the listener as a surprise, as a nostalgic glance at the past. A similar passage is the introduction to the *Andante spianato et grande polonaise*, when the bass turns to E flat minor after the long-held G major field. The same idea is powerfully used by Wagner in the *Rhinegold*, with a similar move from E flat major to C minor, on the words "des Goldes Schlaf". Both cases recall something dysphoric.

Jankélévitch argues that in the Scherzos "le vol de l'imagination est le plus puissant, le plus audacieux... Les symptomes du scherzo – caprice, verve, ironie sombre, liberté – sont présents dans beaucoup d'œuvres de Chopin" ["the flight of imagination is the most powerful, the boldest, the most audacious... The characteristics of the scherzo –

*Ex. 14.* Chopin, Scherzo No. 3 in C sharp minor, bars 155–160.

caprice, verve, dark irony, freedom – are present in many of Chopin's works."] (Jankélévich 1957: 92–93). The scherzo quality is present almost everywhere in Chopin, and it relates to a special *souplesse* in playing style (Jankélévich 1957: 30). Very often it is embodied in cambiata-like figures that are easy to play with a relaxed hand. It appears in the C sharp minor Scherzo in the figure ornamenting the Chorale (Ex. 14). (Also, sometimes new utterance types, like the just-mentioned *chorale*, emerge in the Scherzos.)

The B flat minor Scherzo employs two new types of utterance. It uses the (32) *Faustian question* as its opening phrase (similar to the device used in the C sharp minor Scherzo), which recalls certain Lisztian topics (see Grabócz 1996: 121). The B flat minor Scherzo also makes use of the (33) *heroic gesture*, as in bars 544–553. There, after an intense passage, the music dwindles to mere repetition of the same figure. It finally breaks out of this vicious circle by moving along the circle of fifths, as an heroic solution to the problem. Such moments exhibit a Berliozian aesthetics of the "imprevu", or unexpected. Take, for instance, the B minor scherzo, which opens bombastically, with two chords that are like a sudden outburst or cry (as the symbolist poet Prszybyszewski described them). This utterance of (34) *pathogenic exclamation* rarely occurs in Chopin. Another unique type of utterance would be the (35) *syntagmatic juxtaposition of extremes*, like the "cry" of those two chords immediately followed by a scherzo-like, ironically playful texture. There is certainly nothing effeminate or even organic in such an aesthetics of contrasts. What Jankélévich says about the Scherzos is particularly appropriate here: "Les nerfs sont rudement secoués par cet electro-choc du sombre délire" [One's nerves are rudely shaken by the electical shock of this dismal frenzy.] (1957: 94).

We could continue our inventory until we amass a systematic paradigm of all the utterance types in Chopin. Here we have listed only 35 of them. In some cases, one hears the topics of baroque, classical and romantic music in the background. Of course, the body is always present in any musical utterance, but in some it is marked, and in others it is un-marked. This means that in every utterance we encounter a struggle between the socialized, civilized body – the patriarchal order, so to speak – and the freely pulsating, *khoratic* body. We could go on to study the musical "semes" of these utterances, which would extend our interpretation beyond the level of musical signifieds. But however far we extend our analysis, the richness of such messages will always exceed explanation by any one methodology.

# Part three:
# Social and musical practices

# Chapter 7
# Voice and identity

## 7.1 Voice and signification

Voice is essential to the being and existence of man amidst his *Dasein*. In the first place, voice manifests our desire and will to *express* something. Hence the most important force and energy of the semiotic universe appears in it. This force is the movement from the immanent towards the manifest, in the way that *langue* always strives to appear as *parole*. In its immanence and virtuality, nothing is yet a sign. It becomes one only when it is projected to towards someone. Voice represents just such a fundamental intention, though it is not yet action. Ludwig Klages referred to expression as a metaphor of action: *"Der Ausdruck ist ein Gleichnis der Handlung."* Action always has a specific goal, whereas expression has a more general destination and intention. Klages distinguishes between movement of expression and movement of spontaneous act (*Willkürbewegung*) and represents their relationship with this scheme: A:W = G:U, meaning "Expression is to will as metaphor is to factual statement" (Klages cited in Bühler 1933: 165). The voice can serve both as a tool of expression and as spontaneous act. In the first case, it can be emotive or what Jakobson called "phatic"; in the latter, "conative".

The voice does not just express an emotional state. It seeks to emanate from a subject; it strives to break through the borders of a solipsistic *Dasein*. Voice expresses an attempt to be heard, to be noticed by another *Dasein*. Therefore the voice is essentially an intersubjective entity. In the absentminded reading of a text by oneself or in the humming of a tune, which are autocommunicative acts, the voice is produced only for one's own delight and use. This behaviour differs from a situation in which voice is used to reach other subjects. Singing, as a special, foregrounded use of the voice, as a "marked" activity, is always *eine dar-stellende Kunst*, an art which poses and presents something, which projects the voiced message toward someone.

Gino Stefani (1982) distinguishes several intentions behind what he calls "recitative intonation". The latter can occur just as well when a schoolchild recites his homework as when a monk silently intones a hymn: both abandon themselves to self-oblivion and impersonal recitation. On the other hand, it can be a declaration or a proclamation: a speaker at the railway station, at a crowded meeting, a storyteller, a priest giving a sermon. In music, Verdi's operas make much use of such intonations. All these cases use a vocal expression that features steady pitch and dynamics, and minimal rhythmic articulation.

Peter Ostwald says this about the basic task of human sounds:

> "No person can live alone in isolation from others. Sound is an all-important medium for breaking through one's personal shell to make contact with people. From birth to death the individual screams, gasps, rattles, and calls in order to let others know where he is and what he is doing. Life experience teaches him that sounds are most easily picked up by the ears of other people. He learns to produce noises that are likely to be heard and recognized, so that others may react to him." (Ostwald 1973: 20)

Thus understood, voice is not only autocommunication and more or less symbolic *Ausdruck*, but a means by which to escape the world of *Dasein*, a sign by which the social emerges. Of course, some "silent" communities do exist, as in certain monasteries, where despite their vows of silence the monks and nuns are able to communicate with each other (cf. Thomas and Jean Umiker-Sebeok 1987). Most social life, however, is filled with sound, and particularly human sounds. These may be divided into two types, based on Greimas's "thymic" dyad: *euphoric*, by which man tries to draw others to himself and to influence them by persuasion; and *dysphoric*, whereby one tries to make others go away or keep their distance. By voice and sound we can manipulate people. Ostwald (1973) has diagrammed the continuum that leads from the totally physiological, organic sounds of the body to the most sophisticated social sounds. Language and speaking are of course among such forms of social sound-production, as is singing (except for such autocommunicative cases as mentioned above).

The phenomenology of voice thus indicates that it serves a crucial existential function. In his *Phénoménologie de la perception* (1945), in the chapter "Le corps comme expression et la parole", Merleau-Ponty argues that thinking and language – and one might add, singing – are basic human activities by which man reaches towards the world ("se projette vers le monde"). He argues that the phonetic gesture provides the speaking subject and his listener the articulation of a certain experience, a certain transformation of existence – just as my body furnishes me and its surrounding objects with certain meanings. For Merleau-Ponty the essential thing is not the physiological-anatomical act of speaking. Rather, "the tensions of the throat, pressing the air through tongue and teeth, a certain manner of playing with our body suddenly creates a certain figurative sense and signification which is beyond our body. In order for this miracle to happen it is indispensable that the phonetic gesture employ the already acquired alphabets of signification, that the verbal gesture is realized in a certain panorama common to the speakers, since the understanding of others presupposes a given, common world..." (Merleau-Ponty 1945: 226). Here Merleau-Ponty, in his own phenomenological language, echoes the statement made many years earlier by Saussure, that *langue* precedes *parole*. That is to say, a certain grammar and vocabulary common to the speakers must already be in place, in order for anyone to be able to produce *parole*. This theory of language can easily be extended to cover singing and other uses of the human voice.

Though according to Merleau-Ponty, to vocalize is a trivial physiological event, from a philosophical and existential-semiotical point of view, it forms a crucial moment. What makes man need to establish contact with the world that surrounds him? Why doesn"t the semiotic force of expression occur in all cases? What obstructs its functioning? (Medicine has yet to determine the causes of autism.) Conversely, what enhances voice? What makes it flourish? Does a branch of applied semiotics already exist that focuses on *Ausdruck*?

As mentioned in Chapter 1, Husserl distinguishes two species of signs: *Bedeutungszeichen*, which are, so to say, pre-existent, always already "there", a kind of transcendental sign; and *Ausdruckszeichen*, which in a way are "clothed" inside the *Bedeutungszeichen*, as if dressed in the appropriate costume. Also, Greimas's generative course represents a kind of semiotic "vocal" force that makes meanings emerge from the abstract and achronic semiotic square. Moreover, Bergson argued that every human symbolic activity requires "intellectual effort", a shift from sense to sign: "We move not from sign to sense but from sense to sense through the sign" (Jankélévitch, quoted in Bankov 2000: 97). This is true of voice production as well. Every vocal act contains such a metaphysical effort, without which we would live in a mute, voiceless culture. This effort is the origin of communication. It moves us to take the leap from the *Dasein* of our own identity towards another identity and its *Dasein*; it makes us risk being misunderstood or even being perceived as ridiculous. Nowhere is such a primal act of communication manifested more clearly than when a singer, the producer of the voice, is facing an audience. Moreover, when we recall that the muscular tensions and gesticulations of singing are not always very aesthetic, according to the mimic and proxemic codes of society, then we understand why singers' gestures have been coded in certain canonized forms. Intellectual – and physical – effort appears in singing even more than it does in speech.

Another issue concerns the voice as both bearer and signifier of meanings. If the voice can serve as a sign, then why has it been so little investigated in semiotics? The answer, of course, lies in semioticians' preoccupation with Chomskyan linguistics, which focuses on deep structures of language and tends to ignore phenomena closer to the surface. Still, some histories of voice and its significations have appeared; for example, John Potter's *Vocal Authority* (1998) and Peter F. Ostwald's *The Semiotics of Human Sounds* (1973). It is rewarding to read about music history from the latter book's point of view, which is unique in that the author, Prof. Ostwald, is not a musicologist but a medical scholar. It is sometimes difficult to distinguish the history of voice from the history of vocal *music* itself. Nevertheless, it is quite proper to conceive of voice and singing as constituting the core of all music history.

The antipode of voice is of course instrumentality. Guido Adler, founder of modern style analysis and musicology, argued that all of the fugue-subjects written by J. S. Bach are based on the distinction between the vocal and the instrumental. In some phases of music history, instrumentality predominates, and even singing voices are reduced to playing the role of instruments. "Instrumental voices" have sometimes even been the ideal. For instance, Jean Sibelius considered the Finnish soprano Ida Ekman the most faithful interpreter of his songs because her voice was "instrumental" (unlike the voice of, say, her contemporary Maikki Järnefelt, who was very dramatic and text-bound). This vocal aesthetic originated with Wagner and Wagnerians. By the end of the nineteenth century, the latter started to conceive of all Wagner's operatic music as symphonic – and hence, instrumental – in essence. At the time, however, in the age of romanticism the highest compliment one could pay an instrumentalist was that he or she had a "singing" tone. Piano pedagogues encouraged their pupils to "sing" with their fingers, whatever that meant.

## 7.2 Text

The other counterpole of the voice is the *text*. Some singers and pedagogues emphasize the comprehension and interpretation of the text. For them, everything depends on the verbal text of a song. For instance, in Wagner performances at Bayreuth during the time of Cosima a style emerged which underlined the declamation of text instead of vocal techniques. This led to the vocality of Wagner's music being ignored. We must always remember that Wagner knew the entire opera repertoire of the time and that he explicitly stated, in his essay *Was is deutsch in der Musik,* that Germans had gotten their music from Italy. We must also recall how, at the high points of his operas, *bel canto* blossoms forth, as in the prophecy of Siegfried by Brünnhilde in the last act of *Die Walküre.* Moreover, it was Wagner's habit always to write first, in pencil, the entire vocal part alone, scene by scene, before providing it with harmonic support and ultimately the whole orchestration (see Millington 1992: 245).

Still, the need to understand the sung words has always been the counterpole to the brilliance and foregrounding of the voice itself. Hence the "text" is the anti-subject or antihero in the history of voice. Operatic reforms have often sprung from requirements to understand the text. In *Die Geburt der Tragödie,* when still a young professor of philology, Friedrich Nietzsche wrote that the Socratic, unmusical man is unable to receive the mythical message of tragedy and opera, its "metaphysical consolation", as he put it, precisely *because* such a man wanted to understand the words, which in turn led to such uncreative forms as the recitative. Nietzsche thus took the side of the voice as against text. In the *Fröhliche Wissenschaft* he even claimed that German culture had become impoverished when the text was not longer read aloud. As Michel Perrot notes, by the end of the nineteenth century, reading aloud as family entertainment had almost disappeared and was practiced only by older people (in Ariès and Duby 1987).

## 7.3 Transcendence

The voice has always been a means of communicating with transcendental reality. The voice has been connected to various practices of the sacred, as studied by Iegor Reznikoff 1984: 19–37. In his view, the voice has a connection with our deepest level of consciousness. Prenatal experiences show that man's sensations (exteroceptive signs) both begin and end with voices. Even a person in a deep coma can be reached by the voice. Hence the voice unites the visible and the invisible. Reznikoff connects the voice to five areas of the body: stomach, heart region, throat, mouth, forehead, and head, which in turn correspond to the structure of the cosmos (Reznikoff 1990). Reznikoff is known for his coursies on vocal mediation. One of his exercises shows that the vibrations of the body can be reached if you first utter the vowel "a" and then close your lips, while at the same time keeping your hand on your head. When you close your mouth, you feel in your palm the vibration of you body. This could almost be an empirical proof of Lévi-Strauss's belief that, by music, man becomes conscious of his physiological roots (whereas by myth he realizes the social grounds of his essence). Reznikoff thinks that the voice of the body is related to mythicism and the sacred by two basic forms: prayer and contemplation. Reznikoff has also tried to reconstruct singing methods that predate the Gregorian reforms. In his view, the old, correct, "natural" way of singing was based on the ability of the body to

find the right resonance, the latter being on pure, non-tempered intervals.[9]

All the music of antiquity, and all traditional music, from India
to flamenco to children's music-making, is based on the right vibrations of the body. Reznikoff views are interesting to semiotics because
they intersect with the theory of the modalities, i.e., the ways in
which speakers animate their speech with various wishes, desires and
emotions speech (cf. Ch. 1). Even the modal scales in medieval and
renaissance music were originally viewed as connected with certain
emotional states.

The religious use of the voice is amazingly similar everywhere in
the world. I take two examples. Japanese *shomyo*-singing, as part of
Buddhist ritual, is part of that country's oral culture. *Shomyo* music,
based on Chinese and Sanskrit writings, consists of short melodic
fragments which are put together to form a complete song. It is akin
to and even contemporaneous with Gregorian chant, both of which
feature unaccompanied male voices, similar intonation, free rhythms,
and two styles of singing: declamatory, which follows the text-sylla-
bles, and melismatic. Moreover, both *shomyo* and Gregorian chant use
neume notation. In addition to songs using fixed pitches, one finds passages devoid of scales and notes (see Taikai Takahashi: "How to Sing
Shomyo" 1992, IV: 1–2 . Similar sounds, based on sliding scales or
the complete absence of thereof, are heard in the funeral laments of
Bororo Indians on the other side of the globe, in the Mato Grosso of
Brazil (cf. Ch. 8).

## 7.4 Orality

The previous two cases connect the voice to a religious function, but
at the same time they illustrate *oral* cultures. The latter still exist in the
present electronic age, often called a "new oral age", in which people
are more oriented to the world by spoken language, voice, and visual
signs than by *written* verbal texts. Yoshihiko Tokumaru distinguishes
two kinds of orality: *primary* orality, which prevails in a face-to-face
communication, as in the aforementioned Buddhist and Bororo ritu-

als; and *secondary* orality, which is recorded and mechanically reproduced by telephones, on TV, mobile phones, and the like (Tokumaru and Yamaguti 1986). Secondary orality serves as a surrogate of the primary one and also replaces notation. In Japanese music culture, the use of notation is generally forbidden since music must be learned by heart (as is also the case in some Western pedagogical settings). In Japan, *syoga* occupies the middleground between the oral and the literary. It is a song played by flute, but if the flute breaks, one may continue by singing *syoga*. Such leeway brings to mind a performance of the Schumann Piano Concerto: the flute part was missing, so the conductor sang it. Hence, orality also exists even in the strongly text-bound tradition of Western classical music. With regard to traditional musical cultures, however, Tokumaru points out that authenticity is not guaranteed by recordings (secondary orality), since music is a living sound, and attention must be paid to the means of transmission and not to the result as such.

This view comes close to that of Reznikoff, who believes musical moods are universal and connected to times and mental states: winter, summer, morning, cheerfulness, arrival, waiting, tranquility, courage, etc. The body is different in different states, *Stimmungen* as Heidegger called them, and so is music. The Finnougric *itkuvirsi* is the modality of the lament – only thereafter comes the scale. Thus, if we are seeking the authentic style of Gregorian chant, we must return to the level of the modalities – as still living realities in the traditional music of various countries – and from these experiences draw inferences that are pertinent to contemporary performance practice.

## 7.5 Singing as social identity

In contemporary society, various identities have their equivalent vocal expressions. Various life-styles and life-worlds influence secondary orality. In his book *Distinction* (1984), Pierre Bourdieu has investigated various of these "habituses" among different social classes and *arrondissements* of Paris, each of which has its own musical preferences. Likewise we can recall Adorno's classifications of listener types

(*Hörtypen*), among which is the cultural consumer (*Bildungskonsu-ment*). The latter is enchanted by vocal virtuosity and overall sound, but fails to gain deep insight into the music "itself".

Adorno also maintained a strict division between artistic musical culture and that of entertainment, the latter representing the sour fruits of mass-communication. Can we make the same distinction as to voice types? Do artistic voices differ from popular ones? Doubtless, yes. Still, both artistic and popular voices represent certain types such as "Italian tenors", "Russian sopranos", "Bulgarian and Finnish basses", "German baritones", "American altos" and the like, each of these having its own identity. Their enchantment is often based on the charm of this identity within a broader category. This has been the case ever since ever since the tradition of *bel canto*, some of whose representatives, such as Pasta and Rubini, were physically not particularly appealing. Rather, everything was based on the identity and individuality of their voice. In the same way, popular music aficionados may want to listen just to the voice of Elvis, Ella Fitzgerald, Sinatra, and so on. But the real counterpole to such individual voice-identity is formed by the collective voice, which appears in the various popular traditions.

Stefani's model of musical competence might help explain the situation. His model classifies musical competence on the following levels: work, style, musical technique, social practice, general codes. In *artistic* competence, the individual work is the most important, and the least important level is that of general anthropological codes (such as the descending second as a universal figure of sigh and lament, or the octave as the expression of alertness and attention). Conversely, in *popular* musical competence, general codes are the most important ones, the least important being those of individual creativity. Stefani's model of popular competence does not include popular music in the present media society. Still, it can portray the history of singing and of the voice. The individual work would correspond to some individual's voice, such as that of Pavarotti, Kanawa, Nilsson, Talvela, etc. The style would be realized by various national singing schools or singer types, such as *Lied* singer, chanson singer, and so on. Technique would be represented by the singing styles of performers of *bel canto*, of Wagnerian opera, of operetta, church choirs, rock music, etc. Social practice would be equivalent to genres, such as opera, oratorio, chamber music, lament, liturgy, armed forces, and so on. The general codes would appear in the form of the quasi-physiological foundations of the singing (more on this later). Stefani's distinction between artistic and popular competence, however, may more suitably apply to primary orality, i.e., to the contrast between ethnosemiotic and sociosemiotic societies. Our present, third phase – which I call *technosemiotic society* – emphasises secondary orality, for which Stefani's model may have little pertinence.

In archaic societies, during their ethnosemiotic phase, singing is most closely related to community and communal structures. It is one of the ways by which the members organize themselves and their *Umwelt*. An example would be the Suyá Indians of Mato Grosso, studied by the American anthropologist Anthony Seeger in his book, *Why the Suyá Sing* (1987).[10] When in Brazil, I transcribed some of their songs, called *akias*. In the Suyá tribe, villages are divided into two clans, between which the exogamic principle prevails; i.e., members of clan *x* must marry only those of clan *y*. Then they form two clans or halves of a village, for example, "pumas" and "beavers". When a boy from the pumas marries a girl from the beavers, he must move from his own side to that of the beavers, and he can never return. The only communication between the boy and his sisters, who have remained on the other side, takes place at village feasts, for which every man creates his own *akia*. All of these are sung at the same time, and the overall sound is one of total cacophony. This also explains the musical structure of the *akias*: they all start on as high a pitch as possible, and then sink down. This is done so that his sisters can distinguish his melody. But Suyás can also sing in a more moderate way, particularly when an *akia* is being taught to younger members of the tribe; in that case, the vocal expression is more intimate.

In music, the medium is the message. Thus, when "original" music, such as that of the Suyá, is fitted into "world music" and commercial markets, essential changes take place. The greatest of these changes is the disappearance of the referential function, that is, the loss of the primal community context. The meanings of mass popular culture can no longer be determined or studied from the musical signifier itself, since music has become the same as its mediation (Hennion 1993). John Potter (1998), in turn, says that popular music can no longer be interpreted, only new meanings are added to it. Everything is possible and permitted. On the other hand, herein lies the power of this type of music and culture: we can never predict the meanings it will assume. According to Roland Barthes, there no longer exists a unified, bourgeois sign-system that lays hold on music and subordinates it to its own ideology. Music no longer has a fixed ideology. Musical taste does not coincide with social class.

## 7.6 National voice types

At the sociosemiotic level, however, we can still speak of national identities. The triple distinction of ethno-, socio-, and technosemiotic societies no longer depends very much on time scale. All of these levels can exist at once, since different societies live in different times. For instance, national identity in voice was quite essential recently in the Baltic countries; in their singing "revolution", choral performances were absolutely essential. The choral scenes in Verdi's operas prompted the birth of the Italian nation. And Wagner's *Mastersingers* helped to unify Germany in the mid-nineteenth century. National identities are still heard in voices, but more as picturesque, regional qualities. For example, Taikai Takahashi's recording of the Schubert song *An die Musik* sounds fascinating because we can tell that his basic training was that of a Japanese shomoy singer. The famous opera house at Indiana University in Bloomington once staged a charming performance of Rimsky-Korsakov's *Legend of Tsar Saltan*; it had all the freshness of young voices, but was clearly of a quality that might be called "Indiana Russian style".

Not too long ago, miracles were worked by voice in politics and war. The vocal aspect that carries national ideology is certainly not the semantic level of the text, nor even the chosen language. On this issue, Heloísa Araújo de Duarte Valente, in her dissertation *Os Cantos da Voz*, quotes the Brazilian musicologist, Mario de Andrade: "More than the meaning of the words, it is the general intonation of the idiom, the accentuation and the manner of articulating the words, the timbre of the voices which represent the specific elements of the language of each nation" (Andrade in Valente 1999: 104). Nevertheless, opposing views exist, which consider language itself as always already ideological, as Italian semiotician Ferruccio Rossi-Landi has emphasized (1973). In his *The Art of the Elocutionist* (1932), the British teacher of rhetoric and voice, Guthbert Samuels, had this to say:

> English is fast becoming a universal language: it is a vehicle of thought second to none in lucidity, vitality and energy of expression. There is no imaginative flight beyond its reach, as witness the masterpieces of Shakespeare. It is a noble river, fed by many streams. Its dignity and its noble cadences come from the imperial Latin. Its rapier-like shafts of wit and monosyllabic power come from the Nordic Saxon.

If language carries such obvious ideologies, then certainly the voice, and singing as a marked form of vocal expression, underline them even more.

Voice as a representative of national identity is very problematic, however, for by viewing it as such we risk making a colonialising move. Very early in the twentieth century, Béla Bartók warned that no nation possessed a repertoire comprised purely of its own folksongs, since all of them had been borrowed from other countries. He was more fascinated by the reconstruction of the sound and voice of folk music, which he called the "parlando rubato" style. Still, ethnocentricity can appear even in apparently objective empirical research. Carl Seashore, in his study of vibrations (1948: 42), argues that all the most successful students of singing, well-trained amateurs, and professional singers use vibrato: "Primitive people, such as the uneducated Negro or the Indian, exhibit the vibrato in acceptable form when singing with genuine feeling ... it is probable that vibrato was present in the feeling-filled self-expression of even the most primitive speech and song". In this quotation a certain cultural practice, vibrato, is legitimized as something universal, almost given by nature. And yet, even *bel canto* does not necessarily favour vibrato. I consulted some vocal specialists about this, and none of them spoke about vibrato. Instead, one of them emphasized the continuous shift from chest register to head register.

Another even said that vibrato would be detrimental, because the *bel canto* singer has to be able to sing quick figurations with precision, and vibrato could only obstruct such a task.

Nationality on the level of the voice can appear as a primary orality, as captured by such an expression as "the Finnish singer" or "Russian bass". On the other hand, nationality may be elevated into a marked or foregrounded feature in music. Singers and their voices are sometimes crucial in defining a nation or culture (e.g., Bing Crosby as the "voice of America"). Symptomatic of this fact, Marcel Danesi (1997) has published a course on how to speak Italian, in which one learns the language by singing famous Italian opera arias. Nationality is a kind of fate. It determines to what kind of vocal community people are acculturated and imprints them with that acculturation for the rest of their lives. Moreover, the voice is closely bound to communality, or *Gemeinschaftlichkeit*.

## 7.7 Gender

Roland Barthes is one of the best-known scholars in recent decades to have studied singing in a semiotic way. In his essay, "The Grain of the Voice", he makes a distinction between *genosong* and *phenosong*. As discussed in Chapter 1.41 (thesis 8), genosong refers to the physiological aspect of singing, the corporeal vocal technique that engages the whole body. Phenosong relies on the primacy of language, text and civilisation, the sublimation of the physical level to that of high culture. For Barthes, the French tenor Charles Panzera represented the genosong and Dieter Fischer-Dieskau the phenosong. About the latter, Barthes states that his presence is unfortunately so overwhelming that you had better like Fischer-Dieskau if you want to listen to Schubert's songs, since his renderings are so dominant in the record markets.

Perhaps Barthes's analysis only displayed the Latinate temperament's aversion to everything German. Still if we apply Stefani's model of artistic and popular competences to voice, Barthes's analysis represents a new dichotomy in our history of voice; namely, the dichotomy between general codes (laments, sighs, joy, sorrow, etc.)

and their quasi-physiological signs – i.e., genosong – and codes of mere technique or vocal styling, i.e., phenosong. According to John Potter, Barthes was striving to eroticize the act of singing, even to the point of using it to establish sexual identity. However, Barthes's approach was in fact borrowed from the psychoanalytic views of feminist Julia Kristeva, who in a lecture once said that the most important thing about identity was the feeling of "belonging to something". Barthes's theory of the "grain of the voice" is primarily psychoanalytic, in the same sense as Merleau-Ponty philosophizes about sexual being as the "expression de notre maniere générale de projeter notre milieu". Hence, phenomenologically, sexual identity is a total way of being, which should not be identified with any specific bodily organs.

Gender analysis has also been carried out on vocal music. One well-known attempt known was Alan Lomax's "cantometric" study in the 1960s. Involving several scientists, the study aimed to prove the connection between aspects of singing – particularly pitch – and the sexual morality of a society. Lomax hypothesised that in societies with a very tight sexual morality, music is very high-pitched, whereas in more morally permissive societies, singers favour a lower, less tense quality. Lomax's theory was roundly criticized and ultimately discarded by ethnomusicology. Nevertheless, it was a serious effort to show statistically the connection between vocal style and sexuality.

Of course vocal art has always played with gender identities, starting with the *castrati*, who in performing female operatic roles caused all kinds of confusion in eighteenth-century life. Balzac's famous novella *Sarrasine* provides a lively account of such a case. In Barthes view, Gérard Souzay represented bourgeois vocal art at its purest. Souzay's performance of Reynaldo Hahn's song *l'heure exquise* serves as good illustration of the eroticization of vocal identity. The sensual quality of Zarah Leander's voice tells us much about the culture of the 1920s and 1930s, just as Edith Piaf's voice belongs to the popular competence of French culture.

Identities are not natural phenomena, however, that spring "organically" from just any kind of *Volksgeist* or popular, collective mentality. They are artificial creations to which one is acculturated. If the Western canon of art music is of German origin, then in vocal music, another canon prevails. The latter stems from Italian *bel canto*, and has continued with only slight transformations up to the present day. Hence, (Western) vocal style is Italian in origin, though in the nineteenth century the best *bel canto* was obviously heard outside of Italy. The point to be made here is that even *bel canto* was a cultural construction, which was no doubt based on a certain knowledge of the physiology of singing, but which through the centuries developed into special corporeal and spiritual techniques.

## 7.8 Education

If *bel canto* was based on a systematic educational process, then what happens in education also holds true in the vocal area. One of the most drastic definitions of education is found in John Potter's *Vocal Authority* (1998). The author argues that education is "symbolic violence" which exists in order to legitimate a "certain cultural arbitrary". This definition needs some clarification. First, the idea of education as violence is a more radical version of the general idea, shared by all semioticians, that all signs and sign-usage represent symbolic power. Michel Foucault (1975) radicalized this idea, saying that culture itself is violence, hence so is education, the latter being violence imposed on the dominated people whether they want it or not. Education is thus essentially a *langue* in the form of a collective contract. Still, what justifies Potter's assertion about the "cultural arbitrary"? What does "arbitrary" mean? Again we must turn Saussure to answer this question. In his distinction between the two sides of a sign, signifier and signified, he claimed that their connection was completely conventional or arbitrary. For instance, the English word "song" means vocal expression, whereas the same meaning in German is designated by the word *Gesang*, in French *le chant*, and so on. Similarly, all cultural articulations are just as arbitrary, and people must accept them if they wants to communicate. The same is true when we produce sounds. Certain performance and vocal practices just as arbitrary, but over time have become fixed and developed into rich forms. The voice, in Saussure's paradigm, is located on the level of *parole*. For Saussure

*Figure 12.*   The speech act according to Saussure (1970: 35).

(1916), language was situated on many levels, forming a heterogeneous reality that can be illustrated by the following diagram representing interaction between two speakers (from his *Cours de linguistique
générale*):

Language emerges only in such interaction, and the same can be
said about music.

Nevertheless, we need to know if facts from "nature" – i.e., empirical studies on voice – can limit the arbitrary possibilities from which
various vocal styles have chosen their elements. Moreover, we still
need to consider some special problems which the evidence of the history of voice may provide. First, we cannot remain content merely
with the truth that "every person has a different voice" as being the
source of possible identities. How, for example, does speech influence other vocal expressions, such as singing? And on what level of
reality do we encounter such a thing as vocal identity? When looking
at empirical studies on voice we must remember that this issue is not
new, but has interested music scholars for many centuries. As far back
as 1650 Athanasius Kircher made anatomical comparisons between
men and lower animals and insects, and he noticed that their means of
sound productions were physiologically similar.

Comparison of man's voice to animal sounds is thus nothing new.
Thus, when reading later empirical studies carried out with the aid of
spectrograms and other measuring devices, from Seashore (1938) to
Sundberg (1987), we must remember that they are only one way of
dealing with vocal phenomena. Are such modes of "scientific" inquiry
more real and substantial than are others, such as aesthetic, sociological, phenomenological, existential, literary, or semiotic means of

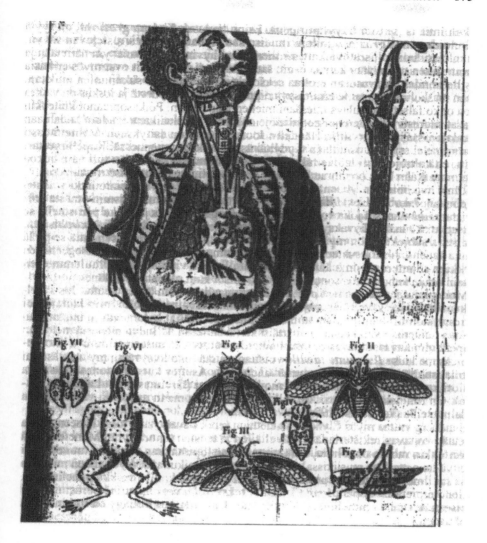

*Figure 13.*　Production of voice in insects, animals and human beings (Kircher 1650).

research? It is difficult answer this question, since as such, it is an epistemological one. Merleau-Ponty states that voice and speech *transcend* our anatomical body: to ourselves, our body is not an object, since we *are* our body. Such a statement supports the general view of singing as the only musical genre in which we are our own instrument. Merleau-Ponty continues: "The way man uses his body transcends his body as a simply biological entity" (1945: 221). It is impossible to consider man's primary level as somehow "natural", on which more cultural and spiritual levels are added. Our behaviours yield significations that transcend anatomical preconditions.


## 7.9 Empirical methods

Johan Sundberg's *The Science of the Singing Voice* (1987) summarizes the central concepts of an empirical approach to the issue. At the same time, his study raises many interesting questions in regard to our paradigm of vocal identities. Sundberg first defines all the major concepts in the field; in English, for instance, *voice* and *sound* are the primary concepts. He examines the production of voice in various registers: the chest, the mid-range, and head register, as one finds in *bel canto* theories dealing with the same issues. In addition, there are other special registers, such as the "Stroh-bass" heard in East European and Russian choral music. Of special interest is the functioning of the reflexive phonation system, which influences muscular contractions in the larynx. This system can be strengthened by training at a young age, but its functioning weakens during the aging process. If the system malfunctions, the muscles either contract too little or too much, which causes the intonation to become unstable. The phonation system can be trained, based on a kind of proprioceptive memory, which singers refer to as "muscle memory".

Articulations takes place in the lips, tongue, jaws, and larynx. The formant frequencies determine the tone quality and timbre of the voice. Sometimes a singer must exaggerate articulation in order to use it as a style feature. For instance, in the song *Violetta grazioso*, the word "grazioso" should be clearly articulated, so as to produce the somewhat precious tinge required at that point. Articulation naturally influences how the words are understood and how the voice projects over the accompaniment

The formants differ among women and men. Hence one can distinguish between "sexolects", i.e., vocal dialects according to gender. The masculinity or femininity depends on the frequency of phonation.

Sometimes it is hard to tell if we are hearing a woman's voice or a male voice singing in falsetto. (The sound of boy sopranos, however, differs greatly from that of women altos.)

All this presents the possibility of applying what Jakob von Uexküll (1940) termed "biosemiotics" to the problem of the voice. As discussed in Chapter 4.1, he proposed that every living organism has its own "*Ich-Ton*" (I-tone), which distinguishes it from other organisms and which decides what sounds and signs it accepts from the surrounding world (*Umwelt*). Every person also has their own I-tone, which determines what they consider to be familiar voices. This I-tone also determines our vocal identities, though in relation to our own voices we can observe those identities only through exo-signs. Our own voice is alien to us, since we hear it through the resonance and vibration of our own body, unlike the way we hear voices sent to us by other bodies.

Many listeners recognize the speaker through the emotional state of the voice. Though pitch, as macrointonation, may be fixed by the composer, singers can express their personal emotions by means of microintonations. According to Vincent d'Indy (1897–1900), melody originated in precisely this manner, that is, by emotional states being transmitted by rhythms and inflections. (These aspects or modalities are what Boris Asafiev later called "intonations".) In this way, syllables become "musicalized". It is obvious that the musicality of music – i.e., its interpretation – depends on these modalizing processes.

Sundberg also refers to Manfred Clynes' famous theory of sentics. In his experiments, Clynes used machines to register his subjects" physical responses, according to which Clynes formulated emotional diagrams of composers and styles (Clynes 1973, 1977; see also, Lidov 1999). Clynes' method has problems, however, such as whether it measures the subjects' reactions to the music itself or those of the performers that play it. Sometimes emotional states are inferred from the gestures that one imagines the speaker to be making when he/she is heard only via telephone. Poulenc's opera, *La voix humaine*, is based on this kind of situation (see also, Fonagy 1983). In a broader sense, however, voices represent social styles. After just a few seconds of listening to a radio reporter's voice, a person in Budapest in the 1970s could tell whether the news was coming from Moscow radio or from the Voice of America, all on the basis of intonation alone.

## 7.10 Conclusion

John Potter's *Vocal Authority* (1998) raises many of the issues we have discussed here, in its detailed history of voice and its ideologies. Yet the question remains, Can the voice itself be reconstructed? Singing styles have certainly been reconstructed, and Reznikoff has used "universal" knowledge of body resonance in his own theories. Yet, to reconstruct a complete style always requires the use of absolute, achronic models. For instance, Lotman and other cultural semioticians of the Tartu School have reconstructed ancient Slavic cultures and artifacts on the basis of the notion that all cultural products are "texts". Lotman's method – with its superimposed levels of a text: symbols, semantics, syntax, phonetics – has not yet been applied to anything so ephemeral as singing styles. Yet the idea of doing so does not seem so farfetched. We could well adopt Potter's view that, "... however singing develops, whether the singer is Mick Jagger or Elisabeth Schwartzkopf, stylistic renewal is driven by a need to find more appropriate ways to deliver a text" (Potter 1998: 2). Potter also presumes that whenever we find music notation along with a verbal text, it means that this text was intended to be sung (1998: 2; see also, Szabolcsi 1965: 199–203). Of course Lotman's conception of text is a greatly expanded notion as compared to that of just the linguistic text. Still, we can ask, as did Barthes, what kind of "text" a song would be.

For Potter, singing is always an ideological activity, a position he defends by the fact that in antiquity the concept of song was denoted by the word *nomos*, i.e., "law". Potter's basic concern is with how singers create meanings. He adopts Jakobson's model of how speaking occurs by means of certain functions: expressive, poetic, conative, phatic, metalinguistic, and referential. But what do these functions mean in vocal music? It is clear that singing is a phatic art, in the sense that the singer is himself/herself at the same time the instrument of transmission. It is also emotive, inasmuch as it often expresses the emotional state of the singer. We have already seen how singing can be conative, particularly in its connections to ideologies and identities. But how might a song be metalinguistic; i.e., how can it ponder its own codes? It seems that singing lacks the metalinguistic ability to model a secondary expression of itself (an issue to be examined next, in Ch. 8). In general, the singer is always serious. Finally, singing is referential precisely when it serves the goals of its society or group.

Does the singer need to become one with his or her song? Such has been the demand ever since the Renaissance. Potter is correct in stating that the singer's ideas and those of the listeners differ from each other radically. This is because the singer, when performing, can strongly focus on the details of the performance itself, whereas the listener can only imagine that he or she is living through this role and the music. Still, today interpretations are no longer as authentic as they once were, because singers no longer understand the words in the same way.[11]

# Chapter 8
## On the semiosis of musical improvisation:
### From *Mastersingers* to Bororo indians

### 8.1 Musical improvisation and semiotics

The idea of developing a theory of existential semiotics (Tarasti 2001) first entered my mind at the same time as I was making observations about improvisation. To illustrate, in Richard Wagner's *Mastersingers* we find a very apt characterisation of the situation in which semiotics now finds itself. We may thus take that opera as a "simulacrum" of the present phase of semiotics.

On the basis of the *Mastersingers* we can delineate three kinds of semiotics. First, the mastersingers themselves were "generativists", in their naive belief that rules could produce "mastersongs". While displaying a mildly ironic attitude toward these enthusiasts of rules, Wagner also casts the young artist Walther von Stolzing, who creates by inspiration, in a somewhat parodising light. If Beckmesser represents a ridiculously meticulous "academic" style, then von Stolzing illustrates a free, improvisatory way of writing, which easily leads to exaggeration (Wagner's performance indication is *anschwellend* in Walther's contest song). Stolzing typifies the music semiotician who creates only by means of the modalities (in the Greimassian sense). Finally, the synthesis of these two characters is Hans von Sachs, who finds a good balance between rules and creativity, *langue* and *parole*, grammar and realization of rules.

One of the most important classics in the study of improvisation is Ernst Ferand's *Die Improvisation in der Musik* (1938). As an example of improvisation, Ferand specifically mentions the scene in Sachs's workshop, when the contest song is created and written: "Es handelt sich hier also um eine den organischen Gesetzen inneren Wachstums gehorchende ... aber doch durchgeformte, ja höchst formvollende Improvisation; dabei vollzieht sich gleichzeitig auch schon der Übergang zur Komposition, indem zwar nicht die Weise, aber doch der Text von Hans Sachs aufgeschrieben wird" (Ferand 1938: 33). [What is involved here is a highly organized and shaped improvisation that fol-lows the organic law of inner growth. As such, it also realizes a transi-tion [from improvisation] to composition; not of the song, but of the text which Hans Sachs had written down (Ferand 1983: 33).]

Let us recall what this improvisation, staged by Wagner, is all about. First, it involves a situation in which the improviser, Walther, has a listener constantly by his side, who interprets and judges his

*Ex. 15. (cont.)*   Richard Wagner: *Meistersinger,* act 3, scene 1.

improvisations. Hence, we have a situation of communication in which Walther serves as the sender and Sachs as the receiver. In terms of Greimas's actantial model, Walther is a subject-hero, who with his auxiliary object, the song, aims to win Eva, Sachs's daughter. Sender and receiver are themselves mastersingers, who determine the rules of the contest and judge the competition. Sachs has taken on the task of being Walther's helper, in which role he encourages the unsure improviser. His opponent, of course, is Beckmesser. On the other hand, Sachs's role is contradictory in that, by helping Walther, he at the same time gives up his daughter. Nevertheless, he does so in order to avoid the fate of King Mark in *Tristan.*

Improvisation occurs here as a particular form of *communication.* Just as in communication the sender and receiver must have codes in common, similarly Walther must follow the rules established by the mastersingers. Walther believes that he cannot formulate his "dream image" by following dry rules, seeing the latter and poetic inspiration as irreconcilable. Nevertheless, Sachs convinces him: "Sind Freunde beid, stehn gern sich bei." When Walther asks how he should start according to the rules, Sachs answers: "Ihr stellt sie selbst und folgt ihr dann." Make the rules yourself, and let Hans Sachs take care of the rest!

Before the improvisation begins, they have a profound discussion about the essence of the generative rules of the songs. Walther asks Sachs how an ordinary, beautiful song differs from a mastersong. Sachs's account of this difference seems almost prophetic, if one thinks of how today computers can produce authentic-sounding Bach

Klagemotiv:
P. 1:1 - 2:6

*Ex. 16.*    Sibelius, First Symphony, clarinet motif from the opening of the 1st
movement.

chorales, children's songs, fiddle tunes, and other kinds of music based
on relatively clear-cut rules, so that not even specialists can distinguish between a "fake" and an "original". In his reply, Sachs returns
to youth, to "springtime", when, as if on its own, a fine song emerges
from the glow of a strong feeling. But if one can still write a beautiful song when autumn comes, followed by winter, when one grows
old and experiences hardships and struggles, then that song is a mastersong. In other words, a mastersong is made according to rules, but
it becomes enriched by a certain life history.

The same could be said about music in general. Tones and sounds
bearing the history of centuries-old technologies are experienced as
richer and more human than are sounds produced synthetically. The
latter always seem less actorial, in semiotic terms. Sachs states that the
"codes" or rules of a mastersong are learned only with time. Still, they
do not appear *ex nihilo*. Walther asks, Who created these rules? Sachs
answers that the creators were spirits worn out by the worries of their
lives, who through song made themselves an image of the spring to
delight their minds. A mastersong was thus a model, a product, which
was detached from life, but with which one could recall a by-gone,
golden age. Walther asks how this image might be kept fresh, after
"spring" has passed; that is, how one could prevent the original spirit
of rules from disappearing, how one could stop the fading of the image
which the song was to convey. Even to this Sachs has a ready answer:
"Er frischt es an, so oft er kann!" The rules have to be renewed as often
as possible. In semiotic terms, the codes have to be checked always
according to the context.

When the improvisation proper starts, Walther comes under the
spell of his emotion; he lets his dream image take shape as a melody.
Hans Sachs, in turn, articulates the melody in the traditional master-

song form: *Stollen, Stollen, und Abgesang*. Sachs halts the improvisation for awhile and gives orders about how to proceed. When the melody is completed he judges it: "Nur mit der Melodei, seid ihr ein wenig frei…" But he does not regard this as a mistake properly speaking, though it might "irritate" the old masters. Then Walther presents the second phrase in its entirety, which satisfies Sachs, though he still misses the true sense of Walther's dream image. At this point the improvisation is interrupted. Everyone familiar with Wagner knows the important function of "interruption" in his narration: it helps to put off the final resolution until the end of the opera, where it serves as the culmination of all that precedes. In sum, this scene from the *Mastersingers*, with its oppositions between rules and free creation, makes an excellent starting-point for the semiotic study of improvisation.

In studying improvisation, semioticians and other scholars have usually attempted to search out the rules hiding beneath the surface, the deep level which can be applied so as to produce an improvised melody. Accordingly, research in this area has become fairly reductionist, in attempts to prove that improvisation is mere illusion, and that what it really involves is a rigorous application of unconscious rules almost in the manner of deductive inference. For example, in Bach's time any organist could improvise a chorale tune; this fact led Italian musicologists Baroni and Jacoboni to find the rules that "generate" such chorales (1978). As explained in Chapter 2.3, Heinrich Schenker argued that from a deep-level contrapuntal structure called the *Ursatz*, the great composers improvised their compositions through the three levels of *Hintergrund, Mittelgrund*, and *Vordergrund* (1956). Inuit songs have also been reduced to their rules (Pelinski 1981). Johan Sundberg has written the deep level grammar for the children's songs by the Swede Alice Tegner (1976). Likewise, the rules for Finnish fiddle music have been formulated (Pekkilä 1988), as well as those of Argentinean tangos, and so on. Consequently, what at first seemed an endlessly rich and varied improvisation and an inexhaustible ability of discovery, has been revealed to be an activity guided by stringent rules. With a machine one can produce "improvisations" that precisely follow a style. But can we call these synthetically-produced melodies improvisations? Do they not lack something essential?

The crucial difference is the *process* of creating, mentioned by Sachs. No machine can invent those rules nor provide them with the historical significations from which their pertinence emerges. Further, rules do not take into account that improvisation concerns not only a *product* (enunciate) but involves the act of improvisation, the *activity* itself (enunciation) (see Ch. 1.4.1, thesis 4). When we speak of improvisation it is essential to clarify which of the two is intended . If the product is meant, then we demand from it such properties as irreversibility and unpredictability. Insofar as the activity itself is concerned, our attention goes mainly to the improviser, the subject of the improvisational act. Correspondingly, we have two different subjects: the subject of the enunciate, which is the subject *in* the text, and the subject of enunciation, who by his or her activity *produces* the text. We thus speak either of the composition, poem, dance and their inner subject; or of the composer, writer, dancer himself.

In some studies of improvisation this distinction is made without awareness of its methodological consequences. For example, in Derek Bailey's *Improvisation: Its Nature and Practice*, the jazz musician and composer Gavin Bryars says the following:

> One of the main reasons I am against improvisation now is that in any improvising position the person creating the music is identified with the music. The two things are seen to be synonymous. The creator is there making the music and is identified with the music and the music with the person. It's like standing a painter next to his picture so that every time you see the painting you see the painter as well and you can"t see it without him. And because of that the music, in improvisation, doesn"t stand alone. It's corporeal. My position, through the study of Zen and Cage, is to stand apart from one's creation. Distancing yourself from what you are doing. Now that becomes impossible in improvisation. (Quoted in Bailey 1980.)

On this view, improvisation is unsatisfactory because the enunciation, the producing, the physical action of the performer is so strongly foregrounded. Someone else, however, might be content with and even aim for this situation. In any case, this quotation serves as a good inverted proof of the crucial role of these two aspects in improvisation.

Both of these viewpoints are also present in the aforementioned scene from the *Mastersingers*. The musical utterance, Walther's contest song, has been surrounded by the activity of producing it and with many evaluative and reflective comments external to the message itself. Such an approach to improvisation proves to be much richer than the mere analysis of a product. In film theory, the music included in the plot of a film is called diegetic. In the opera, Walther's contest song is such a diegetic event, as is the contest itself in the finale. Such a case involves a communication of communication, a representation of representation on stage.

## 8.2 Improvisation as communication

Semiotics can provide theoretical tools for describing both of the above-mentioned aspects. Umberto Eco has divided semiotics into two kinds: semiotics of *communication* and semiotics of *signification* (1976). The former investigates the whole situation of communication, in all its dimensions. The latter examines how meaning is possible at all, how a sign is structured. When we study improvisation as communication, we pay express attention to the improviser and improvisation as a special activity. If we explore the improvisation as a *sign*, we pay attention to the result, the product of this activity. Improvisation as a sign? A sign of what? The sign represents something, refers to something – and of course to somebody.

Improvisation is a sign of a certain existential situation. Heidegger's term *Geworfenheit*, the condition that characterizes the man who tries to define himself amidst the world, also describes the occasion of improvising. It is a sign of the courage to enter into communication without certainty about whether the improvisation – on any level, be it an action or a particular product of this action – will be received, understood, or accepted. In improvisation the existential, temporal, and spatial situation of the improviser always comes to the fore. Improvisation is a particular way in which signs exist. In linguistic terms, improvisation as an utterance is always deictic, that is, an act that points to the moment and place of uttering. Improvisation is a *trace* of a performance situation in the performance itself.

From these preliminary definitions one might already conclude that improvisation always belongs to the semiotics of communication rather than to that of signification. Let us clarify what this means. To do so, we return to the classical diagram by Roman Jakobson (1963: 214):

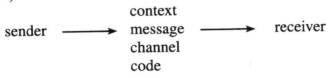

```
                   context
sender  ───────>   message   ───────>   receiver
                   channel
                   code
```

According to Jakobson, communication may emphasize any of the elements in the above diagram, when any one of them becomes so pertinent as to govern the others:

```
                   referential
emotive  ───────>  poetic   ───────>   conative
                   phatic
                   metalinguistic
```

For example, in the just-discussed scene from the *Mastersingers*, the dialogue between Walther and Sachs continually shifts from one "function" to another. The poetic function is involved when they deal with the musical form of the message (Walther's contest song). The conative function operates in the scene in which Sachs as the receiver is moved by the high qualities of the song, and when he says that the melody might irritate the old masters. The phatic function is foregrounded when Sachs urges Walther to take up his pen and paper, and when in the music the preludizing chords "prepare" the beginning, by opening the channel, so to speak. The emotive function is important, among other places, when Walther sings "Ich liebe", thus emphasizing the emotional state of the sender. Moreover, Sachs's story of the golden youth of the mastersingers is emotive in character. The metalinguistic function operates in Walther's questions about the rules, when together with Sachs he ponders the codes of mastersongs. The referential function is saved for the triumphant Midsummerfest of the finale of the last act.

Can Jakobson's theory serve as a basis for a "general theory" of improvisation? Can improvisation, linked with any moment of communication, occur in any part of the above model? Consider the following scenarios:

(1) *A sender improvises*. Here the main emphasis lies on the improviser. It does not matter if the result *sounds* as if it were improvised. The improviser may rely on generative rules to such an extent that the result sounds like a completed composition. For example, an organist improvises a fugue.

(2) *A message is an improvisation*. In this case, the result must sound like an improvisation. Western art music has numerous "traces" of improvisation in written compositions, one example being the notated cadenzas of concertos.

As said above, the difference between sender and message is the same as that between enunciation and enunciate. Often a musical enunciate – such as a passage that sounds improvised or a *topic* in art music – has been created through transference of a sender's activity to the message itself. In such cases one might also speak of improvisation as a *gesture*. The English-horn solo "Hirtenweise" from Wagner's *Tristan* can serve as an illustration. Another is the clarinet solo that opens Sibelius's First Symphony, about which musicologist Ilmari Krohn says the following (1947: 37):

Einleitung vertritt den epischen Erzähler, der ausserdem durch die Bogenform des Strophenbaus und durch die einsam tönende Klarinette charackterisiert ist – die tiefe Frauenstimme eines Klageweibs, wie es noch jetzt in Fernkarelien begegnet ... Das Klagemotive des Hauptstollens ist eine künstlerische Nachbildung der karleischen Klagelieder, die bei Todesfällen oder anderen traurigen Ereignissen von bejahrten frauen anestimmt werden. Auch die zu ähnlichem Zweck im alten Griechenland (und Orient) gebrauchten Klagegesänge (Threnoi) sollen sich in gleicher Weise wie hier von hohem Anfangston allmälich abwärts bewegt haben.

[The introduction portrays an epic narrator, who is moreover characterized by the arch form of the phrase structure and the lonely-sounding clarinet –

the profound female voice of a mourning woman, which still encounters in distant Carelia... The plaintive motive of the main phrase is an artistic imitation of male mourning songs, which at times of death or other sad events is sung by elderly women. Likewise, the mourning songs (Threnoi), used for the same purpose in ancient Greece (and the Orient), have to move in the same manner, from a high beginning tone gradually downwards.]

Of course this does not represent a literal imitation of a lamentation, but rather a symbolic reinterpretation of a folk-music "gesture". In Heitor Villa-Lobos's *Choros*, we encounter an equivalent transition from folk music to art music, from sender to message, from enunciation to enunciate. In these pieces, the improvisatory formal outline, which the composer himself called *une nouvelle forme de la composition*, was based on the nightly serenades given by street musicians of Rio de Janeiro known as *choros* groups, popular at the turn of the century. If one compares original *choros* music, with its virtuosic solos, to, say, Villa-Lobos's *Choros* No. 2 for Flute and Clarinet – the second part of which imitates the technique of the famous *choros* improviser Calado, with melodic leaps of elevenths – this connection becomes quite obvious.

(3) *A receiver improvises.* This process may obtain in certain avantgarde performances in which the art work consists of the audience's reactions to it. Such is the case in Satie's *Vexations* and in certain pieces by Cage. By using excessively scanty messages or an overabundance of signs, the modernists hoped to prompt the audience to react in some spontaneous, more or less improvised way.

(4) *A context becomes the object of improvisation.* This takes place when social situations trigger improvisatory behaviours. Here we encounter extemporized performances, as in a train station, on a trip, at a festival, or under other unusual conditions that precipitate the improvisation. In a broader sense, entire style periods and cultural contexts have leaned toward improvisation, as in French aesthetic culture of the 1910s and 1920s, for which the concept of *jeu*, or play and playfulness, was central.

(5) *A channel is under improvisation.* This can happen, for example, in a theater performance or spectacle, in which anything can serve

as part of the event, as in a samba carnival any object can be used as a percussion instrument.

(6) *A code is improvised.* This situation puts the whole process in jeopardy, since without a certain common minimal code, communication cannot exist. In some avant-garde music, the composer uses graphic notation, whose codes the player must improvise differently each time. In a sense, ambiguous musical situations, which operate with several superimposed levels of meaning, require the listener to discover or create new codes. Thus, improvisation occurs in this respect.

All in all, it does seem possible to approach improvisation as *communication*. To the six situations above, one may add the dimension of "noise". All musical interpretation that takes place spontaneously, at the mercy of the situation, is a kind of disturbance, if one understands "music" to be the unidirectional communication of an idea, from composer to listener. The "noise" can be positive, however. The virtuoso vocal cadenzas of Italian nineteenth-century opera, during which the "normal" course of the music is interrupted, illustrate such positive "noise". Ex. 17 shows one such cadenza, improvised by the famous Finnish-Swedish soprano Jenny Lind, as transcribed by her husband.

## 8.3 Improvisation as signification: A peircean view

The basic unit of signification is, of course, the sign. However, there are many theories about how this sign exists, its structure, how it functions. As discussed in Chapter 1.3, "European semiotics" generally follows Saussure's binary conception of the sign, as divided into signifier and signified, expression and content. By contrast, American philosopher Charles S. Peirce believed that at least three units are needed to define a sign: the sign itself (or representamen), object, and interpretant. Correspondingly, one obtains three species of signs: signs in themselves, signs in relation to their objects, or signs in relation to their interpretants. The best-known of all these categories is that of signs in relation to their objects, which further leads to three classes: *icons*, in which the sign is similar to its object; *indexes*, in which the

*Ex. 17.*   Jenny Lind's improvisation. Transcription by her husband Otto
Goldschmidt (cadenza for 6th cavatina, Bellini: *Beatrice di Tenda*) (quoted
from Holland & Rockstro 1891, Bilaga p. 2)

signs are in a relation of contiguity to their objects; and *symbols*, in
which the relationship is conventional. Peircean semiotics has many
other categories as well, but as an illustration of how to use his theory
in the study of improvisation, I shall utilize only the aforementioned
classes of sign. Using Peirce's ideas we may be able to classify and
analyze almost all signs involved in all kinds of improvisation.

In *iconic*, *indexical*, or *symbolic* improvisation, the latter is interpreted as a sign complex, a series of several signs, a whole text, which
becomes meaningful and assumes its improvisatory character through
its particular relationship to its object, say, to some earlier composition, musical genre, or the like. Improvisation in this case is improvisation from "something", that is, from a given object. The relationship
to this object is that between a sign (representamen) and its object, and
thus iconic, indexical, or symbolic in nature.

A good illustration of iconic improvisation can be found in the
cadenzas of concertos of the eighteenth and nineteenth centuries. Carl
Czerny's *Systematische Anleitung zum Fantasieren auf dem Piano-
forte* Op. 200 (1836) contains many examples of such improvisation.
Almost all cases listed by Czerny deal with improvisation from a given
theme, and hence constitute iconic improvisations. Czerny provides
ready-made models (Peircean legisigns), according to which categories a theme-object can be treated. Among others, Czerny lists allegro, adagio (in serious style), allegretto grazioso (in galant style),
scherzo presto (in capriccio style), rondo vivace, polacca, theme and
variations, fugue and valse écossaise, march and other style genres.
His cadenza to the first movement of Beethoven's C major Piano Concerto is a model of how the theme-objects of the exposition are used
as iconic signs and as unifying elements of the whole. If one compares Czerny's with Beethoven's own cadenza, which is totally different, one notices that the same "objects" can, within certain limits, have
various iconic signs in the "improvisation".

On the other hand, when one goes from a theme to thematic development in the proper sense, the relationship of similarity between
theme-object (the original motive) and its iconic elaboration becomes
so vague that iconicity as an immediate First disappears. In some
musical works such a gradual transformation and dissolution of iconicity forms the central "idea" of the whole piece. This is the case with
Henri Pousseur's *Voyage fantastique*, which little by little and almost
imperceptibly "improvises" from Wagnerian style to that of Richard
Strauss, and from there on to early Schoenberg, atonality, serialism,
and so on. Such examples often operate according to the principle of
*ars combinatoria* – the combining of ready-made elements in a pre-

scribed order. Some scholars view folk-musical improvisation in this way. The singers/players have stored in their minds a repertoire of "elements", from which they then, following certain simple syntactic rules, produce new and "improvised", but still style-congruent music (e.g., as Pekkilä 1988 has shown).

In indexical improvisation, the relationship between the improvised sign and the object from which it emerges is one of contiguity. In this case, sign and object need not be similar. One could hardly imagine a better example than Walther's improvised contest song, discussed above, which emerges as an outburst of a dream image or emotional state. Folk music, too, has many examples of improvisation that stem from a strong feeling, as the latter's spontaneous, indexical signAbove we gave Krohn's interpretation of the clarinet solo from the beginning of Sibelius's First Symphony as an imitation of a funeral lament. Here are three other cases: (1) the funeral lamentation of an old Finnish woman, Donna Huovinen from Ingermanland (recording from 1956); (2) the funeral song by a Bororo Indian from Mato Grosso (recording from the Museu Indio in Rio de Janeiro); and (3) the lament of a Japanese Buddhist priest, in which the text is a fixed unit, and the quasi-musical recitation gives the impression of improvised performance. What is astonishing in all these cases are the similarities of the acoustic form of the indexical signs, in spite of the great differences in cultural context. One is tempted to think that certain ritual situations produce similar reactions in the lamenters by virtue of their mythic-existential context. In literature we have an excellent example of such a ritual improvisation in the final scene of Hermann Hesse's novel, *The Glass-Bead Game*. The scene takes place at sunrise, when young Tito dances spontaneously across the alpine landscape, not knowing that Joseph Knecht is observing him. This precisely represents an archetypal behaviour that may only appear to be improvised. It in fact may be determined by some deep psychic code. We know that improvisation in Indian ragas takes place according to a certain moment of the day and its atmosphere; this, too, is a kind of indexical musical practice.

Symbolic improvisation, in turn, takes its point of departure from some rule, idea, or thought which the improvisation symbolizes. To the degree that Walther's contest song obeys mastersingers' rules, it could be taken as a symbolic improvisation. However, sign classes can intermingle; hence nothing prevents us from speaking about a symbolic-indexical improvisation. A pianist who improvises, say, according to Czerny's style categories, but who constantly alters the musical substance – i.e., the theme-object – would be exercising symbolic improvisation.

All the aforementioned sign classes become mixed in various *intertextual* situations, in which several sign categories function side by side. Only one of them may be improvised, with the others pre-established. Let us illustrate this with a case in which music joins with certain forms of expressive movement. In Finland in the 1950s–60s a system of female gymnastics, developed by Hilma Jalkanen, was at the peak of its popularity. A group of gymnasts from the University of Helsinki traveled around the world giving performances which were said to be recreations of the ideals of Antiquity. The movements in such female gymnastics, according to Jalkanen's system, were completely pre-arranged, yet relied upon certain "natural" principles as a contrast to the continuous tension in the motion-language of ballet. The music, however, was always improvised for each different performance. In a sense, then, the music was a symbolic improvisation. At the same time, it was iconically and indexically connected with certain key moments of the parallel gestural language: iconically, insofar as the music imitated the rhythm of a march, swinging arms, or jumping; and indexically, inasmuch as the music determined the moments for leaps or other bodily motions. A counter-example is provided by the system of motion elaborated by Alexandra and Robert Pierce (1991) in which the music is determined – Chopin, Handel, or written by the authors – but the movements are improvised. Here the movement imitates music through iconic-indexical improvisation. Another good illustration of "improvised" expressive movements coordinated with ready-made music (Beethoven's Pastoral Symphony) occurs in Walt Disney's animated movie *Fantasia*.

What kind of *inference* obtains when improvisation stems from some given basis, be it a theme-object, emotional state, or abstract set of rules? Peirce (1940) speaks of three categories of logical reasoning: *deduction*, *induction*, and *abduction*. Following Czerny's advice, one comes close to deductive reasoning, which always produces "correct" results, though the latter may only be tautologies or trivialities. The same can be said of "improvisation" done by computers: a generative grammar which is fed into a machine leaves no place for freedom, but produces "correct" copies, tokens from given types. Inductive reasoning, in turn, is also foreign to genuine improvisation. In the *Mastersingers*, for example, we meet the unsuccessful improviser, Beckmesser, who proceeds strictly by induction. He tries to compile a mastersong from fragments which he recalls from others' songs, but without success. This would typify "inductive" improvisation. By contrast, Walther's method of improvisation represents the third category of reasoning – abduction. After each *Stollen* he asks with uncertainty whether it was correct regarding the rules of inference or tries to confirm the correctness of his unsure reasoning, and thus finally comes to the right solution, a mastersong. It may be that genuine improvisation can be determined precisely in a Peircean way, as a form of abduction.

## 8.4 Improvisation as signification: A greimassian view

When we examine improvisation as *signification* we need not restrict ourselves to Peircean semiotics. Other theoretical alternatives are available, such as the generative model of A. J. Greimas. Starting from Greimas's theory I have elaborated a model of music analysis, which starts with *isotopies* (fundamental levels of meaning) then progresses to the next phase, in which the process of meaning is articulated according to time, place, and actor. This is followed by the level of *modalities*: "being/doing", "can", "know", "will", "must", and "believe" (see Tarasti 1994).

In the light of this theory, improvisation constitutes its own isotopy, in which its own laws prevail. In musical practices, improvisation is often clearly marked and distinguished from other situations. Just as often, improvisation represents a sphere of chaos or disorganisation, a "carnivalized" domain in Bakhtin's sense (1968). Every receiver understands that the isotopy of improvisation is most often a sphere of particular liberties that would not be permitted elsewhere. Many adherents to creativity doctrines agree that a creative act is a kind of improvisation, which cannot be subordinated to rules or boundaries. Improvisation is like a reserve, where otherwise banished forms of conduct are tolerated and even favoured. But it is an entirely different matter when *everything* is permitted, when nothing is taboo, as occurs, for example, in some avant-garde performances. In that case, the end result is stereotyped and unimaginative, and all such performances seem pretty much the same.

On the next level, the semiosis of improvisation starts to take a clearer shape. One might even argue that improvisation is basically a *temporal* category, which operates according to "unpredictability" and "irreversibility" (Jankélévitch 1974). That is to say, improvisation arises as if from spontaneous caprice, without any anticipation, and its result cannot be repeated as such. Should it recur, it would no longer be improvisation. This is what happens to Walther's contest song at the end of the opera, after we have heard it at the beginning of the third act at the moment of "genuine" improvisation. Thus, nothing is more paradoxical than a notated or recorded improvisation, where we hear or see only the other half of the improvisation: we receive it as an utterance (enunciate), no longer as the *act* of utterance (enunciation).

In the *spatial* sense improvisation appears, as stated above, at a certain place, such as the cadenza of a concerto or the embellishments of an aria. In the *actorial* respect improvisation may be joined either to a certain theme-actor on the level of the enunciate, and also perhaps to the subject of the enunciation. For instance, if we listen to Isaac Albéniz's improvisation on a recording he made in 1903, what interests us about this performance? Probably precisely the fact that the improvisation sounds like "Albéniz". In that case, the object of our interest is actorial, that is, related to a certain person.

What about the *modalities*? All the usual modalities appear in improvisation in its various forms. In an improvised cadenza for a solo concerto, for example, the modalities generally operate as follows: (a) The modality of "know" increases, since the improvised part usually offers new information. Even though improvisation functions iconically in most cadenzas, it is non-redundant. (b) "Must" decreases, since the performer is momentarily freed adhering to the written score.

(c) "Can" increases, since improvisation usually calls for more virtuosity in the technical aspects of the performance. (d) "Will" decreases, because the improvised area is less goal-directed, less teleological than are the other parts of the musical work. Improvisation detaches the listener and performer from the "normal", kinetic-energetic background. Moreover, the tonal tension arising from the "will" towards the tonic is interrupted by the six-four chord. The resolution on the dominant occurs only when the improvisation has ended. (e) "Believe", which is the persuasiveness or "truth value" of the improvisation, is at its smallest level in this section, since improvisation usually attempts to appear as something other than what it really is. Following Greimas's categories, improvisation is a "lie" (it seems to be what it is not) and a "secret" (it does not seem to be what it really is). Composers may, with an improvisatory style, mask the fundamental code of their music-narrative program, concealing the importance of this code in such a way that the listener does not take the improvisatory device so "seriously". The preludizing introduction to Chopin's G minor Ballade is a good illustration. The listener considers this beginning as an introduction to the "event" proper, without knowing that the whole nuclear code of the piece is hidden therein, to be revealed only in the tragic return to G minor at the end. A similar case is that of the listener who hears Sibelius's Fourth Symphony for the first time, and thus cannot anticipate that the tritone motive will be the kernel of the whole work. From the observations just made, it seems that Greimassian concepts are suitable for investigating improvisation as signification.

## 8.5 Conclusion: Improvisation and existential semiotics

At the start of this chapter, I spoke about a particular existential semiotics to which the study of improvisation naturally seems to lead. In such an existential semiotics, all the "classical" sign models remain valid. However, they are joined with *one* factor more: the aspect of situation, as regards the time, history, and future of the object under examination. In brief, we take into account the sign's existential being.

Semioticians have often been accused of being able to reveal only the timeless, the ahistorical, the tasteless and odourless, as it were, strangely pallid functions of signs. Nevertheless, a scholar's viewpoint constantly varies in the temporal process, and the human situation in communication and existence differs from the models that "objectify" it. Existential semiotics rejects a violent analysis that damages phenomena (an ethical-moral principle); the universality of phenomena consists of their being seen *as something*, and in some light; what is said or expressed may be less important than in what sense or mode it is said; as for temporality: the meaning grows denser over time, and is completed in the moment we know we have to give it up. These are the theses of what I call "existential semiotics", as expanded and illustrated in my recent book on the subject (Tarasti 2001). Improvisation automatically includes these aspects. For in the name of improvisation, musicians, actors, reciters, dancers abandon themselves to the mercy of the situation, in the hope that "genius" will not desert such a daredevil.

# Notes

1. In language, for instance if "man" is considered the neutral, non-marked term, then "woman" would be marked the term – although some gender theoreticians would like to turn this situation around. Robert Hatten (1987 and 1994) has convincingly applied markedness theory to music.
2. Iconicity is theoretically very problematic. Eco (1976), among others, has tried to show that there are degrees of similarity, and that in most cases similarity is not automatic but transmitted by cultural conventions (as in certain Arab cultures, which cannot conceive a photograph as an iconic sign of a person).
3. Some scholars (e.g., Lidov 1999: 136), doubt the usefulness of the semiotic square. The reader can look at its applications, most of them available in English, by scholars such as Anne Hénault, Peter Stockinger, Jacques Fontanille, and above all, Greimas himself, to help make up his or her own mind about its utility. For musical applications of the semiotic square, see, among others, the work of Márta Grabócz, Raymond Monelle, and myself.
4. The necessity for "critical distance" was central to Theodor Adorno's (1973) philosophy, and he either praised or condemned composers according to whether or not they met that criterion. By assuming a distanced attitude toward their work, Mahler and Schoenberg were progressive composers, according to Adorno. On the other hand, he considered Sibelius and Stravinsky to be regressive. In his reasoning, Adorno approaches semiotics in the broadest sense, and every phrase he writes about composers such as Mahler or Wagner is rich with meanings. Although Adorno's ideological biases led him astray, to the point of completely "misunderstanding" some composers, his genius nevertheless shines through every sentence he wrote.
5. Barraqué explains the *note-ton/note-son* distinction as follows: "la différence entre une note inclue dans l'harmonie et donc "chiffrable" et une note dont la fonction ressortit avant tout au timbre."
6. Though Meyer excludes them from participation in his notion of style, some musical works imitate pure Firstness, by consisting of detached elements without any cohesive logic for the listener to follow; one such work is John Cage's *Music of Changes*.
7. Some of Barthes's ideas have already been applied to the analysis of music. See, for example, Robert Samuels' book on Mahler's Sixth Symphony (1995).
8. For a detailed analysis of surface modalities, see my essay on Chopin's G minor Ballade, in Tarasti (1994).
9. The myth of "natural" expression pervades the history of singing. According to many singing schools, this quality is gained only by complete relaxation, in which case everything will come naturally and organically. People in the modern world are full of tension and inner turmoil, hence most methods focus on dif-

ferent techniques of relieving such tension. In my view, however, the Finnish pioneer of modern dance and creativity pedagogy, Riitta Vainio, is correct in her view that the worst thing one can say to a tense person is to *demand* that he or she relax, because such a demand induces the very tension one is trying to relieve.

10. Anthony Seeger's grandfather, Charles, was also interested in vocal expression, and he symbolized his system of "moods" and their logic by developing a kind of neumatic notation (Charles Seeger 1960).

11. Wagner was always concerned about how his philosophy was conveyed to the audience, as well as with how the performers understood it. He held no appreciation for performers lacking in philosophical culture.

# References

Aarne, Antti and Stith Thompson
  1961    *The Types of the Folktale: A Classification and Bibliography: Antti
          Aarnes Verzeichnis der Märchentypen.* Helsinki: FF Communications
          3. Translated and expanded by Stith Thompson. Second revised ed.
          Helsinki: FFC 184.
Abbate, Carolyn
  1991    *Unsung Voices. Opera and Musical Narrative in the Nineteenth
          Century.* Princeton, NJ: Princeton University Press.
*Actes du ler congrès international de sémiotique musicale. Beograd, Oct. 17–21,
          1973.* Pesaro: Centro di Iniziativa Culturale.
Adler, Guido
  1885    Umfang, Methode und Ziel der Musikwissenschaft. *Vierte
          Jahresschrift für Musikwissenschaft* 1: 5–20.
  1911    *Der Stil in der Musik.* Leipzig: Breitkopf und Härtel.
  1919    *Methode der Musikgeschichte.* Leipzig: Breitkopf und Härtel.
Adorno, Theodor
  1952    *Versuch für Wagner.* Frankfurt a. M.: Suhrkamp.
  1973    *Philosophy of Modern Music.* London: Sheed & Ward.
Agawu, V. Kofi
  1991    *Playing with Signs: A Semiotic Interpretation of Classic Music.*
          Princeton, NJ: Princeton University Press.
Ambros, August Wilhelm
  1887    *Geschichte der Musik.* Leipzig: Keuckart.
Araújo Duarte Valente, Heloisa de
  1999    *Os Cantos da Voz entre o ruído e o silêncio.* São Paulo: Annablume.
Ariès, Philippe et Georges Duby
  1987    *Histoire de la vie privée.* Paris: Seuil.
Arom, Simha
  1969    Essai d'une notation des monodies à des fins d'analyse. *Revue de
          musicologie* 68: 198–212.
Arrivé, Michel and Jean-Claude Coquet
  1987    *Sémiotiques en jeu: A partir et autour de l'œuvre d'A. J. Greimas.*
          Paris, Amsterdam and Philadelphia: Editions Hades-Benjamins.
Asafiev, Boris
  1977    *Musical Form as a Process.* 3 vols. Transl. and commentary by J. R.
          Tull, diss. Ohio State University.
Bailey, Derek
  1980    *Improvisation: Its Nature and Practice in Music.* Derbyshire:
          Morrland.

Bakhtin, Mikhail
    1973    *Rabelais and His World.* Cambridge, MA: MIT Press.
Bankov, Kristian
    2000    *Intellectual Effort and Linguistic Work. Semiotic and Hermeneutic Aspects of the Philosophy of Bergson.* (Acta Semiotica Fennica IX.) Helsinki: International Semiotics Institute.
Baroni, Mario and Carlo Jacoboni
    1978    *Proposal for a Grammar of Melody: The Bach Chorales.* Montréal: Presses de l'Université de Montréal.
Barthes, Roland
    1957    *Mythologies.* Paris: Seuil.
    1964    *Essais critiques.* Paris: Seuil.
    1970    *S/Z.* Paris: Seuil.
    1977    *Image, Music, Text.* New York: Hill and Wang.
    1986    Rasch. In: *The Rustle of Language.* New York: Hill and Wang.
Bartók, Béla
    1957    *Weg und Werk. Schriften und Briefe.* Zusammengestellt von Bence Szabolcsi. Budapest: Corvina.
Baudrillard, Jean
    1987    *L'autre par lui même: Habilitation.* Paris: Editions Galilée.
Beaumont, Antony
    1985    *Busoni, the Composer.* London: Faber and Faber.
Bengtsson, Ingmar
    1973    *Musikvetenskap: En översikt.* Stockholm: Norstedt.
Bent, Ian
    1987    *Analysis.* London: MacMillan.
Bergson, Henri
    1975    *La pensée et le mouvant.* Paris: Presses Universitaires de France.
Berlioz, Hector and Richard Strauss
    1904    *Instrumentationslehre.* Leipzig: Peters.
Bernstein, Leonard
    1976    *The Unanswered Question: Six Talks at Harvard.* Cambridge MA: Harvard University Press.
Besseler, Heinrich
    1957    Spielfiguren in der Instrumentalmusik. *Deutsches Jahrbuch fir Musikwissenschaft 1956* (ed. W. Vetter). Leipzig: Peters: 12–38.
Blacking, John
    1976    *How Musical is Man?* London: Faber and Faber.
Boiles, Charles
    1973    Les chants instrumentaux des Tepehuas. *Musique en jeu 12:* 81–99.
Boulez, Pierre
    1971    *On Music Today.* Cambridge MA: Harvard University Press.

1986    *Orientations. Collected Writings.* Ed. Jean-Jacques Nattiez.
        Cambridge MA: Harvard University Press.
Bourdieu, Pierre.
1984    *Distinction: A Social Critique of the Judgement of Taste.* Tr. Richard
        Nice. Cambridge, MA: Harvard University Press.
Brelet, Gisèle
1949    *Le temps musical l-II.* Paris: Presses Universitaires de France.
1951    *L'interprétation créatrice III.* Paris: Presses Universitaires de France.
        *Bresil: Le monde sonore des Bororo.* Ivry-sur-Seine: Auvidis.
Bücher, Karl
1909    *Arbeit und Rhythmus.* Leipzig and Berlin: Tuebner.
Buehler, Karl
1933    *Ausdruckstheorie. Das System an der Geschichte aufgezeigt.* Jena:
        Verlag von Gustav Fischer.
Bukofzer, Manfred
1947    *Music in the Baroque Era from Monteverdi to Bach.* New York:
        Norton.
Busoni, Ferruccio
1916    *Entwurf einer neuen Ästhetik der Tonkunst.* Leipzig: Insel.
Camilleri, Lelio
1992    On Music Perception and Cognition: Modularity, Structure and
        Processing. In: Lelio Camilleri (ed.), Music and Cognition. *Minds and
        Machines,* vol. 2. no. 4.
Celletti, Rodolfo
1987    *Histoire du bel canto.* Paris: Fayard.
Chailley, Jacques
1977    *Traité historique d'analyse harmonique.* Paris: Alphonse LeDuc.
Charbonnier, Georges
1970    *Conversations with Claude Lévi-Strauss.* London: Cape.
Charles, Daniel
1981    *For the Birds: John Cage in Conversation with Daniel Charles.*
        Boston and London: Marion Boyars.
1998    *Musiques nomades.* Ecrits réunis et présentés par Christian Hauer.
        Paris: Editions Kimé
2001    *La fiction de la postmodernité selon l'esprit de la musique.* (= Thémis.
        Philosophie.) Paris: Presses Universitaires de France.
Charles, Daniel (ed.)
1987–1988 *John Cage: Revue d'esthétique.* Nouvelle série, nos. 13, 14, 15.
        Toulouse: Editions Privat.
Citron, Marcia J.
1993    *Gender and the Musical Canon.* Cambridge: Cambridge University
        Press.

Clynes, Manfred
    1976    *Sentics: The Touch of Emotion.* 2nd edition. Garden City, N.Y: Anchor
            Press.
Coker, Wilson
    1972    *Music and Meaning: A Theoretical Introduction to Musical Aesthetics.*
            New York: Free Press.
Czerny, Carl
    1983    *A Systematic Introduction to Improvisation on the Pianoforte*, trans.
            and ed. Alice L. Mitchell. New York: Longman. First published in
            1836.
Dalmonte, Rossana
    1981    *Luciano Berio: Entretiens avec Rossana Dalmonte.* Paris: Editions
            Jean-Claude Lattes.
Danesi, Marcel
    1994    *Cool: The Signs and Meanings of Adolescence.* Toronto: University of
            Toronto Press.
    1998    *Sign, Thought, Culture. A Basic Course in Semiotics.* Toronto:
            Canadian Scholar's Press.
Danesi, Marcel and Danila De Sousa
    1998    *Opera Italian! Learn Italian As You Enjoy Italian Opera! For Self-
            Study.* Welland, Ontario: Éditions Soleil, publishing inc.
Delalande, François
    2001    Le Son des musiques. Entre technologie et esthétique. Bibliothèque de
            recherche Musicale. Institut Nationale Audiovisuel. Paris: Buchet/
            Chastel.
Derrida, Jacques
    1967    *De la grammatologie.* Paris: Minuit. (English tr. by G. Ch. Spivak: *Of
            Grammatology.* Baltimore: Johns Hopkins University Press, 1974.)
Descartes, René
    1649    *Les passions de l'âme.* Paris. (New edition ed. by J.-M. Monnoyer.
            Paris: Gallimard, 1988.)
Doubravova, Jarmila
    1982    *Hudba a vytvarné umeni* [*Music and the Fine Arts*]. Prague:
            Academia.
Dougherty, William P.
    1993    The Play of Interpretants: A Peircean Approach to Beethoven's *Lieder.
            The Peirce Seminar Papers: An Annual of Semiotic Analysis.* Oxford:
            Berg.
Duey, Philip A.
    1980    *Bel Canto in Its Golden Age. A Study of its Teaching Concepts.* New
            York: Da Capo Press.

Dunsby, Jonathan and Arnold Whittall
  1988    *Music Analysis in Theory and Practice.* London: Faber.

Eco, Umberto
  1968    *La struttura assente. Introduzione alla nicerca semiologica.* (Nuovi
          saggi italiani 1.) Milano. (Swedish translation: *Den frånvarande
          strukturen.* Lund: Bo Cavefors, 1971.)
  1976    *A Theory of Semiotics.* Bloomington, IN: Indiana University Press.
  1986    *Art and Beauty in the Middle Ages.* New Haven and London: Yale
          University Press.
Eigeldinger, Jean-Jacques
  1979    *Chopin vu par ses élèves.* Neuchatel: Baconnière.
*Eunomio: Parole di Musica.* Rivista semestrale di teoria, analisi a semiologia della
          musica, diretta da Michele Ignelzi a Paolo Rosato. Chieti: Vecchio
          Faggio Editrice.
Ferand, Ernst
  1938    *Die Improvisation in der Musik: Eine entwicklungsgeschictliche und
          psychologische Untersuchung.* Zürich: Rhein Verlag.
Fonagy, Ivan
  1963    Emotional patterns in intonation and music. *Zeitschrift für Phonetik
          und Allgemeine Sprachwissenschaft* 16. 293-313.
Foucault, Michel
  1970    *The Order of Things. An Archaeology of the Human Sciences.* London:
          Tavistock Publications.
  1975    *Surveiller et punir. Naissance de la prison.* Paris: Gallimard.
Frith, Simon
  1978    *The Sociology of Rock.* London: Constable.
  1984    *Sound Effects. Youth, leisure and the politics of rock.* London:
          Constable.
  1988    *Music for Pleasure: Essays in the Sociology of Pop.* Cambridge UK:
          Polity Press.
  1996    *Performing Rites. On the Value of Popular Music.* USA: Oxford
          University Press.
Frith, Simon (ed.)
  1989    *World Music, Politics and Social Change: Papers from the
          International Association for the Study of Pop Music.* Manchester:
          Manchester University Press.
Furtwängler, Wilhelm
  1951    *Keskusteluja musiikista* [Conversations about music]. Ed. Timo
          Mäkinen. Porvoo and Helsinki: WSOY.
Grabócz, Márta
  1986    *Morphologie des œuvres pour piano de Liszt.* Budapest: MTA

Zenetudomanyi Intezet.

1991–1992 La poétique de F.-B. Mache and Esquisse typologique des macrostructures. *Les Cahiers de CIREM*. Rouen: Centre International de Recherches en Esthétique Musicale.

1996    *Morphologie des œuvres pour piano de Liszt*. Paris: Editions Kimé.

Grabócz, Márta (ed.)

1999    *Méthodes nouvelles, Musiques nouvelles. Musicologie et création*. Strasbourg: Presses Universitaires de Strasbourg.

Greimas, Algirdas J.

1966    *Sémantique structurale*. Paris: Larousse.

1970    *Du sens*. Paris: Seuil.

Greimas, Algirdas J. and Joseph Courtes

1979    *Sémiotique. Dictionnaire raisonné de la théorie du langage*. Paris: Hachette.

Greimas, Algirdas J. and Jacques Fontanille

1990    *La sémiotique des passions: Des états des choses aux états d'âme*. Paris: Seuil.

Hanslick, Eduard

1854    *Vom musikalisch Schönen*. Leipzig: Barth.

Hatten, Robert S.

1987    Style, Motivation and Markedness. In: Thomas A. Sebeok and Jean Umiker-Sebeok (eds.), *The Semiotic Web 1986*, 408–429. Berlin and New York: Mouton de Gruyter.

1994    *Musical Meaning in Beethoven. Markedness, Correlation and Interpretation*. Bloomington, Indianapolis: Indiana University Press.

Hennion, Antoine

1994    Institution et marché: Représentations musicales, à propos d'une audition de variétés. In: Hugues Dufourt et Joël-Marie Fauquet: *Musique et Médiations. le métier, l'instrument, l'oreille*, 147–163. Paris: Klinksieck.

Hepokoski, James

1993    *Sibelius: Symphony No. 5*. Cambridge: Cambridge University Press.

Holland, Henry Scott and William Smith Rockstro

1891    *Jenny Lind: Ihre Laufbahn als Künstlerin. 1820 bis 1851. Nach Briefen, Tagebüchern und andern von Otto Goldschmidt gesammelten Schriftstücken*. Leipzig.

Hosokawa, Shuhei

1987    *Der Walkman-Effekt*. Berlin: Merve.

Ignelzi, Michele

1992    ... Nulla da analizzare...". Qualche considerazione sidle prime battute del Preludio del *Tristan and Isolde* di Richard Wagner. *Eunomio 18*: 3–4.

Iivonen, Antti, R. Aulanko, H. Kaskinen and T. Nevalainen
1984    *Intonaatioteorioista.* Helsinki: Helsingin yliopiston fonetiikan laitoksen julkaisuja.
Imberty, Michel
1976    *Signification and Meaning in Music.* Monographies de sémiologie et d'analyses musicales. Faculté de Musique, Université de Montréal.
1981    *Les écritures du temps. Sémantique psychologique de la musique.* Vol. 2. Paris: Dunod.
Indy, Vincent d'
1897–1900 *Cours de composition musicale.* Paris: Durand.
Jakobson, Roman
1963    *Essais de linguistique générale.* Paris: Editions de Minuit.
Jankélévitch, Vladimir
1957    *Le nocturne. Fauré, Chopin et la nuit, Satie et le matin.* Paris: Editions Albin Michel.
1961    *La musique et l'ineffable.* Paris: Armand Colin.
1974    *L'irreversibilité et la nostalgie.* Paris: Flammarion.
1980    *Je Je-ne-sais-quoi et le Presque-rien. 2. La méconnaissance. Le malentendu.* Paris: Editions du Seuil.
Jiranek, Jaroslav
1985    *Zu Grundfragen der musikalischen Semiotik.* Berlin: Verlag Neue Musik.
Kallberg, Jeffrey
1996    *Chopin at the Boundaries: Sex, History, and Musical Genre.* Cambridge and London: Harvard University Press.
Kandinsky, Wassily
1926    *Punkt und Linie zu Fläche. Beitrag zur Analyse der malerischen Elemente.* Munich. (French version: *Point, ligne, plan.* Paris: Editions Denoel, 1970.)
Karbusicky, Vladimir
1986    *Grundriß der musikalischen Semantik.* Darmstadt: Wissenschaftliche Buchgesellschaft.
1992    Zitat and Zitieren in der Musik. *Zeitschrift für Semiotik 14:* 61–78.
Karbusicky, Vladimir (ed.)
1987    Zeichen and Musik. A special issue of *Zeitschrift für Semiotik* (ed. Roland Posner). Band 9, Heft 3–4. Tübingen: Stauffenburg Verlag.
Kielian-Gilbert, Marianne C.
1987    *Course Notes, Exercises and Anthology of Nineteenth-Century Music.* Bloomington IN: Indiana University School of Music.
Kircher, Athanasius
1650    *Musurgia universalis, sive Ars magna consoni et dissoni in X libros digesta.* Rome: Corbelletti.

Kokkonen, Joonas
    1992    *Ihminen ja musiikki. Valittuja kirjoituksia, esitelmiä, puheita ja arvosteluja* [Man and music. Selected writings, papers, speeches and criticisms]. Jyväskylä: Gaudeamus.
Kremer, Joseph-François
    1994    *Les grandes topiques musicales.* Paris: Meridiens Klinksieck

Krims, Adam
    2001    Marxism, Urban Geography, and Classical Recordings: An Alternative to Cultural Studies. *Music Analysis* 20.3: 347–363.
Kristeva, Julia
    1969    Narration et transformation. *Semiotica l:* 422–488.
Krohn, Ilmari
    1945    *Der Stimmungsgehalt der Symphonien von Jean Sibelius*, I. (Annales Academiae Scientiarum Fennicae, B LVII.) Helsinki: Finnische Literaturgesellschaft.
Kurth, Ernst
    1922    *Grundlagen des linearen Kontrapunkts: Bachs melodische Polyphonie.* Berlin: M. Hesse.
    1925    *Bruckner 1-11.* Berlin: Hesse.
    1947    *Musikpsychologie.* Bern: Krompholz.
    1985    *Romantische Harmonik and ihre Krise in Wagners "Tristan".* Hildesheim, Zürich and New York: Georg Olms. First published in 1923.
Langer, Susanne K.
    1942    *Philosophy in a New Key.* Cambridge MA: Harvard University Press.
Larsson, Gunnar
    1986    Näkökulma Chopinin *Barcarolleen* [Aspects of Chopin´s *Barcarolle*]. *Synteesi* 1: 55–60. Helsinki.
LaRue, Jan
    1970    *Guidelines for Style Analysis.* New York: Norton.
Laver, John
    1994    *Principles of Phonetics.* Cambridge: Cambridge University Press.
Le Corbusier
    1951–1958 *Modulor I-11.* London: Faber and Faber. New edition. Cambridge MA: MIT Press.
Leman, Marc
    1992    The Theory of Tone Semantics: Concept, Foundation, and Application. In: *Minds and Machines,* special issue on Music and Cognition, ed. Lelio Camilleri. Vol. 2, no. 4, November. Amsterdam: Kluwer Academic Publishers: 345–363.

Lerdahl, Fred and Ray Jackendoff
   1985   *A Generative Theory of Tonal Music.* Cambridge MA: MIT Press.
Lévi-Strauss, Claude
   1958   *Anthropologie structurale.* Paris: Plon.
   1964   *Mythologiques 1. Le Cru et le Cuit.* Paris: Plon.
   1967–1971 *Mythologiques I–IV.* Paris: Plon.
   1977   *L'Identité. Séminaire dirigé par Claude Lévi-Strauss.* Paris: Bernard
          Grasset.
Lidov, David
   1980   *Musical Structure and Musical Significance,* Part I. Toronto Semiotic
          Circle: Monographs, Working Papers and Prepublications. Toronto:
          Victoria University.
   1999   *Elements of Semiotics.* Semaphores and Signs. New York: St. Martin's
          Press.
Lima, Luiz Fernando Nascimento de
   2001   *Live Samba. Analysis and Interpretation of Brazilian Pagode.* (Acta
          Semiotica Fennica XI.) (Approaches to Musical Semiotics 1.)
          Helsinki: International Semiotics Institute.
Lindblom, Bengt and Johan Sundberg
   1970   Towards a Generative Theory of Melody. *Swedish Journal of
          Musicology 52:* 71–88.
Lisi, Stefania Guerra
   1996   *Sinestesi Arte nella Globalità dei Linguaggi.* Bologna: Editing Gio.
Littlefield, Richard
   2001   *Frames and framing. The Margins of Music Analysis.* (Acta Semiotica
          Fennica XII.) (Approaches to Musical Semiotics 2.) Helsinki:
          International Semiotics Institute.
Lomax, Alan
   1968   *Folk Song Style and Culture.* Washington D.C.: American Association
          for the Advancement of Science.
Lomuto, Michele and Augusto Ponzio
   1997   *Semiotica della musica.* Bari: Edizioni B.A. Graphis.
Lorenz, Alfred
   1924   *Der musikalische Aufbau des Bühnenfestspieles "Der Ring des
          Nibelungen".* Berlin: Max Hesse.
   1924–1933 *Das Geheimnis der Form bei Wagner.* 4 vols. Tutzing: Schneider.
Lotman, Jurij M., B. A. Uspenskij, V. V. Ivanov, V. N. Toporov and A. M.
Pjatigorskij
   1975   Theses on the Semiotic Study of Cultures (as Applied to Slavic
          Texts). In: Thomas A. Sebeok (ed.), *The Tell-Tale Sign: A Survey of
          Semiotics,* 57–84. Lisse: Peter de Ridder Press.

Luyken, Lorenz
  1995    *... aus dem Nichtigen eine Welt schaffen....: Studien zur Dramaturgie im symphonischen Spätwerk von Jean Sibelius.* (Kölner Beiträge zur Musikforschung.) Kassel: Gustav Bosse Verlag.

Mâche, François-Bernard
  1983    *Musique, mythe, et nature ou les dauphins d'Arion.* Paris: Klinksieck.

Mäkelä, Tomi
  1989    *Virtuosität und Werkcharakter: Zur Virtuosität in den Klavierkonzerten der Hochromantik.* (Berliner musikwissenschaftliche Arbeiten, Band 37.) München: Emil Katzbichler.

Marconi, Luca and Gino Stefani
  1987    *Il senso in musica: Antologia di semiotica musicale.* Bologna: C.L.U.E.B.

Martinelli, Dario
  2002    *How Musical Is A Whale?* (Acta Semiotica Fennica XIII.) (Approaches to Musical Semiotics 3.) Helsinki: International Semiotics Institute.

Martinez, Jose Luiz
  1997    *Semiosis in Hindustani Music.* (Acta Semiotica Fennica V.) Helsinki: International Semiotics Institute.

Mead, George Herbert
  1967    *Mind, Self, & Society from the Standpoint of a Social Behaviorist.* Chicago, London: The University of Chicago Press. First published in 1934.

Medushewski, Viatcheslaw
  1989    Lectures at the Music Department, University of Helsinki, November 1989 (unpublished).

Merleau-Ponty, Maurice
  1945    *Phénoménologie de la perception.* Paris: Gallimard.

Meyer, Leonard B.
  1956    *Emotion and Meaning in Music.* Chicago: University of Chicago Press.
  1973    *Explaining Music: Essays and Explorations.* Chicago and London: University of Chicago Press.
  1978    *Explaining Music: Essays and Explorations.* Chicago, IL: University of Chicago Press.
  1989    *Style and Music: Theory, History, and Ideology.* Philadelphia: University of Pennsylvania Press.
  2000    The Spheres of Music. A gathering of Essays. Chicago, London: The University of Chicago Press.

Miereanu, Costin
  1995    *Fuite et conquête du champ musical.* Paris: Editions Méridiens/ Klinksieck

Miereanu, Costin et Xavier Hascher (eds.)
  1998   *Les universaux en musique.* Actes du 4e Congres international sur la
         signification musicale. (Serie Esthetique no 1.) Paris: Publications de
         la Sorbonne.
Millington, Barry (ed.)
  1992   *The Wagner Compendium. A Guide to Wagner's Life and Music.* New
         York: Macmillan Publishing Company.
Mirka, Danuta
  1997   *The Sonoristic Structuralism of Krzysztof Penderecki.* Katowice: The
         Music Academy of Katowice.
Molino, Jean
  1975   Fait musical et sémiologie de la musique. *Musique en jeu 17:* 37–61.
Monelle, Raymond
  1991   Music and the Peircean Trichotomies. *International Review of the
         Aesthetics and Sociology of Music 22:* 99–108.
  1992   *Linguistics and Semiotics in Music* (Contemporary Music Studies. Vol.
         5). Berkshire: Harwood Academic Publishers.
  2000   *The Sense of Music: Semiotic Essays.* Princeton and Oxford: Princeton
         University Press.
Murtomäki, Veijo
  1993   *Symphonic Unity. The Development of Formal Thinking in the
         Symphonies of Sibelius.* (Studia Musicologica Universitatis
         Helsingiensis.) Helsinki: Department of Musicology, University of
         Helsinki.
Narmour, Eugene
  1977   *Beyond Schenkerism: The Need for Alternatives in Music Analysis.*
         Chicago: University of Chicago Press.
Nattiez, Jean-Jacques
  1975   *Fondements d'une sémiologie de la musique.* Paris: Union Générale
         d'Editions.
  1983   *Tétralogies: Wagner, Boulez, Chéreau.* Paris: Bourgois.
  1987   *Musicologie générale et sémiologie.* Paris: Bourgois.
  1990   *Music and Discourse: Toward a Semiology of Music.* Princeton NJ:
         Princeton University Press.
Neumeyer, David
  1988   *Exercise Manual for Schenkerian Analysis.* Bloomington IN: Indiana
         University School of Music.
Newcomb, Anthony
  1984   Once More "Between Absolute and Programme Music": Schumann's
         Second Symphony. *Nineteenth-Century Music 7/3:* 233-250.
Noske, Frits
  1977   *The Signifier and the Signified: Studies in the Operas of Mozart and*

*Verdi*. The Hague: Nijhoff.

Osmond-Smith, David
1975    L'iconisme formel: Pour une typologie des transformations musicales. *Semiotica 15/11*: 33–47.

Ostwald, Peter F.
1973    *The Semiotics of Human Sounds*. The Hague: Mouton.

Peirce, Charles S.
1940    *The Philosophy of Peirce: Selected Writings*, Justus Buchler (ed). London: Kegan Paul.
1955    *Philosophical Writings of Peirce*. Comp., tr., and introduction by Julius Buchler. New York: Dover.

Peirce, Charles S. and Victoria Lady Welby
1977    *Semiotic and Significs. The Correspondence...* edited by Charles S. Hardwick. Bloomington, London: Indiana University Press.

Pekkilä, Erkki
1988    *Musiikki tekstinä. Kuulonvaraisen musiikkikulttuurin analyysiteoria ja -metodi* [Music as Text: A Theory and Method for the Study of Oral Music Culture]. (Acta Musicologica Fennica 17.) Jyväskylä: Gummerus.

Pelinski, Ramón
1981    *La musique des inuit du caribou: Cinq perspectives méthodologiques*. Montréal: Presses de l'Université de Montréal.

Perrot, Michelle (ed.)
1990    *A History of Private Life*. Vol. 4 : From the fires of revolution to the Great War. Cambridge, MA: Harvard University Press.

Pierce, Alexandra and Roger
1991    *Generous Movement. A Practical Guide to Balance in Action*. Redlands (CA): Center of Balance Press.

Pleasants, Henry
1981    *The Great Singers from the Dawn of Opera to Caruso, Callas and Pavarotti*. New York: A Fireside Book.

Ponzio, Augusto
1999    *La comunicazione*. Bari: Edizioni B.A. Graphis.

Potter, John
1998    *Vocal Authority. Singing style and ideology*. Cambridge: Cambridge University Press.

Propp, Vladimir
1928    *Morphology of the Folktale*. Reprint Austin: University of Texas Press, 1970.

Proust, Marcel
1954    *Du côté de chez Swann. A la recherche du temps perdu I-II*. Paris: Gallimard.

Ratner, Leonard C.
  1980    *Classic Music: Expression, Form and Style.* New York: Schirmer.
Reich, Steve
  1981    *Ecrits et entretiens sur la musique.* Paris: Christian Bougois.
Réti, Rudolph
  1962    *The Thematic Process in Mu*sic. New York: MacMillan.
Reznikoff, Iegor
  1984    Fondements de l'art sacré. *Échanges* 180: 19-37
  1990    Lectures at the Department of Musicology, University of Helsinki.
          (Unpublished.)
Ringbom, Nils-Eric
  1955    *Lehr die Deutbarkeit der Tonkunst.* Helsinki: Edition Fazer.
Rosato, Paolo
  1989    Dolcemente dormiva la mia clori: Musica a poesia in un madrigale di
          Tasso e Monteverdi. *Eunomio 14–15:* 3–25.
  1992    Im Westen nichts Neues. Una proposta di modello
          dinamico-diacronico per la lettura dei processi melodici. *Eunomio
          19:* 316.
Rossi-Landi, Ferruccio
  1973    *Ideologies of Linguistic Relativity.* (Approaches to Semiotics 4.) The
          Hague-Paris: Mouton.
Rowell, Lewis
  1983    *Thinking About Music. An Introduction to the Philosophy of Music.*
          Amherst: The University of Massachusetts Press.
Russolo, Luigi
  1975    *L'art des bruits.* Lausanne: Editions l'Age d'Homme.
Ruwet, Nicolas
  1972    *Langage, musique, poésie.* Paris: Seuil.
Salmenhaara, Erkki
  1970    *Tapiola. Sinfoninen runo Tapiola Sibeliuksen myöhäistyylin
          edustajana.* (Acta Musicologica Fennica 4.) Helsinki: Suomen
          Musiikkitieteellinen Seura.
Samuels, Guthbert
  1932    *The art of the elocutionist.* London: Isaac Pitman & Sons.
Samuels, Robert
  1995    *Mahler's Sixth Symphony. A Study in Musical Semiotics.* Cambridge:
          Cambridge University Press.
Saussure, Ferdinand de
  1916    *Cours de linguistique générale.* Paris: Payot.
Schaeffer, Pierre
  1966    *Traité des objets musicaux.* Paris: Seuil.

Schenker, Heinrich
    1956    *Neue musikalische Theorien und Phantasien III: Der freie Satz.*
            Vienna: Universal.
Schering, Arnold
    1936    *Beethoven and die Dichtung.* Berlin: Junker und Dünnhaupt.
Schiller, Friedrich
    1978    *Über naive und sentimentalische Dichtung.* Stuttgart: Reclam. First
            published in 1795.
Schoenberg, Arnold
    1975    *Style and Idea: Selected Writings.* London: Faber and Faber.
Schopenhauer, Arthur
    1879    *Die Welt als Wille und Vorstellung.* 5th edition. Leipzig: Brockhaus.
            First published in 1879.
Scott, Dereck B. (ed.)
    2000    *Music, Culture, and Society. A Reader.* Oxford: Oxford University
            Press
Seashore, Carl E.
    1938    *Psychology of Music.* New York and London: McGraw-Hill Book
            Company.
Sebeok, Thomas A.
    1972    *Perspective in Zoosemiotics.* The Hague: Mouton.
    1981    Prefigurements of Art. *Semiotica* 27:1/2.3–73.
    1991    *Semiotics in the United States.* Bloomington and Indianapolis: Indiana
            University Press.
Seeger, Charles
    1960    On the Moods of a Music Logic. *Journal of the American
            Musicological Society 13:* 224–261.
    1977    *Studies in Musicology 1935–1975.* Berkeley: University of California
            Press.
Solie, Ruth A. (ed.)
    1993    *Musicology and Difference. Gender and Sexuality in Music
            Scholarship.* Berkeley, Los Angeles, London: University of California
            Press.
Stefani, Gino
    1974    *Musica barocca: Poetica e ideologia.* Milan: Bompiani.
    1976    *Introduzione alla semiotica della musica.* Palermo: Sellerio.
    1977    *Insegnare la musica.* Florence: Guaraldi.
    1982    *La competenza musicale.* Bologna: CLUEB.
Stefani, Gino, Luca Marconi and Franca Ferrari
    1990    *Gli intervalli musicali,* Milan: Strumenti Bompiani.
Stefani, Gino, Eero Tarasti and Luca Marconi (eds.)
    1998    *Musical Signification Between Rhetoric and Pragmatics.* Proceedings

of the 5th International Congress on Musical Signification. (Acta Semiotica Fennica VI.) Bologna: CLUEB/International Semiotics Institute.

Stoianova, Ivanka
1978   *Geste, texte, musique,* Paris: Union Générale d'Editions.
1996   *Manuel d'Analyse Musicale. Les formes classiques simples et complexes.* Paris: Minerve

Stravinsky, Igor
1956   *Poetics of Music in the Form of Six Lessons.* New York: Vintage Books. First published in 1947.

Sundberg, Johan
1980   *Röstlära. Fakta om rösten i tal och sång.* Stockholm: Proprius Förlag.
1987   *The Science of the Singing Voice.* Dekalb, Illinois: Northern Illinois University Press.

Sundberg, Johan (ed.)
1992   *Gluing Tones: Grouping in Music Composition, Performance and Listening.* Royal Swedish Academy of Music.

Sundberg, Johan and Bengt Lindblom
1976   Generative Theories in Language and Music Descriptions. *Cognition 4:* 99–122.

Szabolcsi, Bence
1965   *A History of Melody.* New York: St. Martin's Press.

Szondi, Peter
1986   *Theorie des modernen Dramas.* Minneapolis: University of Minnesota Press.

Tagg, Philip
1979   *Kojak, 50 Seconds of Television Music: Toward the Analysis of Affect in Popular Music.* Göteborg: Studies from the Department of Musicology, no. 2.

Takahashi, Taikai
1992   How to Sing Syômyô IV.1–2. In: Kenji Hirano and Taikai Takahashi (eds.), *Hase Rongi.* Tokyo: Toshiba EMI, sleeve notes to booklet accompanying 5 LP discs (THX-90032).

Tarasti, Eero
1979   *Myth and Music. A Semiotic Approach to the Aesthetics of Myth in Music, especially that of Wagner, Sibelius and Stravinsky.* (Approaches to Semiotics 51). Berlin and New York: Mouton de Gruyter.
1987   *Heitor Villa-Lobos ja Brasilian sielu.* Helsinki: Gaudeamus.
1989   L'analyse sémiotique d'un prélude de Debussy: 'La terrasse des audiences du clair de lune". La mise en evidence d'un parcours narratif. *Analyse musicale 16,* Juin: 67–74.
1991   Beethoven's *Waldstein* and the Generative Course. *Indiana Theory*

*Review 12:* 99–140.

1994a   *A Theory of Musical Semiotics.* Bloomington, Indianapolis: Indiana University Press.

1994b   *Heitor Villa-Lobos.* Jefferson NC: McFarland.

2001    *Existential Semiotics.* Bloomington and Indianapolis: Indiana University Press.

Tarasti, Eero (ed.)

1987    Basic Concepts of Studies in Musical Signification: A Report on a New International Research Project in Semiotics of Music. In: Thomas A. Sebeok and Jean Umiker-Sebeok (eds.), *The Semiotic Web 1986.* Berlin and New York: Mouton de Gruyter: 405–581.

1991    La sémiotique finlandaise. Numero spécial de *Degrés 19.* Bruxelles.

1993    *Musical Signification: Essays on the Semiotics of Music.* An Anthology with 40 contributions. Berlin and New York: Mouton de Gruyter.

Taruskin, Richard

1997    *Defining Russia Musically. Historical and Hermeneutical Essays.* Princeton, New Jersey: Princeton University Press.

Tawaststjerna, Erik

1978    *Jean Sibelius 4.* Helsinki: Otava.

Taylor, Charles

1989    *Sources of the Self: The Making of the Modern Identity.* Cambridge, MA: Harvard University Press.

Tokumaru, Yoshihiko and Osamu Yamaguti (eds.)

1986    *The Oral and the Literate in Music.* Tokyo: Academia Music.

Uexküll, Jakob von

1940    *Bedeutungslehre.* Leipzig: Barth.

Ujfalussy, Jozsef

1968    *Az esztetika alapjai es a zene* [The Foundations of Musical Aesthetics]. Budapest: Tankönyvkiado.

Umiker-Sebeok, Jean and Thomas A. Sebeok

1987    *Monastic Sign Languages.* Berlin and New York: Mouton de Gruyter.

Vecchione, Bernard

1986    Les techniques scientifiques d'analyse musicale. *Analyse musicale 5,* Octobre: 49.

1987    Eléments d'analyse du mouvement musical. *Analyse musicale 8,* Juin: 17–23.

Veilhan, Jean-Claude

1977    *Les règles de l'interprétation musicale à l'époque baroque (XVlle-XVllle s.) générales a tous les instruments.* Paris: Alphonse LeDuc.

Voss, Egon
  1970   *Studien zur Instrumentation Richard Wagners.* Regensburg: Bosse.
Wagner, Richard
  (no date) *Gesammelte Schriften I-XIV.* Ed. Julius Kapp. Leipzig:
       Hesse and Becker.
  1963   *Mein Leben.* Vollständige, kommentierte Ausgabe. Ed. Martin
       Gregor-Dellin. Munich: List.
Walker, Alan
  1966   *Chopin, Profiles of the Man and the Musician.* London: Barrie and
       Rockliff.
Weiner, Marc A.
  1997   *Richard Wagner and the Anti-Semitic Imagination.* Lincoln and
       London: University of Nebraska Press.

# Name index

Printed in Poland
by Amazon Fulfillment
Poland Sp. z o.o., Wrocław